CCEA

GCSE ENGLISH LANGUAGE

THIRD EDITION

Amanda Barr
John Andrews
Jenny Lendrum
Aidan Lennon
Pauline Wylie

Whilst the publisher has taken all reasonable care in the preparation of this book CCEA makes no representation, express or implied, with regard to the accuracy of the information contained in this book. CCEA does not accept any legal responsibility or liability for any errors or omissions from the book or the consequences thereof.

The publisher would like to thank the following for permission to reproduce copyright material:

Acknowledgments can be found on page 225.

Photo credits:

p.3 © Ahmet Emre YILMAZ / 123rf; p.4 Becker – Fotolia; p.5 top Peter Atkins – Fotolia; p.5 bottom © Wavebreak Media Ltd / 123RF.com; p.7 auremar – 123RF; p.8 lculig – 123RF; p.11 © jan kranendonk / Shutterstock.com; p.13 freshidea – Fotolia; p.14 © Shutterstock / s_bukley; p.17 © malcolm romain / iStockphoto.com; p.19 © Laurence Gough – Fotolia; p.20 © ViewApart - Fotolia; p.23 Getty Images / iStockphoto / Thinkstock; p.26 top © Nerthuz / iStock / Thinkstock / Getty Images; p.26 bottom Brian Jackson – Fotolia; p.28 © 2005 / TopFoto; p.29 Christophe Fouquin – Fotolia; p.30 Nejron Photo – Fotolia; p.31 © Imagestate Media (John Foxx) / Education SS121; p.32 © iriska – Fotolia.com; p.34 © Woodmansterne / TopFoto; p.35 © Pefkos – Fotolia.com; p.39 Artwork © Random House From Mud, Sweat and Tears by Bear Grylls Published by Channel 4 Books Reprinted by permission of The Random House Group Limited; p.40 Ronald Grant Archive / TopFoto; p.42 Siegfried Schnepf – Fotolia; p.44 © michele galli / iStockphoto.com; p.47 © jrwasserman – Fotolia.com; p.49 left vinx83 – Fotolia; p.49 middle © Shutterstock / tornadoflight; p.49 right © Fyle - Fotolia; pp. 51, 54 and 55 Cover © Stripes Publishing Ltd 2011 Cover image © iStockphoto.com 2011 Image from Gravenhunger by Harriet Goodwin, published by Stripes Publishing Ltd; p.53 Anne Baek Photography / Fotolia; p.58 2005 TopFoto / ImageWorks; p.62 Animal Aid; p.65 rikilo – Fotolia; p.66 Rido – Fotolia; p.69 © Jenner – Fotolia.com; p.70 © Shutterstock / Syda Productions; p.71 © Xavier Arnau/E+/Getty Images; p.73 micromonkey – Fotolia; p.75 Anthony Shaw – Fotolia; p.78 © Getty Images/Stockbyte/Thinkstock; p.81 D. Hurst / Alamy; p.82 Stockbyte / Photolibrary Group Ltd / Big Business SD101; p.84 Laz'e-Pete – Fotolia; p.85 left winston – Fotolia.com; p.85 right © Getty Images / Thinkstock / Stockphoto / UberImages; p.85 bottom 1tjf – 123RF; pp.86 and 87 studiom1 – 123RF; p.88 Sergey Lysenkov – 123RF; p.89 Roman Fedin – 123RF; p.91 Getty Images / iStockphoto / Thinkstock; p.92 Dominik Bruhn – 123RF; p.93 © Christopher Dilts / Bloomberg via Getty Images; p.94 © Trinity Mirror / Mirrorpix / Alamy Stock Photo; p.95 Dan Mullin / Getty Images; p.96 © Stephen Barnes / Northern Ireland News / Alamy Stock Photo; p.97 Steve Meddle / ITV / REX / Shutterstock; p.100 michaeljung – Fotolia; p.104 Lance Bellers – Fotolia; p.105 dominic dibbs / Alamy Stock Photo; p.106 Alastair Muir / REX / Shutterstock; p.109 Johan Persson / ArenaPAL; p.110 © Buyenlarge / Getty Images; p.112 Clark Nobby / ArenaPAL; p.114 iofoto – Fotolia; p.115 Marek Uliasz – 123RF; p.116 © federicofoto – 123RF; p.124 © Shutterstock / Atomazul; p.129 Noppasinw – Fotolia; p.130 everst – 123RF; p.131 MediaPunch / REX / Shutterstock; p.133 Robert Wilson – 123RF; p.136 © Wavebreak Media Ltd /123RF.com; p.139 © Vadim Tsuprik – Fotolia.com; p.142 © alexskopje – Fotolia.com; p.144 © violetkaipa – Fotolia; p.146 © Shutterstock / Mat Hayward; p.148 © Shutterstock / Martin Novak; p.149 © Shutterstock / Prasit Rodphan; p.151 © Martinan – Fotolia; p.154 © Shutterstock / Juhku; p.156 © Shutterstock / Ruslan Ivantsov; p.157 top © Shutterstock / Pierpaolo Pulinas; p.157 bottom far left © Jacob Ammentorp Lund / 123RF; p.157 bottom middle left © Shutterstock / Adrian Pluskota; p.157 bottom middle right © Getty Images / iStockphoto / Thinkstock; p.157 bottom far right © Shutterstock / New Punisher; p.158 © Patryk Galka / iStockphoto.com; p.159 © grandfailure / 123RF.com; p.164 © michaeljung – Fotolia; p.167 © Shutterstock / studiovin, p.170 © Shutterstock / villorejo; p.171 © Johan Persson / ArenaPAL / Topfoto.co.uk; p.172 © alphaspirit – Fotolia, p.173 © Susanne Bauernfeind – 123RF; p.174 © Imagestate Media (John Foxx) / Unique Images of Animals SS17; p.175 © Getty Images / PhotoObjects.net / Thinkstock; p.180 © PaylessImages – 123RF; p.184 © Stockdisc / Corbis / Legal SD176; p.185 © vlue – 123RF; p.188 © Hemis / Alamy Stock Photo; p.191 © Ryan Rodrick Beiler / iStockphoto / Thinkstock; p.194 © KCphotography / Alamy Stock Photo; p.199 © Shutterstock / BonNontawat; p.201 © anni94 – Fotolia.com; pp.202 and 203 From the work Burn by Paula Weston, first published in the UK by Orion Children's Books, an imprint of Hachette Children's Books, Carmelite House, 50 Victoria Embankment, London EC4Y 0DZ; p.204 © moonlight_bgd - Fotolia; p.205 © Imagestate Media (John Foxx).

Every effort has been made to trace all copyright holders, but if any have been inadvertently overlooked, the Publishers will be pleased to make the necessary arrangements at the first opportunity.

Although every effort has been made to ensure that website addresses are correct at time of going to press, Hodder Education cannot be held responsible for the content of any website mentioned. It is sometimes possible to find a relocated web page by typing in the address of the home page for a website in the URL window of your browser.

Orders: please contact Bookpoint Ltd, 130 Milton Park, Abingdon, Oxon OX14 4SB. Telephone: (44) 01235 827720. Fax: (44) 01235 400454. Lines are open 9:00–17:00, Monday to Saturday, with a 24-hour message answering service. Visit our website at www.hoddereducation.co.uk

ISBN 9781471888649

© Amanda Barr, John Andrews, Jenny Lendrum, Aidan Lennon, Pauline Wylie 2017

First published in 2017 by

Hodder Education

An Hachette UK Company,

Carmelite House, 50 Victoria Embankment

London EC4Y 0DZ

Impression number	5	4	3	2	1
Year	2021	2020	2019	2018	2017

All rights reserved. Apart from any use permitted under UK copyright law, no part of this publication may be reproduced or transmitted in any form or by any means, electronic or mechanical, including photocopying and recording, or held within any information storage and retrieval system, without permission in writing from the publisher or under licence from the Copyright Licensing Agency Limited. Further details of such licences (for reprographic reproduction) may be obtained from the Copyright Licensing Agency Limited, Saffron House, 6–10 Kirby Street, London EC1N 8TS.

Cover photo © Sébastien Bonaimé/Thinkstock/Getty Images

Illustrations by Integra Software Services Pvt. Ltd., Pondicherry, India

Typeset in Caecilia LT Std 10/12pt by Integra Software Services Pvt. Ltd., Pondicherry, India

Printed in Italy

A catalogue record for this title is available from the British Library

CONTENTS

Introduction — viii

UNIT 1

Section A: Writing for purpose and audience — 1

Introduction to writing for purpose and audience — 1
Planning for the task — 2
    What are you writing? — 2
    Why are you writing? — 4
    Whom are you writing for? — 6
Getting the form right — 10
Using appropriate techniques — 11
    Emotive language — 11
    Persuasive language — 12
    Fact and opinion — 12
    Counter-arguing — 14
Structuring effectively — 16
    Linking ideas — 16
    Sentence structures and forms — 16
    Punctuation — 17
Getting the right tone — 18
Ensuring accuracy — 19
    Check your writing to get the best possible mark — 19
Writing for purpose and audience: target success — 20
    Practice question: writing for purpose and audience — 20
Writing for purpose and audience: key to success — 23

Section B: Reading to access non-fiction and media texts — 25

Introduction to reading to access non-fiction and media texts — 25
Non-fiction and media texts — 26
    Why are things written? — 26
    How are things written? — 28
Analysing language closely — 29
    Point. Evidence. Explain. — 29
    Focusing on words and phrases — 29
    Responding to autobiographical writing — 30
    Analysing language techniques — 32
Analysing structure — 36
    Choice of tense — 36
    Using sequence and time — 36
    Effect of sentence structures — 37

Contents

Extracting meaning	38
The extracting meaning task	38
Supporting interpretations	40
The supporting interpretations task	40
Putting it into practice: reading to access non-fiction texts	42
The 'Analyse' task	42
The 'Extracting and interpreting meaning' task	43
Responding to media texts	43
Identifying purpose and audience	44
Analysing presentational devices	46
Colour	47
Layout	48
Images	48
Font	50
Analysing language	52
Promotional language	52
Media texts structure	52
Tone	53
Putting it into practice: reading to access media texts	54
Reading to access non-fiction and media texts: target success	57
Practice question: reading to access non-fiction texts	58
Practice question: reading to access media texts	60
Reading to access non-fiction and media texts: key to success	63

UNIT 2
Speaking and listening — 64

Introduction to speaking and listening	64
'I can speak and I can listen…'	66
Preparing to speak	66
Preparing to listen	67
Individual presentation and interaction	68
Presenting	68
Interacting	70
Discussion	71
Chairing a discussion	71
Participating in a discussion	72
Role play	74
Getting the best from role play	74
Speaking and listening: controlled assessment: target success	76
Assessing speaking and listening tasks	77

UNIT 3

Task 1: The study of spoken language — 80

Introduction to the study of spoken language	80
The skills of spoken language	81
The characteristics of spoken language	82
Spoken and written language	83
Factors affecting spoken language	85
Spoken language terms	86
Idiolect	88
Accent and dialect	88
Context and register	88
Your idiolect	89
Formal vs informal speech	90
Standard English	90
Spontaneous vs scripted speech	92
Prosodic features	92
Contexts for spoken language	94
Interviews	94
Commentaries	95
Presentations	97
Occupational talk	97
Analysing spoken language texts	98
The study of spoken language: controlled assessment: target success	101
The study of spoken language: key to success	102

Task 2: The study of written language — 103

Introduction to the study of written language	103
Drama	104
The key features of drama	104
Prose	110
The key features of prose texts	110
Point. Evidence. Explain.	112
Insight into characters	113
Language and style	113
Themes	114
Poetry	115
Poetic language and structure	115
Analysing a poem	117
Key features of poetic techniques	117
Writing about literary texts	118
The study of written language: controlled assessment: target success	120
The study of written language: key to success	121

Contents

UNIT 4

Section A: Personal or Creative Writing — 123

Introduction to Personal or Creative Writing — 123
Planning for writing — 124
    The three Ws — 124
    Why plan? — 124
    How to plan effectively — 125
Using an appropriate form of writing — 127
    Structuring your writing — 128
Personal Writing — 129
    Introducing your Personal Writing essay — 129
    Developing your Personal Writing and adding interest — 129
    Concluding your Personal Writing — 134
Creative Writing — 136
    Selecting an appropriate form — 137
    Selecting an appropriate perspective — 139
    Beginnings and endings — 140
    Creating narrative — 143
    Creative characters — 145
    Creating dialogue — 148
    Creating empathy — 150
    Creating setting — 152
    Creating atmosphere — 155
    Writing a theme-based narrative — 157
    Editing tips — 158
Personal and Creative Writing: target success — 159
    Practice question: Personal Writing — 159
    Practice question: Creative Writing — 159
Personal and Creative Writing: key to success — 164

Section B: Reading literary and non-fiction texts — 166

Introduction to reading literary and non-fiction texts — 166
Literary and non-fiction texts — 167
    Why are things written? — 168
    How are things written? — 168
Writer's craft — 169
    Style — 169
    Linguistic techniques — 170
    Studying words and phrases — 173
    Studying sentence structure and punctuation — 174
    Tone — 176
Comparing literary texts — 177
    Language to compare and contrast — 178
Responding to literary and non-fiction texts — 179
    Point. Evidence. Explanation. — 181

Putting it into practice: reading literary texts	183
The comparative question	183
Putting it into practice: reading non-fiction texts	186
Reading literary and non-fiction texts: target success	190
Practice question: reading literary fiction	190
Practice question: reading non-fiction	194
Reading literary and non-fiction texts: key to success	198
Exam practice: putting your skills into practice	199
Mark schemes	208

INTRODUCTION

Welcome to CCEA GCSE English Language

This book focuses on helping you understand the requirements of CCEA's GCSE Specification for English Language. Although some students will naturally find this subject area easier than others, this book will show you that – no matter what your skill level at the start of the course – you can improve and do well. It will develop your skills in reading, writing, speaking and listening, and the study of spoken language.

This book has three main aims:

- ▶ To help you become familiar with the four different units of the English Language course.
- ▶ To create an awareness of what exactly will be tested within the four units.
- ▶ To offer a step-by-step approach to developing the combination of skills, knowledge and techniques that will allow you to maximise your potential in the examinations and in the Controlled Assessment tasks.

Below is a detailed outline of the Specification and the Assessment Objectives. These provide a clear overview of what you will be learning and the skills you will need to develop to fulfil your potential in this course.

The units in this Student Book provide guidance on how to tackle each element of your GCSE course. This guidance is intended to support you, but your teacher may encourage you to explore other approaches to discover methods that work for you and help you develop your target skills.

- ▶ The **Reading-based units** will help you build up essential skills and techniques. There are opportunities to read and study a range of fiction, non-fiction and media texts to enhance your analytical skills. Sample questions and textual annotations will prove helpful in focusing your thinking and analytical skills.
- ▶ In the **Writing-based units**, you will study a range of extracts to help you understand how certain effects are achieved to interest and engage an audience. You will find a selection of tasks to encourage you to consider your own craft in writing and to prepare you for responding in many different writing forms. Practice tasks, including those for the new Creative Writing assessment, which uses visual stimuli to encourage creativity, will ensure you are prepared to write creatively, to write from experience and to write for audience and purpose.
- ▶ The **Speaking and listening unit** offers a variety of Controlled Assessment tasks, with specific advice on the requirement to interact as part of an individual presentation.
- ▶ In the **Written and spoken language Controlled Assessment unit** you will find advice on responding to spoken language and support with analysing spoken language texts. In addition, this section also offers guidance on responding to poetry, prose and drama, as well as general instruction on how to secure a strong performance in both Controlled Assessment tasks.

Introduction

▶ **Putting it into practice** and **Target success** sections at the end of the units offer a chance to try exam-style tasks and questions, and to look in detail at questions using sample student responses and level indicators.

▶ Across all the sections you will find engaging activities that allow you to apply your skills to real-life situations. Activities guiding you in evaluating your work and in sharing your responses with others, will allow you to track your progression and to set individual targets. Model responses are also provided so you can get a feel for how you should be answering.

▶ The **Putting your skills into practice** section on page 199 provides exam-style resources to be used under timed conditions in the lead-up to your exam, with guidance on how to mark your own responses.

With the combination of all the targeted support and advice provided in this book, the guidance of your teacher, and your own efforts and preparations, your GCSE English Language course should be both enjoyable and rewarding. The more positive your approach and the more thorough your preparation, the better you will do.

English Language: at a glance

The table below outlines what you will be working on for the next two years in GCSE English Language. While the course will be demanding, it will hopefully also be engaging and rewarding. You can use this table for reference from time to time so that you can see what you have completed and what remains to be done.

While the various elements of the exam are displayed below in numerical order, this is not necessarily the order in which you will cover these in school.

Unit	Unit description	Content of each unit	Assessment options
Unit 1	External examination: 1 hour 45 minutes, worth 30 per cent of your final GCSE grade	Section A: Writing for purpose and audience Section B: Reading to access non-fiction and media texts	Every summer from 2018 and every January from 2019
Unit 2	Controlled Assessment: worth 20 per cent of your final GCSE grade	Speaking and listening Task 1: Individual presentation and interaction Task 2: Discussion Task 3: Role play	Every summer from 2018 and every January from 2019
Unit 3	Controlled Assessment: worth 20 per cent of your final GCSE grade	Studying spoken and written language Task 1: The study of spoken language Task 2: The study of written language	Every summer from 2019 and every January from 2020
Unit 4	External examination: 1 hour 45 minutes, worth 30 per cent of your final GCSE grade	Section A: Personal or Creative Writing Section B: Reading literary and non-fiction texts	Every summer from 2019 and every January from 2020

The Assessment Objectives and their role in the examining process

The English Language Specification sets out to test four Assessment Objectives (AOs). Your ability to use the English Language AOs will be tested in the four units of the course.

The four Assessment Objectives

AO1 Speaking and Listening

i Speak to communicate clearly and purposefully – this will require you to structure and sustain talk; adapt it to different situations and audiences; and use Standard English and a variety of techniques as appropriate.
ii Listen and respond to speakers' ideas and perspectives, and how they present meaning.
iii Interact with others shaping meanings through suggestions, comments and questions, and drawing ideas together.
iv Create and sustain different roles.

AO2 Study of Spoken Language

i Understand variations in spoken language, explaining why language changes in relation to contexts.
ii Evaluate the impact of spoken language choices in your own and others' uses.

AO3 Studying Written Language (Reading)

i Read and understand texts, selecting material appropriate to purpose, collating from different sources and making comparisons and cross-references as appropriate.
ii Develop and sustain interpretations of writers' ideas and perspectives.
iii Explain and evaluate how writers use linguistic, structural and presentational features to achieve effects and to engage and influence the reader.

AO4 Writing

i Write to communicate clearly, effectively and imaginatively, using and adapting forms and selecting vocabulary appropriate to task and purpose in ways that engage the reader.
ii Organise information and ideas into structured and sequenced sentences, paragraphs and whole texts, using a variety of linguistic and structural features to support cohesion and overall coherence.
iii Use a range of sentence structures for clarity, purpose and effect, with accurate spelling, punctuation and grammar.

Introduction

Where the Assessment Objectives are assessed within the four units

The table below shows where the individual AOs are assessed and the overall weightings for each AO.

Assessment Objective	Component weighting: External assessment Unit 1	Component weighting: Controlled Assessment Unit 2	Component weighting: Controlled Assessment Unit 3 Task 1	Component weighting: Controlled Assessment Unit 3 Task 2	Component weighting: External assessment Unit 4	Overall weighting
AO1	–	20%	–	–	–	20%
AO2	–	–	10%	–	–	10%
AO3	12.5%	–	–	10%	12.5%	35%
AO4	17.5%	–	–	–	17.5%	35%
Total weighting	30%	20%	10%	10%	30%	100%

Functional English

Functional English provides students with the skills, knowledge and understanding to use English in everyday, real-life situations.

The functional aspects of English are concentrated in:

▶ **Unit 1**: Writing for purpose and audience and Reading to access non-fiction and media texts; and

▶ **Unit 2**: Speaking and listening.

Students who complete these units will have the opportunity to achieve an endorsement for Functional English recorded on their GCSE certificate.

UNIT 1

Section A: Writing for purpose and audience

Introduction to writing for purpose and audience

Unit 1 is externally examined and is made up of two sections. The first section is Section A and it assesses writing for purpose and audience.

Target outcome: Clearly ordered writing that displays an appropriate sense of audience and purpose.

Target skills

The target skills you will learn about in this section will enable you to:
- ✓ write accurately and effectively
- ✓ use an appropriate writing form
- ✓ express ideas and information precisely and accurately
- ✓ select vocabulary to persuade and/or inform the reader
- ✓ use accurate grammar, spelling and punctuation.

Assessment Objectives

Your Assessment Objectives in this section are:

i   Communicate clearly and effectively using and adapting forms and selecting vocabulary appropriate to task and purpose in ways that engage the reader.

ii Organise information and ideas into structured and sequenced sentences, paragraphs and whole texts, using a variety of linguistic and structural features to support cohesion and overall coherence.

iii Use a range of sentence structures for clarity, purpose and effect, with accurate spelling, punctuation and grammar.

Exam question ❓

There is one task to complete in Section A.
You will have 55 minutes to produce an extended written response on a given topic.
It is advised that you spend 15 minutes planning your response, 30 minutes writing and 10 minutes checking and editing your work.

AO4 i, ii Planning for the task

The task will invite you to write on a specified topic, for example:

Write an article for your school magazine in which you try to persuade your audience of the benefits of homework.

Getting started is always the most difficult part of the writing process, but it may help you to know that even the most talented of writers find this a daunting task. The time allocated to this section includes time for thinking and planning, so use it wisely.

To produce an effective piece of writing in the time provided you must be clear about:

- **What** you are going to write – you must show an awareness of the specified subject and form.
- **Why** you are writing – you must show an understanding of your purpose.
- **Whom** you are writing for – you must show an awareness of your audience.

What are you writing?

Effective planning is the foundation for successful written work. Firstly, you must **generate ideas** relevant to the specified topic. Thinking under pressure can be challenging so you will need to practise your planning techniques. You will also benefit from discussing and debating issues in class and with your peers so that you develop strong personal opinions on a range of issues. In this section, being opinionated is an advantage!

You may wish to record your initial thoughts in table form, as a bulletpoint list or spider diagram. For example:

Agree	Disagree
Homework consolidates classroom learning.	Students do not do their best work at home.
Homework involves parents in their child's education.	Few homeworks are completed at home.
Homework develops good habits.	Homework increases stress.

Or:

- Homework lets teachers assess students' understanding.
- Homework helps students develop good habits.
- Homework makes a valuable contribution to student learning.

Or something like the spider diagram opposite.

Do not worry about writing neatly in your plan and at this stage there is no need to record ideas in full sentences – bullet points will do the job!

Activity

Work experience is a waste of time

Generate your own ideas on this new topic using one of the planning methods suggested on this page, or a method of your own that helps you organise your ideas.

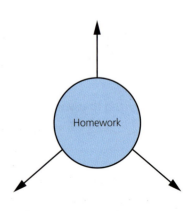

Planning for the task

Beginnings and endings

A successful **introduction** will:
- show understanding of audience, purpose and form
- be brief and concise
- be confident
- engage the audience.

Here are some of the different techniques you could use to achieve a strong introduction:
- **Humour**, e.g. 'Whoever invented homework clearly had no social life!'
- **Making your view clear immediately**, e.g. 'If you ask me, homework is child cruelty!'
- **A shocking statistic**, e.g. 'A whopping 89 per cent of 16-year-olds own more than one mobile device…'
- **Emotive language**, e.g. 'One must have sympathy for young people who are forced to endure six torturous hours in school and then waste their precious time slaving over a mountain of meaningless homework.'
- **A list**, e.g. 'Algebra, poetry, the periodic table, the causes of WWI… this is what your average GCSE student has to confront after six hours of school!'
- **A direct appeal to the audience**, e.g. 'I urge you to reclaim your social life and reconnect with your friends.'
- **An emphatic or provocative statement**, e.g. 'Homework sucks!'
- **A question**, e.g. 'Is homework really necessary?'
- **An anecdote**, e.g. 'Yesterday I left school with a heavy heart, and an equally heavy schoolbag. My "kind" teachers had gifted me a huge volume of homework and I'm not afraid to admit that when I got home, I cracked! Homework had reduced me to a snivelling mess!'

Activity

Identify the strengths and weaknesses of these three introductions.

> My name is Mark and today I will be talking about social media. Some people think social media is evil and others think it is the greatest thing ever invented. I will be telling you what I think…

> 'Social media does more harm than good'? What a ludicrous statement and clearly an opinion held by one who has yet to discover the wonders of Facebook, the joys of Snapchat and the thrills of Twitter. My friends, we all know social media is a force for good!

> Allow me to begin with a confession… I loathe Facebook, I detest Snapchat and I twitch at the very thought of Tweeting! For me social media is dangerous, unnecessary and desired only by those who are in fact unsociable.

Write three different introductions to the task:

Write a speech that you will deliver to your classmates, persuading them to spend less time on social media.

Share your strongest introduction with your class and vote for the best overall introduction.

3

UNIT 1 SECTION A: WRITING FOR PURPOSE AND AUDIENCE

Conclusions

Conclusions should also be planned, so they leave a lasting impression on your audience. Without effective planning you run the risk of relying on a predictable or flat ending, so you should be working to engage your reader right to the very last punctuation mark!

Ways to conclude include:

- Posing a question to encourage your reader to reflect on the issue, e.g. 'It has been said that this is the first generation of kids who will die before their parents. Surely we cannot allow this to happen?'
- Ending with a call to action to try to motivate your audience, e.g. 'Let's all do something about this – before it really is too late!'
- Ending with an emphatic statement to conclude confidently and assertively, e.g. 'The time has come to put this debate to rest once and for all; mobile phones have no place in classrooms!'
- Appealing to the heart and mind of your audience, e.g. 'Today, the future is in our hands and together we can create a better tomorrow.'

Look out for interesting and inspiring openings and conclusions. Good places to find them are: the school library, newspaper and magazine articles, biographies and autobiographies.

Why are you writing?

Every piece of writing has a **purpose**, in other words a **reason why** it was written. This is also referred to as the writer's **intention**.

A piece of writing may have **more than one** purpose. The writer's intention may be to:

- persuade
- stimulate
- inform
- advertise or sell
- entertain
- explain
- motivate
- argue a point of view
- express feelings
- provoke emotions
- challenge or confront
- warn
- inspire
- deliberately shock.

Developing ideas to achieve purpose

Once you have planned successfully you will know what points you wish to make, but to achieve your purpose you must be able to develop and expand upon each of your chosen points.

Activity

Look back at the initial ideas that you generated on page 2 to complete the following task:

'Work experience is a waste of time.'[1] ← [1] Topic.

[2] Form. → Write a speech[2] for young people,[3] in which you outline your views[4] on the benefits of work experience. ← [3] Audience.

[4] Purpose – in this instance you are arguing a point of view.

Planning for the task

Below one student has commenced their planning by generating points that could be made when responding to the task on the previous page.

Disagree
- It helps young people acquire a real understanding of the workplace.
- It helps young people make more informed career choices.
- Employers nowadays look for more than qualifications.

Work experience is a waste of time

Agree
- Too many students are disappointed by their placement.
- It can be impossible to get placements for certain careers.
- Students see it as nothing more than a week out of school.

Alone, these points would not be enough to begin writing. Before you begin writing you must:

1 be certain you can successfully expand upon each point
2 identify the strongest points that will enhance your response by engaging your reader and even convincing them to agree with you
3 identify the order in which you will make your points.

Once you have a range of ideas, you are ready to expand your thinking by developing each point in sufficient detail. You cannot convincingly make an audience engage with your ideas in one sentence, so you must successfully develop each point in sufficient detail.

The planning statements in the diagram above can function as **topic sentences**. These are sentences, often placed at the beginning of a paragraph, that indicate what main idea will be addressed in that paragraph. Topic sentences **inform** your reader of your thoughts, that is, **what** you think about the issue. To achieve your purpose, you will need to **explain** further in order to let the reader know **why** you hold a particular view.

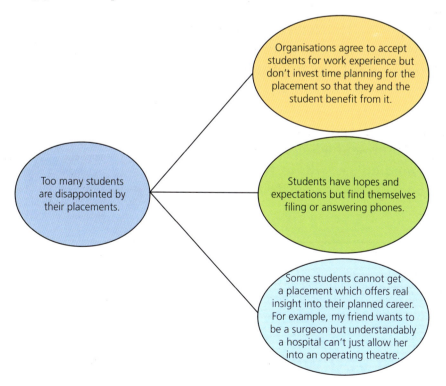

UNIT 1 SECTION A: WRITING FOR PURPOSE AND AUDIENCE

Once you are satisfied that your initial planning ideas can be developed, you should decide which points are most important and rank them in order, starting with the strongest. Remember you have only 30 minutes to write your answer, so you may need to abandon some of your initial ideas. Aim to have five or six points that you will use in the essay.

You can see on the previous page how one initial idea can be expanded and developed. In the example below, the opening topic sentence outlines how this paragraph will discuss the fact that many students are disappointed by work experience. It **informs** the reader of the writer's viewpoint. In the remainder of the paragraph the writer **argues a point of view** by **explaining why** they believe that work experience is a waste of time for many. They also share **persuasive** anecdotal evidence with the reader to support this point of view:

It is no secret that a significant number of students are totally let down by their work experience placement and return to school feeling dejected and demotivated.[1] I firmly believe[2] the fault lies with the host organisations, as too many willingly accept these students but fail to invest in any prior planning[3] to ensure the experience is an enriching[4] one that benefits both student and organisation. Instead, they ignorantly assume one placement student is as useless as the next; good for nothing other than making tea, answering phones and filing.[5] As each hour passes, the enthusiasm and ambitions of the student shrink and boredom sets in.[6] What's worse is that those high-flying students, with the greatest ambitions, are often denied entry into their chosen workplace. For as long as I can remember my friend Jenny has longed to be a surgeon; while the rest of us were singing into our hairbrushes she was trawling through medical encyclopaedias.[7] You[8] can imagine her utter[9] disappointment when she was tasked with filing reports in medical records as the theatre was strictly out of bounds. What a waste of talent![10]

---

[1] Topic sentence makes clear that this paragraph will explore how students are let down by work experience.

[3] Use of alliteration to inject liveliness.

[6] Developed explanation that convincingly argues a point of view using language to engage the reader.

[7] Use of anecdote to make the argument more convincing.

[9] Adjective 'utter' to emphasise the extent of her disappointment.

[2] Confident expression, beginning an explanation that concentrates on the responsibility of hosts who accept students for work experience.

[4] Impressive vocabulary.

[5] List of three emphasises the variety of boring tasks that are demanded of work experience students.

[8] 'You' used as a direct address to the reader to establish a connection.

[10] Strong emphatic statement to close the paragraph with valid use of exclamation mark.

Activity

Look back at your initial planning on the topic of work experience. Take each of your ideas and plan how you would develop it to successfully achieve your purpose. Then write two detailed paragraphs in which you argue your point of view.

Whom are you writing for?

As well as identifying clear reasons why you are writing, you need to consider the **intended audience** for whom you are writing.

Planning for the task

For example, your intended audience might be:
- newspaper readers
- your classmates
- a specific audience, e.g. parents of teenagers
- a particular age group, e.g. adults or young children
- people with a specific interest, e.g. in sport.

Purpose and audience are closely linked. You must keep both in mind when you plan what you will write and how you are going to write it.

Your audience will influence your language choices but you should be aware that in an exam situation you should always use formal language and adopt an appropriate tone.

Activity

Read through the texts below, which are all about exam pressure. Working in pairs or small groups, identify:
- the target audience for each text
- the purpose of each text
- how the writer of each text has used language to achieve their purpose.

Then, compile a list of techniques that writers use to connect with their audience.

Text A

Are exams causing you stress?

If so, remember you are not alone. Many young people find examinations a source of stress and anxiety. Stress affects individuals differently and can impact on many aspects of our lives. Did you know that your appetite can be affected by your emotions? Did you know that stress limits your ability to concentrate? While stress can be, well, stressful, a little dose of it now and then is actually good for us! Whatever your stress levels, the important thing is to acknowledge your feelings and learn how to manage your stress. There are lots of organisations that want to help you cope with stress...

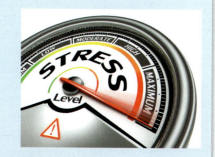

Text B

Dear parent,

As your son or daughter prepares to sit important GCSE examinations, we want to support you in encouraging your child to develop good habits to prevent any stress that might be caused by the experience of sitting examinations. Our young people deserve to succeed and we have a shared responsibility to support them during the coming months. As experts in education we understand the various stress triggers, how stress affects our young people and, more importantly, strategies to help them manage their stress.

Text C

It is estimated that 3 million teenagers will be sitting exams this summer, but recent research reveals concerning statistics about soaring levels of examination stress. A survey conducted by children's charity T.E.E.N. revealed that an alarming 93 per cent of 16-year-olds admitted to experiencing high levels of anxiety related to school exams. What is more concerning is that 54 per cent of those surveyed felt they had not received any support or advice on how to deal with their stress.

To discover more, click on the link below and view our short video on ways to conquer examination stress: www.teentrust.co.uk/conquer.stress

UNIT 1 SECTION A: WRITING FOR PURPOSE AND AUDIENCE

Establishing a positive rapport

There are various ways to connect with your audience and you should use a variety of approaches throughout your writing.

- Address your reader directly – the personal pronoun 'you' can be effective in making your reader feel that your text is relevant to them.
- Use inclusive language – words such as 'we', 'us' and 'our' give your reader the impression they are involved.
- Use imperatives – imperatives make your writing seem confident and assertive, e.g. 'Think about the improvements that could be made if…'
- Ask questions to engage your reader, e.g. 'When did you last exercise?'
- Use emotive language to appeal to the heart and mind of your reader, e.g. 'Unless you use social media sensibly, you are at real risk of encountering some cruel comments from cowards who set out to shatter your self-confidence.'

Adding authority

To make your reader believe in what you say, you must make your writing convincing. Apart from expressing your ideas confidently, introducing other sources will add weight to your writing. Ways you could do this include:

- Using statistics to give the impression you are informed about the topic and to endorse your claims, e.g. 'A whopping 78 per cent of teenagers have a part-time job.' If you feel a statistic will enhance your writing, remember to make it sound credible.
- Disguising your opinion as fact, e.g. 'Social media is poisoning the minds of our youth!' If you promote your opinions strongly, it can make it difficult to disagree with them. Readers will be swayed by confident assertions, but don't overdo it!
- Referring to an expert – readers will accept the word of an 'expert', especially when it supports what you are saying, e.g. 'My concern about the use of technology in the classroom is shared by Professor Kelly from Queen's University, Belfast who is on record as saying, "overuse of technology can contribute to low concentration levels in learners."'

Activity

The following extract has been taken from a response in which the student is arguing that registering for organ donorship should be compulsory. Read through it in pairs and discuss the prompt questions, which encourage you to think about how the student has achieved their purpose and established a rapport with their audience.

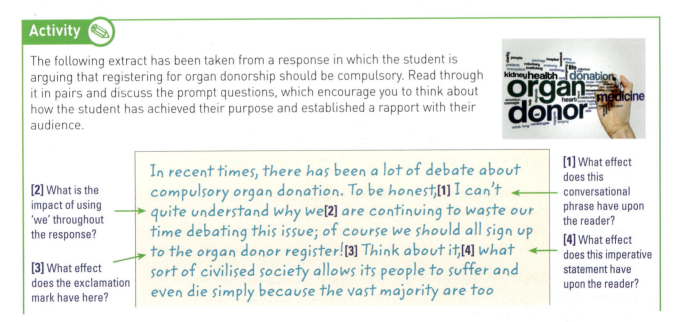

[1] What effect does this conversational phrase have upon the reader?

[2] What is the impact of using 'we' throughout the response?

[3] What effect does the exclamation mark have here?

[4] What effect does this imperative statement have upon the reader?

> In recent times, there has been a lot of debate about compulsory organ donation. To be honest,[1] I can't quite understand why we[2] are continuing to waste our time debating this issue; of course we should all sign up to the organ donor register![3] Think about it,[4] what sort of civilised society allows its people to suffer and even die simply because the vast majority are too

Planning for the task

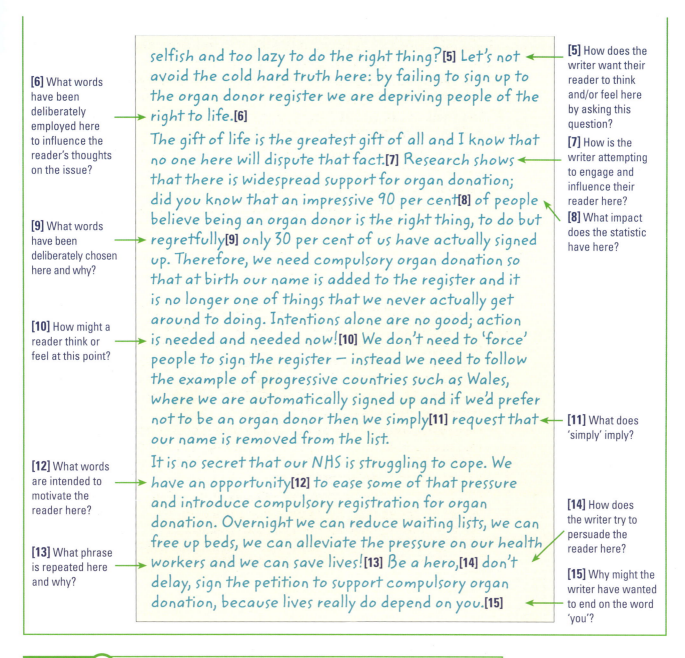

[6] What words have been deliberately employed here to influence the reader's thoughts on the issue?

[9] What words have been deliberately chosen here and why?

[10] How might a reader think or feel at this point?

[12] What words are intended to motivate the reader here?

[13] What phrase is repeated here and why?

selfish and too lazy to do the right thing? **[5]** Let's not avoid the cold hard truth here: by failing to sign up to the organ donor register we are depriving people of the right to life. **[6]**

The gift of life is the greatest gift of all and I know that no one here will dispute that fact. **[7]** Research shows that there is widespread support for organ donation; did you know that an impressive 90 per cent**[8]** of people believe being an organ donor is the right thing, to do but regretfully**[9]** only 30 per cent of us have actually signed up. Therefore, we need compulsory organ donation so that at birth our name is added to the register and it is no longer one of things that we never actually get around to doing. Intentions alone are no good; action is needed and needed now! **[10]** We don't need to 'force' people to sign the register — instead we need to follow the example of progressive countries such as Wales, where we are automatically signed up and if we'd prefer not to be an organ donor then we simply**[11]** request that our name is removed from the list.

It is no secret that our NHS is struggling to cope. We have an opportunity**[12]** to ease some of that pressure and introduce compulsory registration for organ donation. Overnight we can reduce waiting lists, we can free up beds, we can alleviate the pressure on our health workers and we can save lives! **[13]** Be a hero, **[14]** don't delay, sign the petition to support compulsory organ donation, because lives really do depend on you. **[15]**

[5] How does the writer want their reader to think and/or feel here by asking this question?

[7] How is the writer attempting to engage and influence their reader here?

[8] What impact does the statistic have here?

[11] What does 'simply' imply?

[14] How does the writer try to persuade the reader here?

[15] Why might the writer have wanted to end on the word 'you'?

Activity

Select one of the tasks below. Write two paragraphs in which you promote your point of view and use a range of techniques to engage and convince your reader.

'To succeed, you must read.' Write a speech persuading your classmates of the benefits of reading.

Write a blog in which you present your views on the following statement, 'Tattoos and piercings do not belong in the workplace.'

Swap with a partner and evaluate each other's writing by identifying strengths and areas for improvement.

Once you have planned your response and have a clear idea about the points you are making in your writing, you must turn your attention to the form that your writing will take.

AO4 i Getting the form right

Your writing for purpose and audience task is likely to ask you to write in one of the following forms:
- A speech
- A letter
- A magazine or newspaper article
- A blog.

You should demonstrate your understanding of form early on in your response. The identified form might also influence how you conclude, for example a speech will conclude very differently from a letter.

Activity

Study the extracts below and identify the form of each from the list above:

> What is with teachers who think they exist just to dish out homework? What really makes my blood boil is that tomorrow the teachers will briefly scan the page, mark a small tick and move on to the next student. All they will know is they succeeded in making me a captive in my own bedroom, robbed me of the privilege of watching my favourite programmes and denied me any meaningful conversation with family and friends!

> Good morning classmates, without wanting to offend anyone, can I just say how exhausted you all look this morning? I'm guessing that like me, most of you were up late last night slaving over horrific homework. Am I right?

> Dear Principal Jones, on behalf of the student body I wish to outline our strong objection to the current homework policy within our school. As you are aware, it is common practice for students to have an additional three hours of home study to complete every night…

> Down with homework! Homework has often been regarded as a necessary evil, something to ensure a student has sufficiently understood their classroom learning, but increasingly many schools are reviewing their homework policies and asking, does homework really improve standards?

Whatever form is stated, you should concentrate on the content and tone of your writing rather than trying to capture the appearance of a specific form. For example, if writing an article you may wish to include a headline or subheadings, but there is no need to write in columns or to include images and captions. If writing a letter, you do not need to include addresses.

Activity

For each of the introductory paragraphs above, compose a suitable concluding paragraph that demonstrates your appreciation of the form. For a reminder of the different types of conclusions you might use, see page 4.

Using appropriate techniques

AO4 i, ii

On page 8 you learned about techniques that could be used to connect with your audience and add authority to your writing. Regardless of the topic and the form, you should strive to produce writing that is interesting and lively, which is not always as easy as it seems. As the extract below demonstrates, writing that is overly reliant on statistical or factual information can become dull for the reader.

> About 106,000 people in the UK die each year due to smoking. Smoking-related deaths are mainly due to cancers, COPD (chronic obstructive pulmonary disease) and heart disease.
>
> Cigarette smoke contains over 4,000 chemicals, including over fifty known carcinogens (causes of cancer).
>
> About 30,000 people in the UK die from lung cancer each year. More than 80 per cent of these deaths are directly related to smoking.
>
> (www.nhs.uk/smokefree/why-quit/smoking-health-problems)

Activity

Use the information above to write a paragraph that warns the audience of the dangers associated with smoking. You should convey the information in a more engaging style.

Emotive language

While the information about smoking stated above is concerning, it is not expressed in a way that engages us or invites us to read on. To avoid boring your reader, you should ensure you use a variety of language techniques that will add interest and hold the attention of your reader. Your choice of words can trigger an emotional response in your audience. As the short extract that follows shows, particular **adjectives** and **adverbs** can influence how your audience feel.

> We all love a **gloriously hot** summer's day, the sort of day that brings a heat so **intense** and so **stifling** that it demands you do nothing else but get outdoors and soak it up. The sort of day that brings the idiots out in droves. You know who I'm referring to, those sun-seekers who **carelessly** lounge on the sun bed, inviting the **punishing** sun to roast their **fair, freckled** skin, **totally oblivious** to the risks they are taking.

UNIT 1 SECTION A: WRITING FOR PURPOSE AND AUDIENCE

> **Activity**
>
> Practise using persuasive techniques by selecting a television advert that you think is very persuasive (charity adverts are usually a popular choice here!).
>
> Imagine you are a scriptwriter. Compose a new voiceover for the advert. Your words, phrases and techniques should leave an impression upon your audience and add meaning to the visuals on screen.
>
> Read your script to the class over your chosen advert with the volume muted. Vote for the most persuasive voiceover and be able to explain why it is a worthy winner.

Persuasive language

Advertisers are experts at selecting and manipulating words in order to **persuade** their target audiences. You too can use these techniques in your written work.

Emotive language, like that in the example above, is often used in adverts, but other types of vocabulary are also employed:

- Flattering adjectives – to increase reader engagement, e.g. 'As an intelligent individual, you will know that…'
- Imperatives – special words that guide or instruct the audience, e.g. 'Look at this!'
- Descriptive details – to entice the audience to buy the product/support the cause, e.g. 'This chance-of-a-lifetime experience…'
- The personal pronoun 'you' – for direct appeal, e.g. 'You won't be able to take your eyes off…'
- Verbs in the present tense – to convey immediacy or excitement, e.g. 'It's thrilling to be telling you about…'
- Informal language – to communicate friendliness, e.g. 'Hey, what are you waiting for?' or 'So, don't hang about…'
- Modal verbs – to make suggestions and offer advice, e.g. 'Giving up smoking *would* be a good idea as this habit will affect your health.'
- Puns and other forms of wordplay – often for humorous effect.
- Figures of speech – such as similes, hyperbole/exaggeration and alliteration.

Fact and opinion

Supporting your arguments with information, evidence and/or opinion, reinforces your viewpoint and is highly persuasive to the audience.

If you follow this with **further explanation** and/or use **rhetorical devices** to emphasise your key points, then you will be well on your way to creating effective persuasive writing. For example:

- 'Eighty per cent of people who smoke twenty cigarettes a day for twenty years will have a smoking-related disease. Fact! Half of them will die of cancer. Fact! Want to hear more? Probably not, if you're a smoker – but I make no apology for what I am about to say next.'
- 'Couch potatoes, hoodies, druggies, layabouts, vandals, hoodlums – just some of the labels teenagers today have been branded with. Is this fair, I ask you?'

Expressing **opinions that appear to be facts** is an effective way to provoke a reaction from an audience and can be most persuasive:

- 'The truth is that most football fans are thugs!'
- 'Everybody knows that women are better drivers than men.'

Facts and opinions integrated into and combined with a **variety of sentence constructions** can have powerfully persuasive results:

- 'Smoking kills. It's as simple as that!'
- 'No less shocking is the fact that…'

Using appropriate techniques

Activity

Write a 250-word article for your school magazine entitled 'You are what you eat', which gives advice and warns about the dangers of consuming too much sugar and junk food.

Read the 'facts and figures' and opinions below, and consider how you might integrate these into your article.

Facts and figures
The average child consumes thirty teaspoons of sugar a day.
The average can of juice has ten teaspoons of sugar.
In the past decade sugar consumption increased by 23 per cent.
Eating a large hamburger meal with a cola takes about six minutes to eat, but you'll have to walk for over six hours at a brisk pace to burn off all the calories.
Eighty-five per cent of 16-year-olds admit they would be unable to cook themselves a meal.
An unhealthy diet that contains high quantities of sugar, salt and processed food, increases your risk of diabetes, heart disease and stroke.

Opinions
It costs more to eat healthily; junk food is much cheaper and more convenient.
Food labels are too confusing to read.
It's my body so I should be free to eat what I enjoy!

Many students like devising acronyms to help them remember key techniques to make their writing interesting and to help them engage with their audience. A common acrostic is:

- **I** Imperatives
- **N** Name an expert
- **A** Alliteration
- **F** Facts
- **O** Opinions
- **R** Rhetorical devices
- **E** Emotive language
- **S** Statistics
- **T** Triples/lists of three

While these can be useful, there are many more techniques than those listed here and you should aim to employ a wide variety.

UNIT 1 SECTION A: WRITING FOR PURPOSE AND AUDIENCE

Counter-arguing

When you are writing to promote your opinion, you should always be mindful that there will be others who hold an opposing point of view. It is sometimes necessary to acknowledge this fact and engage with your opponent's view. To signal this, you could state:

- 'My opponents will claim…'
- 'I know there are those individuals who will have you believe that…'
- 'Some of you may challenge my views here, even going so far as to state…'
- 'There will be many who will criticise my stance and instead they believe…'

While it is good to show an awareness of your opposition's view, there is no need to go into it in any great detail. Instead you should work on your ability to **counter-argue**. This means that you reject their claims and expose the weaknesses in their argument. You can show your skill at doing this by using phrases such as:

- '…but this argument is weak as…'
- 'These people are misinformed as…'
- 'I totally reject these claims as…'
- 'There may be some validity to these claims but what they fail to consider is…'

Read the example below and see how one student, writing on the topic 'Reality television is cruel television', has demonstrated an awareness of their opposition and composed a suitable counter-argument:

> Now, I know there are people out there who will claim that those who appear on reality television shows, such as The X Factor and Big Brother, know exactly what they are letting themselves in for. My opponents will argue that by appearing on these shows, the contestants are inviting public humiliation, but this is a weak argument! The truth is that many of these contestants find themselves figures of ridicule because of one person — the cruel, ratings-hungry editor who does not care what happens to the contestants once their five minutes of fame has ended.

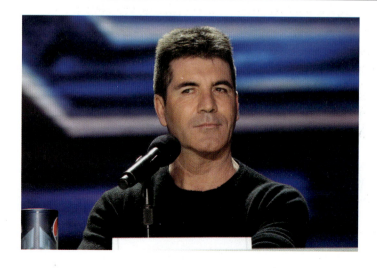

14

Using appropriate techniques

> **Activity**
>
> Practise your counter-arguing skills by completing each of the statements below:
> 1. 'My critics will have you believe that abolishing homework will make school students more motivated during school hours…'
> 2. 'There will be people here today who think footballers deserve these extortionate salaries, but…'
> 3. 'My opponents will claim that boxing is not a safe sport and should be banned…'

> **Activity**
>
> Read the letter below, which states the case for lengthening the school day. Write a response in which you promote your views.
>
> Use language to connect ideas, to add authority, and to engage and connect with your reader.
>
> Acknowledge your opposition and compose a suitable counter-argument.
>
> ---
>
> Dear Student,
>
> To improve upon the already high standards achieved by students at Hartswood College, I am proposing an extension to the school day, which will see us continue our studies every day until 5 o'clock.
>
> I assure you this decision has been made in the best interests of students so you may have the best chance of excelling in your examinations. As you are aware, Hartswood College is already the top-performing school in this community, and I want us to continue to deliver the very best learning opportunities. In fact, should this proposal go ahead it will require significant financial investment to fund additional running costs and staff wages, but the management team believe you are worth that investment.
>
> We propose that the extended school day will commence next academic year, and while it may require some getting used to, I believe the majority of staff and students will experience a smooth transition given that already every day staff and students are on premises well after 3:15, attending revision classes, studying in the library and participating in sports clubs. As your principal, I take great pride in the fact that there is a strong desire to continue the school experience beyond 3:15 and I want to deliver that to all our students.
>
> An initial survey of parents has confirmed there is large-scale support for this exciting proposal, with over 90 per cent welcoming an extension to the school day. Your parents recognise us as leading the way and I am confident it is only a matter of time before other schools follow our example.
>
> At this stage I wish to consult more widely. So as a valued student of Hartswood College, I invite you personally to respond with your views on this exciting proposal. All submissions should be emailed to me by next Friday.
>
> Yours,
>
> Principal Peters

AO4 ii, iii — Structuring effectively

In order to **communicate** your ideas successfully, you need to develop your point of view in a series of convincing persuasive arguments and express these in a **confident** manner.

Developing your ideas fluently is all about effective structuring – in other words **how** you present your thoughts to your audience. Structure is the skeleton of a piece of writing – it gives shape to the 'body' of your ideas!

To make your written work coherent, your ideas and arguments need to be organised into paragraphs. Remember, the basic rule is to keep one main idea to one paragraph. Your introductory paragraph should be fairly short but engaging. The main section of your writing then consists of several detailed paragraphs that demonstrate your ability to use language and to maintain your audience's interest to achieve your purpose.

Point. Evidence. Explanation.

The Point, Evidence, Explanation (P.E.E.) technique is a useful strategy for developing individual paragraphs.

- Keep to one key **Point** per paragraph.
- Support the point with **Evidence**, to add weight to your opinion.
- Then offer **Explanation** to further reinforce your viewpoint.

Here is an example of one point made using the P.E.E. technique:

> Obesity in children has reached epidemic proportions. Sir Liam Donaldson, the Chief Medical Officer, recently described obesity as 'a time bomb' waiting to explode. Today, one in twelve 6-year-olds is obese. Among older children the proportion is even higher: here the figure is one in seven 15-year-olds. These are figures that should shock us all but, more importantly, should shock irresponsible parents into changing disastrous diets to healthier options for their children. After all, it is only what they deserve!

Linking ideas

If you have planned effectively you will know the order in which you will promote your ideas. It is also vital, however, to link your ideas so that one paragraph 'flows' fluently into the next. There are two ways to achieve this connection:

1. Use discourse markers, e.g. 'furthermore', 'however', 'moreover', 'although', 'despite', 'nevertheless'.
2. Use linking sentences so that each paragraph connects with what has just been stated but develops your point of view further, e.g. 'As well as benefiting your physical health, regular exercise can also improve your mental health…'

Activity

Select one of the linking sentences below and write the paragraph that would go before and the one that would follow on from your chosen linking sentence:

- 'As well as being expensive, school uniform also is impractical.'
- 'Of course, exams are not the only pressure facing young people today.'
- 'Poor behaviour is not the only problem that comes with introducing technology into classrooms.'
- 'Not only is it unfair for schools to forbid parents to take their children on holiday during term time, it is also hypocritical as many school trips take place during term time.'

Sentence structures and forms

You should also try to make your writing livelier by using a variety of sentence lengths:

- Short sentences can be used for impact and to convey strength of feeling, e.g. 'That's disgusting!'
- Longer sentences can be used to convey either several linked ideas or detailed information to your reader, or to emphasise a point.

Structuring effectively

You should work on using a combination of long and short sentences in your writing to keep the reader engaged with your topic.

In addition to varying sentence lengths, you should aim to use a variety of sentence forms. Questions can be used to engage your reader by encouraging them to think. Direct speech can make your writing interesting, e.g. '"The decisions you make today determine your tomorrow." If I had a pound for every time my dad speaks those words, I'd be able to retire comfortably. What is it with parents who think they know it all?'

Activity

Improve the paragraph below by re-writing the sentences so that the ideas are expressed so as to make a greater impact upon the reader:

> I really think if someone wants to succeed that they should always do their homework. Homework is not always easy. Homework is not always fun. Homework is not always interesting. Homework is essential. When I complain about homework my mum tells me to think of it as short-term pain for long-term gain.

Punctuation

Accurate punctuation is an essential part of any written response, but you can also use it in particular ways to demonstrate your ability to use it to enhance meaning:

- **Exclamation marks (!)** can be an effective way of conveying strong feelings and a forceful tone, e.g. 'Do I believe young people today have it too easy? Absolutely!' Be careful not to overuse the exclamation mark or it will lose its impact.
- **Ellipses (...)** can be used to create anticipation and entice your reader to read on. For example:

> Young people today face enormous pressure from school. Let me explain... the youth of today are constantly told that qualifications are no longer enough and that on top of school work they must volunteer, mentor and gain experience through part-time work.

- **Semi colons (;)** are used to separate longer items in a list. For example:

> On a daily basis a typical teen gets through: two cans of fizzy juice; three packets of crisps; two bars of chocolate; one packet of chewing gum and half a packet of biscuits. Or to put that another way, over thirty tablespoons of sugar.

The semi-colon can also be used to link two independent clauses that are closely connected. Remember, whatever comes before and after the semi-colon should be able to stand alone as individual sentences, but by using the semi-colon you are stressing the connection. For example:
- 'Some people are in favour of school uniform; others want it abolished.'
- 'I have a Science test tomorrow; I simply can't go out tonight.'

AO4 i, ii, iii — Getting the right tone

Consider the differences in tone in these sentences:
- 'Please be quiet.'
- 'Shut your mouth!'
- 'Would you ever shut that gob of yours?'

Each speaker wants someone to stop talking, but the choice of words makes all the difference to whether the effect is intended to be respectful, rude or insulting.

The tone you use can vary. In fact, tonal shifts in a piece of writing can add interest – humorous touches are often appropriate and appreciated by an audience, even if the subject matter is serious.

Your tone should always be appropriate to the task. A sense of outrage is fine but there is no need to be inappropriate or abusive, even when expressing strong views. This would never persuade an audience to agree with your viewpoint – quite the reverse. It is important to be aware of your tone as this has an effect on the audience. Be assertive but never aggressive.

If you choose words that convey a sense of liveliness and inject an enthusiastic tone into your writing, the audience is more likely to empathise with your views.

Informal language is more conversational in tone and can sometimes be put to good use in written work:
- 'So, come on, let's think about this.'
- 'But, hang on a moment. What exactly are we talking about here?'

Activity

Read the text below, in which an agony aunt has responded to a reader seeking advice before going on a first date. As you read, identify the tonal changes and consider how these are achieved.

> Dear reader,
>
> Firstly, please be aware that your anxieties are completely normal. It is common to feel nervous before a first date but, rather than dwell on these feelings, focus on the fact that this person asked you out because they like you. That is an excellent starting point for any friendship or relationship!
>
> You raised concerns about what to wear. It's great to want to make a good impression, but your clothes are not the reason you are going on a date so do not over-think things. Wear something comfortable and which makes you feel good about yourself. If you feel good, you will be confident and in control. I would recommend finding out where you are going as you might feel foolish paintballing in a dress and high heels! You don't want to feel self-conscious or uncomfortable as I guarantee this will come across and might stop you enjoying yourself.
>
> Above all else, relax and be aware that your date is also likely to be feeling anxious. Think over what you both have in common and perhaps prepare a few conversation topics to help put you both at ease. It is always a good idea to spend a first date in a place where there are other people around and to let a friend or a parent know where you are going. Finally, the most important thing of all is to be yourself – you are an amazing individual!

Activity

Write a letter of advice to a student who is nervous about starting GCSE studies. Be sure to use appropriate tones and language that reassure and engage your reader.

Ensuring accuracy

AO4 i, ii, iii

You have learnt how important it is to think about:
- what you are going to write
- whom you are writing for
- why you are writing
- the form your writing is going to take
- how you are going to express your views
- how you are going to use language to achieve your purpose.

This list is about the planning and writing process, but reviewing and checking your work for accuracy is also essential if you are to communicate your ideas as effectively as possible.

Be sure to leave yourself at least ten minutes in which to review and check what you have put down on paper. This is something you must always do if you want to maximise your performance!

Check your writing to get the best possible mark

- Have you structured the piece adequately?
- Is there sufficient variety in sentence construction?
- Does it all make sense – do any sections require reorganising so that the meaning is clear?
- Are your word choices precise enough?

Activity

Look back at your response to the proposal to extend the school day (p.15). Assess this piece by listing three strengths of your response. Identify what you need to work on to improve your writing. Locate a section within the response where this weakness is apparent and re-write it, making the necessary improvements.

UNIT 1

Writing for purpose and audience: target success

Matching grades to writing for purpose and audience

In Section A the essential qualities that will be required are highlighted at the important grade boundaries. Read these descriptions *carefully*; they tell you what your answer should be like.

Grade C writing displays:
- ✔ successful adaptation of form
- ✔ an appropriate sense of audience and purpose
- ✔ clearly structured and increasingly fluent writing
- ✔ a range of sentence structures, and varied vocabulary to create different effects and engage the reader's interest
- ✔ effective paragraphing for clear development of ideas
- ✔ accurate spelling and punctuation.

Grade A/A* writing displays:
- ✔ confident and assured control of form and style appropriate to task and purpose
- ✔ a positive rapport with the audience through logical argument or persuasive force
- ✔ linguistic and structural features used skilfully to achieve coherence
- ✔ a wide range of accurate sentence structures
- ✔ choices of vocabulary, punctuation and spelling that are ambitious and largely correct, with errors limited to one-off mistakes.

Practice question

Respond to this sample writing for purpose and audience task:

Write an article for your local paper in which you challenge the claim that 'young people today have it too easy'.

Response time: 55 minutes.
15 minutes thinking and planning
30 minutes writing
10 minutes checking your writing

Target success

Sample student response

Do 'young people have it too easy'?[1]

I challenge anyone to walk in my shoes for a day and still claim that young people today have it too easy![2] I'm not an extraordinary young person, in fact I'm quite content to be 'average' because, believe me, holding on to that label is pretty tough given the endless homework, the crippling pressure to secure that all-important impressive GCSE profile and, of course, the strength required to survive the world of social media.[3] Honestly, there's nothing 'easy' about being a teen in the twenty-first century.[4]

Homework is not a twenty-first century phenomenon but it is increasing in its demands and swallowing up[5] our precious free time. After an intensive day of study the last thing we students need is a further dose of essay writing and problem solving. We want to be outdoors, socialising and remembering what it is to have a childhood. We want to indulge in our favourite foods and lounge on the sofa watching our favourite programmes. We want[6] rest and relaxation and we deserve it. What adds to our frustration here is that we are increasingly told that qualifications are no longer enough![7] Oh no, now we must be volunteering to gain insight into the adult workplace or we must acquire additional skills such as first aid or coaching. That's fine, except all these things demand time and young people do not live in an alternate time zone, we get the same 24 hours as adults[8] and we have more than enough going in our already chaotic[9] lives to fill it, thanks very much.

Pressure is not exclusive to school[10] because, as we all know, life outside of the classroom can be stressful. Young people embrace technology; we do not fear it.[11] The smart phone is an essential piece of tech for any teenager and you're no one unless you're on social media. I myself was lured into the world of social media a few years ago; long before I was actually old enough to have an account and without the consent of my parents. But, well, we all appreciate how easy

[1] Headline demonstrates clear appreciation of form.

[2] Engaging introduction that demonstrates awareness of audience and purpose.

[3] Long sentence to emphasise the pressures faced by young people.

[4] Emphatic statement to close introduction and establish a confident tone.

[5] Exaggeration for emotive effect.

[6] Repetition of 'we want' emphasises the longings of young people. Inclusive use of 'we' implies the writer is speaking on behalf of all young people.

[7] Punctuation for impact.

[8] Use of humour to add interest and a welcome change of tone.

[9] Adjective chosen to make the reader appreciate just how busy the life of a young person can be.

[10] Effective linking between paragraphs and clear sense of progression.

[11] Use of semi-colon to link ideas within a sentence.

21

UNIT 1 SECTION A: WRITING FOR PURPOSE AND AUDIENCE

it is to become part of that world, don't we?[12] All it takes are a few creative lies and a quick click of the mouse and you're in, a member of an exclusive group and desperate to attract 'likes' and 'friends'. In reality, you need skin like titanium[13] to withstand the judgemental comments, the body shaming and the cyber-bullying[14] that take place on social media. Some will say I'm overreacting and claim that it's easy to remove yourself from unpleasant experiences on social media sites,[15] but that's not actually true. Turning off a computer or a mobile phone does not end your pain. Erasing a comment or a person does not erase your hurt.[16] 'Sticks and stones will break your bones but names will never hurt you.'[17] That's what my grandmother used to say, and for her that may have been true but words do hurt and they do scar, especially if you are an impressionable and vulnerable young person. Did you know that an alarming 68 per cent of teenagers have experienced cyber-bullying? That's shocking![18] Dr Ben Lewis, an expert in mental health, confirms that young people are suffering increasing levels of anxiety and low self-esteem, which is made worse by their online experiences. He states, 'It's a worrying trend but the internet is here to stay and we must take action to educate our young people to use social media responsibly and safely.'[19]

So let's shatter this myth that young people today have it too easy! Let's give our young people the credit they deserve and recognise that every day they are growing a little more resilient, they are moving a little closer to their goals and working a little harder to get through that mountain of homework.[20]

[12] Engaging conversational tone established through use of question.

[13] Original use of simile.

[14] List of three to emphasise the unpleasant side of social media.

[15] Awareness of opposition.

[16] Develops a convincing counter-argument.

[17] Direct speech as anecdotal evidence.

[18] Statistical evidence presented as a question to engage the audience, followed by an emphatic supporting statement.

[19] Expert opinion used to add weight to the writer's concerns about social media.

[20] Effective conclusion, motivating the reader through repetition of inclusive statements beginning 'Let's…'

This answer demonstrates:
- ✓ effective paragraphing
- ✓ confident development of ideas that maintain the reader's attention
- ✓ appropriate sense of audience
- ✓ increasingly fluent and persuasive style
- ✓ varied sentence structures
- ✓ accurate use of punctuation
- ✓ strong conclusion, attempting to leave a lasting impression.

Writing for purpose and audience: key to success

POINTS TO REMEMBER

Read these pointers and then complete the practice question below.

▶ The best writing results from the following process: **Think, Plan, Write.** Resist the temptation to start immediately; taking the time to think and plan is essential to producing work that has a strong opening, demonstrates a clear train of thought and presents an effective conclusion.

▶ Begin with the three key questions: **Why, What and Who?** This will set you off on the correct pathway.

▶ Where appropriate, make your writing lively and engaging. Let your personality come through in the writing – the last thing the person marking your work wants is to read something dull! Your tone and vocabulary choice needs to match the audience and purpose.

▶ Remember you have only 55 minutes in which to complete the writing process.

▶ There are no prizes for finishing first so use all of the time wisely – the only reward for finishing early could be a low grade if you do not make the most of the time available.

▶ Review your finished work – you *must* review your work to get the most out of your answer because *everyone* makes mistakes when they are working quickly and under pressure. Remember too that there are no marks for extreme neatness – it is much better that your work is accurate even if it contains a few corrections. As you check your work, consider the following questions and correct any mistakes you find:

i Have you paragraphed your writing?
ii Have you used a range of sentence lengths?
iii Have you varied the sentence openings?
iv Have you used a varied vocabulary?
v Have you left out any words or are there any sentences where the meaning is less than clear?
vi Finally, does it all make sense – do any sections require re-organising so that the meaning is clear? Is your word choice precise enough?

UNIT 1 SECTION A: WRITING FOR PURPOSE AND AUDIENCE

Here is an acrostic to help you remember the key messages:

- **P** Planning/Purpose
- **E** Emotive language
- **R** Rhetorical devices
- **S** Structure/Selecting vocabulary/Supporting your points
- **U** Using factual information
- **A** Audience/Anecdotes/Arguments
- **D** Direct appeal
- **E** Empathy/Expressing opinions and feelings

> **Practice question**
>
> Plan and write a speech to be delivered to your class in which you present your views on the following topic:
>
> **'Technology is destroying our youth'**
>
> *Response time: 55 minutes*
>
> Re-read your answer and check it against the checklists for success below.

Checklist for success: working towards Grade C	
Have you developed your response in a manner that will hold the reader's interest?	
Have you clearly planned, organised and structured the writing so that you've presented your ideas in a fluent manner?	
Have you tried to maintain an appropriate sense of audience and kept your focus on the purpose (it could be a speech or an article)?	
Is the piece paragraphed and does each paragraph have a topic sentence?	
Have you used some stylistic devices (rhetorical questions, emotive language, etc.) that are in keeping with the purpose and audience and that help to hold your audience's attention?	
Have you used a range of appropriate vocabulary, some of which is used to create effect?	
Have you used clear punctuation and does it create variety and clarify meaning?	
Is there appropriate variety in the sentence structuring?	
Have you checked your spelling and tried to use some ambitious vocabulary?	

Checklist for success: working towards Grade A/A*	
Does your writing develop the topic in a sophisticated manner?	
Does your writing positively engage and confidently hold the reader's attention?	
Has your writing created a positive rapport with your reader?	
Does your writing demonstrate an assured use of structure and a confident style?	
Have you used a range of stylistic devices (rhetorical questions, emotive language, etc.) that are adapted to purpose and audience?	
Have you used a wide range of appropriate, extended vocabulary and is it used to create an effect or to convey a precise meaning?	
Have you used confident and effective variation of sentence structures, making use of simple, compound and complex sentences to achieve particular effects?	
Have you used accurate punctuation to vary pace, clarify meaning and avoid ambiguity, and is it used to create deliberate effects?	
Is virtually all spelling, including that of complex irregular words, correct?	

UNIT 1

Section B: Reading to access non-fiction and media texts

Introduction to reading to access non-fiction and media texts

Unit 1 is externally examined and is made up of two sections. The second section is Section B and it assesses reading to access non-fiction and media texts.

Target outcome: An understanding of writers' ideas and how various linguistic, structural and presentational devices have been used to influence the reader.

Target skills

The target skills you will learn about in this reading section will enable you to:
- ✔ read and understand texts
- ✔ recognise the effects of language choices
- ✔ develop interpretations of writers' ideas
- ✔ explain and evaluate how writers use linguistic, grammatical and structural features to influence the reader.

Assessment Objectives

Your Assessment Objectives in this section are:
i   Read and understand texts, selecting material appropriate to purpose and collating from different sources.
ii Develop and sustain interpretations of writers' ideas and perspectives.
iii Explain and evaluate how writers use linguistic, structural and presentational features to achieve effects and to engage and influence the reader.

The exam questions

You will have 50 minutes in which to read two texts and answer four questions. Two tasks will focus on your understanding of non-fiction texts and how writers convey ideas.
The remaining two tasks will focus on how media texts influence a reader through language and presentational features.

AO3 i — Non-fiction and media texts

The term 'text' has a very broad meaning. Texts include not only:
- picture books
- novels
- newspapers
- letters
- conversations
- speeches
- plays
- feature films
- TV programmes
- computer graphics, and
- advertisements;

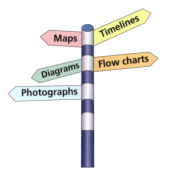

they include also:
- maps
- charts
- diagrams
- graphs
- timelines
- databases
- flow charts
- concept maps, and
- photographs.

When you encounter any text, you must be clear about:
- **Why** the text has been written – its **purpose**.
- **Whom** the text is aimed at – its **audience**.

Why are things written?

Non-fiction texts are commonly written to:

| Argue | Persuade | Advise |

| Inform | Explain | Describe |

Of course, it is possible for a text to have more than one purpose. For example:

- A **newspaper article** might **inform** the reader about a serious crime, **describe** the events that occurred, and **advise** the public on how they can help police catch the culprit.
- A **charity advert** has the **primary purpose** of **persuading** a reader to donate time or money, but to successfully achieve this aim the text will also **inform** the reader about the charity's cause and **explain** how the involvement of the reader can help things improve.

Activity

1. Copy and complete the table below, identifying the different purposes of each text:

Text	Purpose(s)
A school report	
A fast food brochure	
A film poster	
A leaflet about flu	
A magazine article about online safety	
A chapter from an autobiography about the writer's experiences of travelling in Australia	

2. Copy and complete the table below by providing another example of a text that fulfills the identified purpose:

Text purpose	Example 1	Example 2
To argue	A debate speech where you speak in support of parents having the freedom to take their children on holiday during term time.	
To persuade	A letter to your Principal to encourage him/her to give permission for a school trip.	
To advise	A letter to a primary school student who is joining your school in September.	
To inform	Written directions from the bus station to the local shopping centre.	
To explain	An essay discussing reasons for the outbreak of war in 1914.	
To describe	A blog to share your holiday adventures.	

UNIT 1 SECTION B: READING TO ACCESS NON-FICTION AND MEDIA TEXTS

How are things written?

To fully appreciate the audience and purpose of a text you will have to examine the language and layout of the text.

Before beginning your analysis of a text you should be aware that you are looking at a final version and that, in crafting the text, the writer has had to make many decisions about their choice of words and phrases, their use of language techniques and any presentational devices or layout features.

Language

When studying the language of a text you are likely to begin by considering the type of language used. This means thinking about the complexity of the language and asking yourself: is it straightforward and easy to follow or does it use a lot of complex or specialist language? Answering this question can help you identify the **intended audience** of a text, for example, a text aimed at primary school children will use more straightforward language and simpler sentence structures than a text for adult readers.

A writer's choice of words and phrases is not random, so pick out words and phrases that have an impact on you as a reader and that therefore help the writer achieve their purpose.

Writers also use a variety of language devices to help them achieve their purpose, so a text that is written to inform might include a lot of statistics whereas a text that is devised to persuade will rely more on emotive language.

Layout

How a text looks on the page can also provide clues about its intended audience and purpose.

A **non-fiction** text such as an autobiography will be organised into paragraphs of varying lengths and will look like prose fiction, but an article in a newspaper or magazine will use conventions like text columns, sub-headings and pictures with captions.

Activity

Gather a range of non-fiction and media texts, such as pages from textbooks, newspaper articles, advertisements, extracts from biographies or autobiographies, and extracts from travel blogs.

In a small group, identify the purpose and target audience of each text. Explain briefly how the language or layout of each text influenced your decision-making.

A **media** text such as an advert can usually be easily recognised because it uses the conventions of this type of text: features like slogans, logos, images and written text. It may have headings or sub-headings and the written text may be presented using bullet points or placed in text boxes.

By reading on and completing the learning activities in this section, you will gain confidence in analysing a range of texts and in writing about the impact of language and layout features.

Analysing language closely

AO3 iii

The word 'analyse' means to examine something in close detail. A task that demands you analyse usually contains the word 'how'.
For example, tasks relating to a non-fiction text about a tsunami might ask:

Analyse how the writer emphasises his feelings of fear to engage the reader.

Or:

Explain how the writer conveys the devastating effects of the tsunami.

Analysing the **language** of a text requires you to be able to pick out words, phrases, techniques and sentences that have an impact upon you as a reader and therefore help the writer achieve their purpose.

Point. Evidence. Explain.

Point. Evidence. Explain. (P.E.E.) is useful when writing about non-fiction texts, as this example demonstrates:

Point	Make a point about the text.	e.g. 'The writer emphasises the devastation by using emotive language.'
Evidence	Provide evidence from the text to illustrate.	e.g. 'This is used in the opening sentence when he states, "It was hellish. The entire village had vanished under water!"'
Explain	Explain the effect by considering: • how your evidence makes the reader think/feel • how your evidence helps the writer achieve his/her purpose.	e.g. 'The reader is forced to think that the tsunami was like a nightmare experience as the word "hellish" makes it seem like the tsunami had totally transformed their world. The writer wants us to appreciate how their lives have been ruined as he includes the word "entire", making us realise they had lost everything and the situation was hopeless.'

As you can see from the example above it is in the 'explanation' that you show your analytical skills. Analysing requires you to be able to interpret and explain using your own words.

Focusing on words and phrases

Writers have a wide range of words at their disposal. Some words, however, are more powerful than others. For example, using the **verb** 'said' in a sentence tells a reader very little, e.g. '"I'm starving!" said the boy.' In this instance the words of the boy have very little impact upon the reader. Changing the verb can create impact, e.g. '"I'm starving!" **whimpered** the boy.' The verb 'whimpered' is much more powerful and encourages the reader to feel sympathy for the boy.

29

UNIT 1 SECTION B: READING TO ACCESS NON-FICTION AND MEDIA TEXTS

Activity

Re-write each of the sentences below, substituting the coloured verb with a more powerful alternative:

- 'My legs ached as I walked up the steep hill.'

- '"Please help me," said the girl.'
- 'The striker kicked the ball right into the back of the net.'
- 'With a grumbling stomach, I took a seat at the table and began to eat my feast.'

In addition to verb choices, in your analysis you should give consideration to a writer's choice of **adjectives** and **adverbs**. Sentences do not require adjectives or adverbs, but when used carefully they add interest and create impact.

Responding to autobiographical writing

Autobiographies are non-fiction texts in which an individual writes about their own life experiences. To make their writing vivid and detailed they will often use adjectives and adverbs to help the reader visualise the scene.

Analysing language closely

In the short autobiographical extract below, the writer recalls their first day at school. As you read, consider the questions around it:

[1] What does the adverb 'timidly' suggest about the writer's feelings on her first day at school?

[2] Why might the writer have repeated the adjective 'small'?

[3] What does the verb 'detested' emphasise?

[4] What impression does the adjective 'vast' create about how the young child viewed her classroom?

[5] How do the adjectives in this sentence enhance the description of the box of pencils?

[6] What word does the adverb 'especially' emphasise?

[7] What does the adjective 'fascinating' tell us about how the child viewed the sharpener?

[8] Why might the writer include this description in her autobiography?

I remember sitting timidly**[1]** in a small red seat at a small**[2]** wooden table with a cold metal shelf underneath where I would store all my books. I detested**[3]** that shelf; I repeatedly banged my knees on it and for the first month my mother was puzzled by the purple and yellow bruises that covered my knees like an ugly stain. I remember nothing about my teacher on that first day, she was only a voice at the front of the room and I was more fascinated by the vast**[4]** library of books just waiting to be discovered and the heavy rainbow box of chunky**[5]** colouring-in pencils that were just crying out to me to create a masterpiece. I was especially**[6]** excited at the thought of getting to use the giant orange pencil sharpener that was clamped to the side of the teacher's desk — it was certainly a fascinating**[7]** machine. Its black handle would soon be spinning and the fine pencil sharpenings would tumble inside and gather in the little compartment.**[8]**

On that first day, the classroom was new and exciting and I already knew I was going to love my time here.

Activity

1. Write a short paragraph (up to twelve sentences) about a memorable primary school classroom and use words, phrases and description that help your reader imagine it and understand your feelings relating to that setting.
   Swap your paragraph with a partner and highlight any words, phrases or descriptions in their work that are effective in visualising the room or in providing clues about their feelings.
2. Based on your partner's work, practise using P.E.E. by writing a two-paragraph response to the following question:
   Analyse how the writer creates a vivid description of their classroom.

UNIT 1 SECTION B: READING TO ACCESS NON-FICTION AND MEDIA TEXTS

Analysing language techniques

As well as making deliberate decisions about their choice of words and phrases, writers will also use a range of language techniques to help them achieve their purpose and leave an impression upon the reader.

Fact and opinion

You need to able to tell the difference between fact and opinion; this is an essential skill.

- A **fact** is something that is known for certain to have happened or to be true or exist. A fact can be supported by evidence.
- An **opinion** is normally a personal statement or viewpoint, which can be the result of an emotion or an individual interpretation of a situation or fact. Opinions are *believed* to have happened or to be true or exist, and cannot be supported by evidence.

For example:

Fact: 'December is the month after November.'

Opinion: 'December is the best month of the year.'

Persuasive use of fact and opinion

Fact and opinion can be combined to 'colour' the information being conveyed. For example: 'A worrying 17 per cent of children are overweight.'

The fact in this sentence is '17 per cent of children are overweight'. The element of persuasive opinion comes in the word 'worrying'. This offers the writer's view on this statistic, which tries to influence the reader by implying that they too should be concerned by this percentage.

> **Activity**
>
> Practise making persuasive use of fact by re-writing these statements so that your reader feels the emotion identified in brackets:
>
> - '54 per cent of 16-year-olds have part-time jobs.' (concern)
> - 'The average teen spends three hours a day playing computer games.' (alarm)
>
>
>
> - 'Last year the school donated £10,000 to local charities.' (impressed)
> - 'For one week only, 50 per cent off all stock.' (enticed)

Analysing language closely

Writers may also use one or more of the following persuasive techniques.

- **Direct address** engages the reader and therefore retains their interest in the writing because it seems directly relevant to them, e.g. 'I ask you…' or 'Don't you agree that…?' Indirect involvement with the reader can also be effective through imperatives, e.g. 'Imagine a time when…' or 'Consider the following advice…'
- **Emotive language** is used to influence how the reader thinks and feels as they read through the text, e.g. 'This was the very place where thousands of brave soldiers had been slaughtered by enemy troops.'
- **Imagery** paints a picture for the reader or can generate emotion to support the mood of the writing, e.g. anger, fear, pity, joy. **Metaphors** can be used in this way and they also say a lot through their connotations, e.g. 'The sea was a ferocious beast, snarling at us and tossing our boat' makes the experience seem dramatic and dangerous.
- **Creating a rapport with readers** makes it seem that the writer is on the same side as the reader, e.g. 'Friends…' or 'Fellow students…'. Psychologically, this makes it more difficult for the reader to disagree with the writer.
- **Repetition** creates drama and impact and can be used to make a point memorable, e.g. 'Nobody called. Nobody came to find me. Nobody cared.' Repetition is often used like this in **groups of three** (**triads**). These can be three sentences or three words, e.g. 'Life, liberty and pursuit of happiness.'
- **Rhetorical questions** are used simply to emphasise a point, e.g. 'Isn't it true that…?'
- **Assertive language** is forceful and confident so it makes your point seem indisputable. It also makes your opinion sound as if it is a widespread belief, e.g. 'Everyone knows…' or 'It is abundantly clear that…'
- **Hyperbole** is the use of exaggeration to create an effect, e.g. 'He has a brain the size of a pea.' **Superlatives**, such as 'best' or 'greatest', are often a feature of hyperbole, e.g. 'He was the most handsome man on Earth.'
- **Alliteration** is the repetition of consonant sounds at the beginnings of words in close succession and makes the point more memorable, e.g. 'Nerds can naturally make nukes from nickels.'
- **Appeal to greater authority** means referring to experts or research to support a viewpoint, which adds credibility to what the writer is saying and can make opinion sound like fact, e.g. 'Scientists believe that…'
- **Humour**, in the right context, can lighten the tone, establish a closer rapport between writer and reader, and add variety to help maintain interest.
- **Personal anecdote** may convince the reader of the authenticity of the writer's views. Autobiographical writing or travel writing is often strongly anecdotal as the interest comes from reading about the personal experiences of the writer.

UNIT 1 SECTION B: READING TO ACCESS NON-FICTION AND MEDIA TEXTS

- **Tone** can be adapted according to the point being made and the reaction that the writer wants to generate in the reader. Here are examples of comments that are sincere, sarcastic and envious in tone:
  - 'She rose from her chair when I came in and exclaimed with a smile, "Wow! Nice outfit!"'
  - 'She gave me one look and said, with a short laugh, "Yeah, right! Nice outfit!"'
  - 'She glanced at me quickly and muttered reluctantly, "Um, yeah… Nice outfit."'
- **Contrast** can be an effective way of highlighting difference or dissimilarity, e.g. 'I'd imagined a sparkling top-of-the-range saloon, instead I was delivered a rusting old hatchback.'

Activity

The extract below is taken from a piece of travel writing, in which Bill Bryson shares his experience of visiting Blackpool. Read it and answer the questions, which invite you to analyse how the writer emphasises his feelings of disappointment during his visit to the resort.

[1] What does this phrase suggest about the writer's expectations?

[2] What does this verb choice emphasise?

[3] What impact do these adjectives have? What does the alliteration add here?

[6] What effect does the humour have upon the reader?

[7] What words or phrases emphasise his dislike in this closing sentence?

It was the illuminations that brought me there. I had been hearing and reading about them for so long, that I was genuinely keen[1] to see them. I rushed[2] to the sea-front in a sense of expectation. Well, I could not see what all the fuss was about – Blackpool's illuminations were dreary and dismal.[3] There is, of course, always the danger of disappointment when you finally experience something you have wanted to see for a long time, but in terms of let-down, it would be hard to exceed Blackpool's light show.[4] I thought there would be lasers sweeping the sky, strobe lights tattooing the clouds and other gasp-making dazzlements. Instead there was just a rumbling procession of old trams decorated as rocket ships or Christmas crackers and several miles of pathetic decorations on lamp posts.[5] I suppose if you had never seen electricity in action it would be pretty breathtaking, but I'm not sure of that.[6] It all just seemed tacky on a rather grand scale, like Blackpool itself.[7]

(Bill Bryson, *Notes from a Small Island*)

[4] What tone does the writer convey in this sentence?

[5] What is the effect of contrast here across two sentences?

Activity

Below is a section from one student's analysis of the Blackpool extract. Read it to find examples of P.E.E. and to identify the different techniques analysed by the student.

> The writer begins by using language to convey his positive expectations. For example, he recounts that the attraction was the 'illuminations' and how he was 'genuinely keen' to see them. Through the adverb 'genuinely' the reader acknowledges his enthusiasm and high expectations that he is about to witness something special.
>
> The writer then describes the reality and his language becomes very negative. He states that the illuminations were 'dreary and dismal.' By using two negative adjectives he is emphasising to the reader how unimpressed he was, and the alliteration adds to his tone of disappointment.
>
> It is clear that he could not find a single thing to like about Blackpool's illuminations. He goes as far as saying 'in terms of let-down, it would be hard to exceed Blackpool's light show.' This is stated in a convincing downhearted tone and impresses on the reader that this experience has been one of the biggest disappointments of his life.
>
> The writer uses contrast to emphasise the real extent of his disappointment. He shares how he expected 'gasp-making dazzlements', implying he had hoped to witness a real spectacle that would leave him open-mouthed in wonder. Instead he saw 'a rumbling procession of old trams', with the words 'rumbling' and 'old' suggesting it appeared tired and unimpressive.

Activity

Below are another two paragraphs from the Bryson account of Blackpool. Write a three-paragraph response to the following task:

Analyse how the writer emphasises his dislike for Blackpool.

What was no less amazing were the crowds of people who had come to witness this miserable show. Traffic along the front was bumper to bumper, with childish faces pressed to the windows of every creeping car, and there were masses of people walking happily along the spacious promenade. I once read that half of all visitors to Blackpool have been there at least ten times. Goodness knows what they find in the place.

In the morning I got up early to give Blackpool another chance. It wasn't much better by daylight. One of the sights that I knew would stick firmly in my mind was the long promenade and the three piers at Blackpool. I will long remember the people sitting in deck chairs underneath a dark sky, some with their shirts off, some with their mouths open and clutching copies of the daily papers. Tomorrow they would be using them for wrapping fish and chips. They were waiting for the sun to shine, but the forecast was rain for the next five months! I escaped from Blackpool as soon as I could.

(Bill Bryson, *Notes from a Small Island*)

AO3 iii Analysing structure

As well as analysing the language of a text, you should also consider how the writer has structured the text. The primary techniques to consider when analysing structure are:

▶ The tense in which the text is written.
▶ The sequence in which the events or experiences are told.
▶ The use of sentence structures to enhance meaning at key moments in the text.

Choice of tense

When a writer is recounting an event or experience, they will usually write in the past tense and so be able to write in great detail about what occurred and reflect upon their feelings. Sometimes, however, they may opt to use the present tense to bring a sense of immediacy to their writing. Consider the difference between these two accounts:

> **Text A**
> I was shocked by the scale of the devastation. I stood still, not knowing what to do. I felt hopeless.

> **Text B**
> Emerging from the shelter I stop suddenly to absorb the sheer devastation. I can do nothing but stare, it all seems so hopeless.

In Text A the writer recounts the events with a sense of detachment, but in Text B the use of present tense draws attention to his sudden feelings of shock and helplessness. It helps the reader empathise because the experience feels so immediate.

Using sequence and time

Writers must also make decisions about the order in which events or experiences are recounted and about when to move swiftly on or to dwell and describe.

In the extract below Bear Grylls, a famous explorer, recalls a dramatic experience.

> The air temperature is minus twenty degrees. I wiggle my fingers but they're still freezing cold. Old frostnip injuries never let you forget. I blame Everest for that.
>
> 'You set, buddy?' cameraman Simon asks me, smiling. His rig is all prepped and ready.
>
> I smile back. I am unusually nervous. Something doesn't quite feel right. But I don't listen to the inner voice. It is time to go to work.
>
> The crew tell me that the crisp northern Canadian Rockies look spectacular this morning. I don't really notice.
>
> It is time to get into my secret space. A rare part of me that is focused, clear, brave, precise. It is the part of me I know the best but visit the least.

Analysing structure

> I only like to use it sparingly. Like now.
>
> Beneath me is three hundred feet of steep snow and ice. Steep but manageable.
>
> I have done this sort of fast descent many, many times. Never be complacent, the voice says. The voice is always right.
>
> A last deep breath. A look to Simon. A silent acknowledgment back.
>
> Yet we have cut a vital corner. I know it. But I do nothing.
>
> I leap.
>
> (Bear Grylls, *Mud, Sweat and Tears: The Autobiography*)

In the extract above the final sentence 'I leap' is made all the more dramatic because the writer has described the minutes before in fine detail, building a sense of his unease. In deciding to write about this event, the writer recognised the need to share the few minutes leading up to the jump. This episode has been crafted deliberately using present tense and a chronological structure, where the events develop minute by minute, to create tension and make it dramatic.

Effect of sentence structures

Writers work hard to secure and maintain the interest of their reader by varying their use of sentences. Skilled writers will also use sentence structures to enhance meaning.

Consider again the Bear Grylls extract. You will notice that the writer has used short sentences at various points in the text. Let's look closely at paragraph 3:

> I smile back. I am unusually nervous. Something doesn't quite feel right. But I don't listen to the inner voice. It is time to go to work.

This paragraph consists of five short sentences. While the words on the page convey his nerves, the concise sentences also contribute to the tense atmosphere by emphasising his unease and therefore making the account more emotive and convincing.

This next extract is taken from *Touching the Void*, which tells of a near-fatal mountaineering expedition. As you read, consider the questions, which encourage you to think about the structure of the text.

[1] What mood is established at the beginning through this simple sentence?

[2] What effect do the shortening sentence lengths have here?

[3] Here the writer is describing what he sees. What effect does the longer sentence have?

> The wind swung me in a gentle circle.**[1]** I looked at the crevasse beneath me, waiting for me. It was big.**[2]** Twenty feet wide at least. I guessed that I was hanging fifty feet above it. It stretched along the base of the ice cliff. Below me it was covered with a roof of snow, but to the right it opened out and a dark space yawned there.**[3]** Bottomless, I thought idly. No.**[4]** They're never bottomless. I wonder how deep I will go? To the bottom… to the water at the bottom? God! I hope not.**[5]**
>
> (Joe Simpson, *Touching the Void*)

[4] What emotion do you detect through the use of a one-word sentence here?

[5] What effect does the short sentence have at the end of the extract?

Activity

Using P.E.E., write a three-paragraph response to the following task:

Explain how the writer communicates his changing emotions in the extract from *Touching the Void*.

In your answer consider:

- words or phrases that are used to convey his feelings
- language techniques used to convey his awareness of danger
- sentence structures that help convey the writer's changing feelings.

AO3 i, ii — Extracting meaning

Not every reader reads to analyse; many read for pleasure and enjoyment or to find information. Not all texts offer the same level of challenge, but as you become a more experienced reader, try exploring more challenging texts that require you to work a little harder to extract meaning.

The extracting meaning task

Tasks that ask you to show an understanding of what you have read usually require you to summarise using your own words. It is vital, however, that your summary is relevant to the set task.

To be certain that your interpretation of a text is valid you must be able to support it by providing evidence from the text. It is best to select short relevant quotations that you can embed into your own sentences.

Let's look at another extract from Bear Grylls, where he describes what happened after he leapt off the mountainside. As you read, discuss the questions around it with a partner.

Simon, his heavy wooden sled, plus solid metal camera housing, piles straight into my left thigh. He is doing in excess of 45 mph.**[1]**

There is an instant explosion of pain and noise and white.**[2]**

It is like a freight train.**[3]** And I am thrown down the mountain like a doll.**[4]** Life stands still.**[5]** I feel and see it all in slow motion.

Yet in that split second I have only one realisation: a one-degree different course and the sled's impact would have been with my head. Without doubt, it would have been my last living thought.**[6]**

Instead, I am in agony, writhing. I am crying. They are tears of relief. I am injured, but I am alive.**[7]**

(Bear Grylls, *Mud, Sweat and Tears: The Autobiography*)

---

[1] What information here lets us appreciate that this is a painful collision?

[2] What word in this sentence emphasises the dramatic and painful nature of the collision? Explain.

[3] What effect does this simile have in making the collision seem dramatic?

[4] What effect does this simile have in emphasising his helplessness and vulnerability?

[5] What effect does this short sentence have upon the reader?

[6] Summarise what Bear Grylls realises here.

[7] What is his strongest emotion at the end of the extract, and why?

Activity

Referring only to the extract above, answer this question:

In your own words, write down what causes Bear Grylls to feel intensely emotional? **Present supporting evidence.**

Extracting meaning

To answer this question successfully, you must first identify where in the extract Bear Grylls feels intensely emotional; the key word here is 'intensely' and it should inform your selection.

If you look at the end of the text it is clear that a range of **intense** emotions is expressed here:

> I am in agony, writhing. I am crying. They are tears of relief. I am injured, but I am alive.

Activity

Once you have identified the intense emotions in the extract, re-read it up to this point, finding three or four points that show 'What causes' these emotions, embedding direct quotations as evidence in your own short explanations.

Below is one student's response to the above task:

> Bear Grylls feels intensely emotional because he has just had a near-death experience as he realises that pure luck has meant the sled avoided his head and instead collided with his thigh.**[1]** It is clear that the collision is intense as he refers to it as 'an explosion' and he experiences a lot of pain as he is 'writhing', but it is obvious at the end of the passage that his strongest and most intense emotion is relief as he claims 'I am still alive' through his 'tears of relief'.**[2]**

[1] Point effectively summarises why the writer feels intensely emotional.

[2] Evidence from the text is brief, relevant and integrated into the student's response.

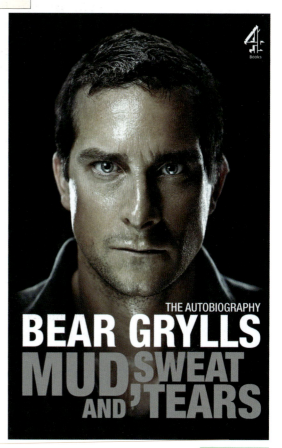

AO3 i, ii, iii — Supporting interpretations

The supporting interpretations task

To prove the validity of your interpretation you must comment on your evidence, explaining **how** it supports your interpretation as well as considering the impact upon a reader.

Read the short extract below:

> We were minutes away from boarding the plane when my fear revealed itself in an ugly sweat, a dry mouth and uncontrollable fidgeting.
>
> 'What's up with you?' asked my wife. 'For goodness sake stand still! And smile, you're going on holiday.' She turned back to looking out on to the runway.
>
> 'I'm terrified.' I whispered.
>
> She spun, as though I'd just admitted to murder. She studied me for a second, rubbed her hand up and down my arm then broke into a fit a laughter; cruel mocking laughter.

Activity

Below are three things we learn from the above extract. For each point, find supporting evidence and explain how it supports the point:
- The husband is a reluctant flyer.
- The husband feels embarrassed about confessing his fear.
- The wife is unsympathetic.

Read the short extract below from *I Am Malala* (which inspired the documentary *He named me Malala*), the autobiography of the educational campaigner, who as a young girl was shot by the Taliban on her way home from school.

> Our street could not be reached by car. I would get off the bus on the road below, go through an iron gate and up a flight of steps. Sometimes I'd imagine that a terrorist might jump out and shoot me on those steps. I wondered what I would do. Maybe I'd take off my shoes and hit him. But then I'd think that if I did that, there would be no difference between me and a terrorist. It would be better to plead, 'Okay, shoot me, but first listen to me. What you are doing is wrong. I'm not against you personally. I just want every girl to go to school.'
>
> (Malala Yousafzai, *I am Malala*)

Activity

For each of the points to the right, find a suitable quotation from the text to support the statement.

From this extract the reader understands that Malala:
- lives in a dangerous place
- does not support violence
- values education for girls.

On the next page is one student's response to the task:

In your own words, write down two things that cause Malala to feel uneasy as she journeys home from school. **Present supporting evidence.**

Supporting interpretations

> **First reason**
> Malala finds it concerning that her street is cut off from a road and inaccessible to cars as this means she has to walk home, which clearly makes her feel vulnerable.
>
> **Supporting evidence**
> This is obvious as she states that, 'Our street could not be reached by car...'
>
> **Second reason**
> Malala's own imagination also causes her to feel uneasy as her vulnerability causes her to think of bad things that could happen to her. It is clear that she feels her journey home is a risky one.
>
> **Supporting evidence**
> Evidence to support the fact she believes her journey is potentially dangerous is, 'Sometimes I'd imagine that a terrorist might jump out and shoot me.'

This student's response demonstrates an ability to:
- ✔ extract meaning
- ✔ select relevant quotations
- ✔ support and validate their interpretation by explaining the impact of certain words upon a reader.

This task requires you to **identify the source** of Malala's uneasy feelings and demonstrate your understanding by responding using your own words, which this student does successfully in the first sentence of each paragraph above. In the second sentence of each they provide a suitable quotation.

In your own words, write down two reasons the writer gives to explain why she is prepared to risk her life. **Present supporting evidence**.

> **First reason**
> Malala is prepared to risk her life because she refuses to give in to terrorists.[1] This is clear when she states that she has imagined how she would react if she encountered a terrorist, but that she would not resort to any violence as to hit back would be to behave like the terrorists. Malala lives like this because she believes in doing what is right.[2]
>
> **Supporting evidence**
> Malala states that to respond violently would mean there was 'no difference between me and a terrorist'.[3]
>
> **Second reason**
> Malala is prepared to risk her life because she believes it is vital that girls have access to education. She strongly believes in education and is prepared to risk her life for it. She will not let anyone prevent her from going to school and instead carries on living with her uneasy feelings.[4]
>
> **Supporting evidence**
> At the end of the extract she states, 'It would be better to plead... I just want every girl to go to school.'

[1] Point demonstrates understanding of the causes of Malala's unease.

[2] 'Explanation which considers what meaning the reader extracts from the text.'

[3] Brief, relevant quotation to illustrate.

[4] Develops the explanation that Malala lives like this because she believes so strongly in education.

AO3 i, ii, iii — Putting it into practice: reading to access non-fiction texts

You now know that when responding to non-fiction texts at GCSE you must be able to demonstrate an ability:

- to analyse a text by commenting on the writer's use of words and phrases, language techniques and structural features
- to extract meaning
- to select relevant evidence to support your interpretation of a given text
- to explain the impact of the writer's choices upon a reader.

The 'Analyse' task

Analysis questions will usually start 'Analyse how the writer…' or 'Explain how the writer…'. These tasks require you to show an appreciation of **how** the writer achieves a certain effect or conveys meaning through their use of language. Analysing a text demands close study of words and phrases, language techniques and structural features.

Read the extract below and consider the prompt questions, which will help you gather ideas on how to respond to this task:

Explain how the writer emphasises the pleasant experience of visiting the marketplace to engage the reader.

My purse is heaving with coins and my pocket is stuffed with bags[1] that will soon be carrying all sorts of intriguing trinkets and original souvenirs[2] snapped up at bargain prices. No matter where in the world I travel, I make it my business to seek out the local market, not the market for tourists but the authentic market, the market run by locals for locals.[3] Experience had taught me that this was where the real treasures were to be discovered.[4]

On an early August morning I find myself among a throng[5] of people who are making the same pilgrimage[6] to the marketplace. Even before entering the market compound, I can feel the anticipation fizzing in my stomach. The market itself does not disappoint; it is a feast for the senses![7] A gentle breeze carries the aroma of rich spices and delicate perfumes. Giant cauldron-sized pots bubble with culinary delights in various shades of yellow and orange. Small prints in golden frames depict some of the exotic landscapes I have witnessed during my stay and I just can't resist purchasing my own precious masterpiece.[8] Adoringly, I place it in my bag and carry on my mission.[9]

[1] What do the writer's verb choices reveal about her intentions?

[2] What do the adjectives suggest about her reasons for going to this market?

[3] What is the effect of the writer repeating the word 'locals'?

[4] What does the verb 'discovered' make us think about the writer's experience?

[5] What does the word 'throng' suggest?

[6] What is the effect of the writer referring to her journey as a 'pilgrimage'?

[7] How does the writer use punctuation to emphasise her feelings here?

[8] What do the adjectives in this sentence suggest about the marketplace?

[9] What words in the final sentence convey the writer's pleasure?

42

Below is the beginning to one student's response to the task:

> The writer begins by making clear that she is preparing herself for a successful and busy experience. The verbs 'heaving' and 'stuffed' confirm that she is keen to immerse herself in the buying experience at the marketplace. She emphasises how her pleasure for the market comes from the fact she can purchase 'all sorts of intriguing trinkets and original souvenirs'. The adjectives 'intriguing' and 'original' demonstrate that the marketplace is a pleasurable place as it offers the buyer plenty of choice and the opportunity to purchase things that cannot be got elsewhere.

Activity

Using the ideas generated from your own reading of the extract, continue the analysis of this text by writing three more paragraphs.

The 'extracting and interpreting meaning' task

This question requires you to show understanding of **what** you have read. Your response should communicate your understanding in your own words and provide evidence from the text to support your point.

Using the extract below, answer the question:

In your own words, write down two reasons the writer feels suddenly surprised. Provide evidence from the passage to support your answer.

> While taking a well-earned rest I am suddenly less interested in the array of wares on offer and instead my attention is fixed on the people. While they are all very welcoming and extend a smile as they bustle past with bulging bags, I realise they see me as an outsider. With my brightly coloured clothes and untamed auburn hair, I stand out a mile. I may as well have 'TOURIST' stamped on my forehead. I don't recall feeling like this before, but it is not an unpleasant realisation and I quickly laugh it off. And then I wonder how they manage to do it! Just how do they succeed in preventing other outsiders like me coming in their droves? I don't manage to find an answer but I know why they do it; they know this place is sacred.

To answer this question successfully, you must find the point in the extract where the writer expresses her surprise. Now read around that part to find the source of her surprise.

Activity

Below, one student has identified the evidence they feel is needed to answer this question. Use this evidence to write a full response:

> 'I realise they see me as an outsider.'
> 'I wonder how they manage to do it!'

Responding to media texts

Media texts are also non-fiction texts but they rely on more than one method of communicating with a reader. In addition to language and structural features, media texts can convey meaning through presentational devices such as colour, images and layout features. Look at the introduction to Unit 1B on page 26 to review the list of types of non-fiction texts – included in this list are examples of media texts.

By working through the activities in this section you will come to appreciate how language and presentational features work together to create an impression upon a reader.

Identifying purpose and audience

AO3 i, iii

We often encounter media texts by chance. For example: we hear them on the radio; we watch them on the television; they drop through our letter-boxes; we read them in newspapers and magazines; we pick them up from shop counters or notice them on billboards. They are everywhere and we are so frequently exposed to them that it takes a really special media text to catch our attention.

Like many non-fiction texts, media texts will often be multi-purpose texts that are targeting a wide and varied audience. When we identify the audience and purpose of a media text we must be as specific as possible and avoid making general statements. For example, if we looked at a poster advertisement for a new expensive lipstick, we should avoid comments such as:

> This text is aimed at women and it is promoting a new product.

Instead we might say:

> This advertisement is aimed at **women who have an interest in beauty** and who like high-end products. Its primary purpose is **to persuade** customers to purchase the product, and to achieve this aim **it informs** the audience of its superior long-lasting quality and moisturising benefits.

Activity

Read about the different organisations below that have recently produced media texts. Identify the purpose of each text and its target audience, trying to be as specific as you can.

i   A new playbarn has opened in your area with attractions suitable for children aged 3–10. To attract trade, the owner has an opening offer of 50 per cent off. He has produced a brochure for distribution to 2000 local addresses.

> **ii** A city centre cinema has just displayed a poster about a new science-fiction film opening next week. The film has a 15 certificate and its leading man is Hollywood star Mike Mickleson.
>
> **iii** A local animal charity needs more people to adopt abandoned dogs. It has launched its campaign through the local press.

To identify the audience and purpose of a media text accurately requires an examination of language and layout features.

Media texts, such as leaflets, brochures and book covers, are expensive to produce. This means the creators are faced with the challenge of trying to appeal to a wide audience and to meet several purposes. Those who produce media texts are also aware that we do not all 'read' the same way.

- **Visual readers:** We all started life as visual readers, relying on images to convey meaning. The creators of media texts know that 'a picture can paint a thousand words' and that many readers will be attracted to texts with a strong visual appeal.

- **Skim–scan readers:** Rather than stopping to read the entire text as we pass by it, we may instead skim and scan it to get a general gist of what the text is about before deciding if it appeals to us. For this reason, the creator of a media text may include features that will appeal to the 'skim–scan' reader and that try to encourage them to engage further with the most important parts of the text. Movie trailers, posters and book covers appeal to 'skim–scan' readers as they give a flavour of what the text is about, with the ultimate aim that they persuade you to pay to see the entire movie or read the book.

- **Comprehensive readers:** Many readers will read the text in full and draw meaning from language and presentational features.

The truth is, *how* we read media texts is not fixed; if something catches our eye, like a book blurb, we might read it and then go on to read the whole novel. In contrast, a leaflet that drops through our letterbox may get a quick scan that tells us enough to know it is not directly relevant and to recycle it.

For GCSE English you are required to study a range of media texts, so while you may recognise features that appeal to visual readers or to skim–scan readers, you must always read the full text.

AO3 i, iii — Analysing presentational devices

Presentational devices are those features that determine the appearance of a text. There is often much to consider when studying the use of presentational devices, but remember that you are analysing so you must always explain the effect upon the reader.

You should be aware that all media texts will have a specific subject, which means the presentational devices are often used to communicate ideas about the subject. For example, a holiday brochure may favour bright colours such as yellow and orange, which have connotations of sunshine and warmth so the choice of colour is appropriate for the subject of the text.

One way of analysing presentational devices is to use the mnemonic C.L.I.F.:

Colour	• Which colours have been used and why? Does one colour dominate? • What tones have been used – bright and vibrant or more muted tones? • What feelings or emotions might a reader associate with specific colours?
Layout	• Does the text look 'busy' or well spaced out? • What stands out and why? • Is meaning conveyed more effectively through words or images? • Is the information organised into paragraphs? • Does the text include headings or sub-headings? • Have certain parts of the text been underlined or emboldened to stand out?
Image(s)	• What do the images show and what do they suggest about the subject of the text? • Are the images real life or animations? • Consider whether there is a dominant image or several that are used to communicate different ideas. • How do the words and images interact to convey meaning? • How is the reader encouraged to think or feel when they look at certain images?
Font	• Is there a range of font styles and sizes used? • Where is the title positioned and how does it look? Distinctive? Modern? Traditional?

You should accept that you not going to be able to analyse everything that could possibly be said about a given text. You will usually be expected to analyse **two** presentational devices, so when making decisions about what to write about you should be certain that you can explain:

▶ **What?** What does the specific device suggest about the subject of the text? For example, a leaflet for a local museum might feature an image of a family all exiting the attraction with smiles on their faces. This suggests the museum is suitable for a family day out and that it will satisfy people of different ages with different interests.

▶ **How?** How does the writer make the reader think or feel a particular way about the subject of the text? For example, a text promoting an adventure park might use lots of bright colours to encourage the reader to think positively about the place itself and to suggest that their experience will be a colourful one with lots to see and do.

▶ **Who?** Whom does your chosen feature appeal to? For example, a movie poster depicting an image of a ghostly figure suggests the genre of the movie is horror and therefore it will have particular appeal to horror enthusiasts.

Colour

When analysing colour you need to be aware of the subtle and not-so-subtle effects that different colours have on us. To analyse colour successfully it is important you consider the most likely interpretation, rather than listing all the possible reasons a certain colour can be used. Remember, with any presentational device you are analysing its use *within the text in front of you* and so your analysis should always be valid and specific.

Each colour can have several **connotations** or associated meanings. Here is a breakdown of their possible effects:

Colour	Connotations
Grey	gloomy, depressing, bland, wisdom, old age, boredom, decay, dullness, dust, pollution, neutrality, mourning
White	purity, neutrality, cleanliness, truth, snow, winter, coldness, peace, innocence, simplicity, surrender, cowardice, fearfulness, unimaginative, bland, empty
Black	death, funerals, evil, power, sophistication, formality, elegance, mystery, style, fear, seriousness, rebellion, slimming quality (fashion)
Red	passion, strength, energy, fire, love, excitement, arrogance, ambition, power, danger, blood, war, anger, aggression, summer, stop, communism
Blue	seas, men, harmony, sadness, tranquillity, calmness, coolness, water, ice, cleanliness, depression, coldness, strength, friendliness
Green	nature, eco-friendly, spring, fertility, youth, environment, wealth, money (US), good luck, vigour, generosity, go, aggression, jealousy, illness, greed, envy, renewal, growth, health, calming
Yellow	sunlight, joy, happiness, wealth (gold), summer, hope, air, liberalism, cowardice, illness, hazards, weakness
Purple	royalty, wisdom, nobility, spirituality, creativity, wealth, ceremony, flamboyance, mourning, riches, romanticism (light purple), delicacy (light purple), penance, bravery (Purple Heart)
Orange	energy, enthusiasm, happiness, balance, heat, fire, flamboyance, playfulness, warning, danger, autumn
Brown	boldness, depth, nature, richness, rustic, stability, tradition, filth, poverty, roughness, down-to-earth, wholesomeness, steadfastness, dependability
Pink	femininity, sympathy, homosexuality, health, love, marriage, joy

Activity

Consider what colour choices you would make if asked to produce media texts for each of the following:
- A magazine advertisement for a new toothpaste.
- A poster for a new romantic comedy.
- A leaflet to persuade people to recycle.
- An advertisement for a new sports drink.

UNIT 1 SECTION B: READING TO ACCESS NON-FICTION AND MEDIA TEXTS

> **Activity**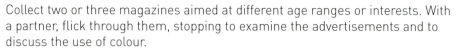
>
> Collect two or three magazines aimed at different age ranges or interests. With a partner, flick through them, stopping to examine the advertisements and to discuss the use of colour.
>
> Select one advertisement. Identify the purpose and target audience, and analyse the use of colour. Display these together on a 'Colour wall' to help your class appreciate how different colours are used within media texts.

Layout

Layout is concerned with the arrangement of information on the page. Given that when we encounter media texts as part of our daily lives we do not often read them in the same way we would a novel or a newspaper article, producers of these texts know that they need to make them look appealing to a reader. It is no surprise therefore that they make careful decisions about how to organise the information and ensure it appears reader-friendly.

Common layout features that help make a text appear reader-friendly include:

- **Lists and bullet points**, which allow the reader to quickly read the information.
- **Paragraphs**, which are usually rather short, often only one or two sentences, allowing the reader to digest the information easily.
- **Headings and sub-headings**, which allow the reader to navigate the text and to locate information quickly.
- **Text boxes and borders**, which are effective in drawing the reader's attention to important information within the text.

The appearance of a text will also provide clues about the target audience, for example if a text is aimed at younger children it will probably rely more on images and have very little copy or words. A text aimed at adults, on the other hand, may have more copy and fewer images.

A busy page can suggest lots to see and do, whereas a text that is well spaced out might promote a calmer, more leisurely experience or suggest the company is organised and professional.

> **Activity**
>
> With a partner or in a small group, study a range of media texts such as leaflets, advertisements or posters and discuss the layout features. Select one text and write a short analysis of its layout. Share your response as a class.

Images

Images can be a powerful way of communicating meaning. Obvious reasons why media texts include images are that they add interest, make the text attractive and help catch the attention of the reader. Remember, though, that while this is true of most media texts, you want to demonstrate your appreciation of how and why images have been used in the **text in front of you**.

You do need to acknowledge what is depicted in the images, but this is basic-level analysis. Be aware that an image can have different **connotations** or associated meanings. For example, an image of a child could connote innocence, curiosity or even playfulness. When deciding which interpretation is most relevant, you cannot analyse the image in isolation. The important thing is that your analysis of a given image is in keeping with the overall purpose and subject of the text. A successful analysis will show an understanding of how the image or images that are displayed work as part of the wider text. To develop your response further, always consider what impression the image has upon the reader.

Analysing presentational devices

If a text has more than one image you should of course acknowledge this, but you should then focus on one or two key images and analyse them in finer detail. If the text has a clear dominant image, then that image demands examination.

Zooming in

When you study an image, do not simply consider its content; you should also consider its arrangement. This means thinking about:

▶ **The angle or perspective:** for example, a text promoting an outdoor activity in a park might include an image giving a bird's eye view to show how vast the place is, making the reader appreciate that there will be lots to explore. An eye-level shot makes the reader feel they are looking directly at a subject. A low-level shot might be used to capture an image of a building or mountain, with the shot taken looking upwards to emphasise the height or majesty of the subject.

▶ **The framing:**
  ▶ **Long shots** are used to capture a scene or a full body shot.
  ▶ **Medium shots** usually capture people from the waist upwards and encourage us to examine their reactions and interactions. For example, elsewhere in the activity park leaflet there might be an image showing a family sitting at a picnic table, interacting, relaxing and smiling. The effect would be to make the reader think that this a place for the family to enjoy one another's company.
  ▶ **Close-up shots** show very little background and instead often show one subject, for example the final image on the activity park text might be of a small squirrel to show it is a place to observe wildlife.

Activity

The following images have all been used to promote a wildlife park. Using the descriptions above, identify which angle or framing shot has been used in each of the images.

Below is one student's analysis of one of the images. Read it carefully and identify which image is being analysed:

> The image is striking and immediately grabs the attention of the reader due to the use of a close-up shot. Many readers will not see animals like this at such close range and the image makes them think a visit to the park will allow them to experience sights like this up close. The reader begins to think that this is a place where they can experience surprising and privileged encounters with wildlife.

Select two different images and write an analysis of each that identifies the angle or framing shot used and the impact upon the reader.

Font

Font refers to the style and size of the writing or copy within a text. Most media texts use a range of font sizes to appeal to their reader, with the most important information or headings and sub-headings presented in a larger font to assist with the organisation and location of information.

Titles or product names often have a different font size from the rest of the words in the text. You should study the font style of a title closely as it is often in keeping with the subject of the text. Font styles that are very sharp and angular might be described as modern or masculine or striking, whereas a style that is more curvaceous and fluid might be described as sophisticated or feminine. Of course, font styles carry different connotations for different readers. When you are writing about font styles, try to select a suitable adjective to describe it and consider how the chosen style complements the subject matter of the media text.

Words that could be used to describe font styles include:

- Modern
- Tribal
- Arresting
- Traditional
- Unique
- Bold
- Distinctive
- Masculine
- Striking
- Gothic
- Feminine
- Sophisticated

Activity

Consider this heading, taken from a text to promote a theme park. With a partner, discuss what impression the reader forms about the park based on the font style:

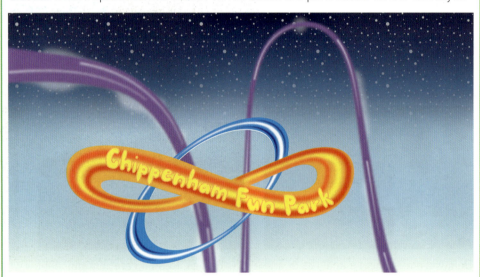

Analysing presentational devices

Activity

Discuss the cover below with a partner, using the prompt questions. Think about how presentational devices have been used to communicate meaning and to leave an impression upon the reader.

[1] Layout: The author's name is positioned at the top of the text. What impression might this give to a reader about the quality of her work? What is the first thing to capture the attention of a reader and how is this achieved? Based on the layout of the text, what can you say about its purpose and target audience?

[2] Font: How would you describe this font style? What expectation does it establish about the book itself in terms of genre or plot?

[3] Colours: How appropriate are the chosen colours? What do they suggest about the book?

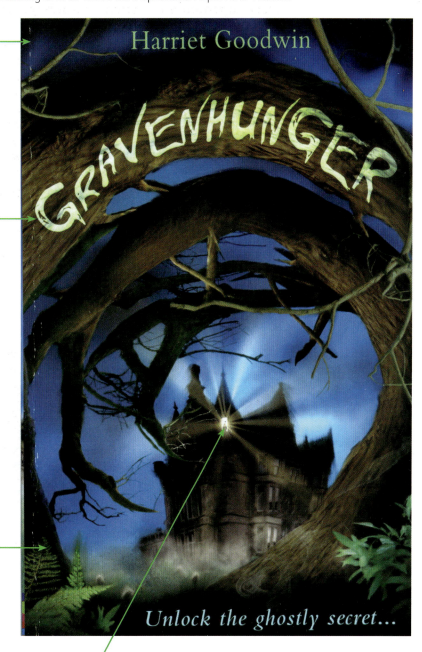

[4] Images: What is suggested by framing the image of the house with branches? What does the image make the reader think or feel about the book? What expectations does it create? Zoom in on the window of the house; how might a reader respond to this detail within the image?

AO3 i, ii, iii Analysing language

To really understand how media texts work, you must appreciate the connection or interplay between presentational devices and the writer's language choices.

When analysing language we must always consider:
- words and phrases
- language techniques.

We must also appreciate how structural features such as sentence structures and punctuation can be used to enhance meaning.

Language and structural features were covered on pages 28–37, dealing with non-fiction texts. Many of these points also apply to media texts, so refer to those pages to remind yourself of what you must consider when analysing language.

The purpose of a text will influence the language used and the desired tone. As media texts often have more than one purpose, they will make use of a range of language features to achieve different aims within the text.

Promotional language

Many media texts are produced to promote products, experiences or places. Organisations are competing for the reader's custom and their money, and for this reason media texts employ language that is used to persuade or entice the reader.

You might expect to see some of the following within media texts:

- **Reviews** from satisfied customers, readers or audiences. These are often included to support the positive claims made within the text. For example, a poster for a new horror film might include a quotation from a film review, e.g. 'Utterly terrifying!' If this is from a respectable source, then the reader is encouraged to have high expectations and to trust the claims made elsewhere on the poster.

- **Endorsements** for a product or a campaign, for example from celebrities. These are often used to encourage the reader to purchase a new product or to try out new experiences. Companies know that fans will be keen to emulate their celebrity idols by purchasing these. For example, a company specialising in laser eye surgery may use endorsement from a figure whom the public admire and trust in order to promote their service and reassure customers.

- **Offers and promotions** have strong appeal because they make the audience believe they are saving money or getting value for money. New products or businesses often have introductory offers or promotions to attract a customer base. For example: 'For a limited time only, visit our attraction and get a free Family Pass valid for one year.'

Media texts structure

As well as examining tense and sentence structures, you should pay careful attention to how the text begins as this is usually crafted to hook or engage the reader. Equally important is the ending of the text as it will be crafted to leave a lasting impression upon the reader. So study it carefully to see how this has been achieved.

Analysing language

Common techniques that engage and leave a lasting impression upon a reader include:

- **Inclusive language or direct address** to make the reader feel the text is directly relevant to them, e.g. 'If you're tired of the same old food, why not try…' or 'At Arlo's Diner, we believe our customers deserve the very best, that's why you recently voted us your number one diner.'
- **Rhetorical questions** to encourage the reader to think, e.g. 'Are you really safe online?'
- **Superlatives** that establish high or positive expectations in the reader, e.g. 'For the *best* value in Belfast visit Arlo's Diner' or 'The *funniest* comedy for decades!'
- **Imperatives** to try to compel the reader to take action based on what they have read, e.g. 'Visit Belfast! Don't delay, book today!' or 'Find out more by logging on to…'

Tone

Often when we read we detect a certain attitude or emotion within the text. This is conveyed by the writer's choice of words and phrases, the use of language techniques and punctuation. These all work together to create **tone**.

The tone of a text can change as the text progresses, for example an advert for a new beauty product may begin with a question e.g. 'Are you fed up with dull, lifeless hair?' This question is used to create a conversational and engaging tone.

The text might then share some statistics to show how satisfied customers are with its new product, e.g. '89% of customers who participated in our trial reported smoother, shinier hair within two days.' This statistic is used to create an informative tone, making the reader feel more informed about the benefits of using this product.

Finally, the text might state, 'Buy now at the introductory price of just £1.99.' The imperative 'Buy now' is used to create an urgent tone intended to call the reader to action to snap up the offer.

Activity

Read the short statements below, which have all been taken from media texts. Identify the purpose of each text, the techniques used and their effect upon a reader. Then describe the tone conveyed in each statement.

> Book your ticket today!

> If you find yourself a victim of online fraud, report it immediately by calling 02045 187 648.

> Sadly, too many animals lose their life to neglect but with your help we can change that.

Activity

Schools also produce media texts to attract new students. With a partner, study your school website or prospectus. Identify the purpose(s) of your chosen text and consider the target audience(s).

- Analyse the images used and consider what impression they give of your school. Select two images that you feel are most effective and explain why.
- Analyse the language and consider how the words and phrases, language techniques, structural features and tones are used to ensure the text fulfils its purpose.

AO3 i, ii, iii
Putting it into practice: reading to access media texts

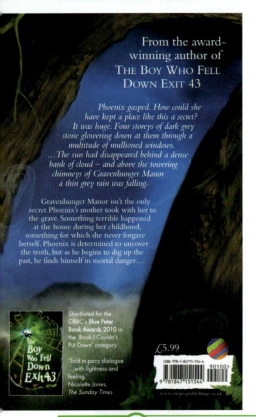

By now you should realise that to analyse a media text successfully you must be able to:

- identify its purpose and audience by considering the language and layout
- analyse language, including structural features and tone, by providing evidence and explaining effects upon the reader
- comment on presentational devices and explain their impact upon a reader.

Let's look at the blurb on the back cover of *Gravenhunger* (see opposite).

Activity

Consider the use of colour, layout, image and font on the back cover of *Gravenhunger*.

- Begin by devising five questions that you will ask a partner to get them thinking analytically about the use of presentational devices.
- Swap your questions and discuss your responses.
- Individually, write an analysis of how presentational devices have been used on the back cover of the text. Remember to use C.L.I.F (see page 46).

Now you will begin to analyse how language has been used in the blurb, which has been reprinted below.

Activity

As you read the text, record your response to each of the prompts, which encourage you to think about how language and structural features have been used to suggest this book is an entertaining read.

[2] What effect does this abrupt first sentence have upon the reader and what tone does it convey?

[4] What does this description suggest about the house? Which words or phrases are successful in capturing the interest of the reader?

> From the award-winning author of *The Boy Who Fell Down Exit 43*.**[1]**
>
> Phoenix gasped.**[2]** How could she have kept a place like this a secret?**[3]** It was huge. Four storeys of dark grey stone glowering down at them through a multitude of mullioned windows.**[4]**
>
> …The sun had disappeared behind a dense bank of cloud – and above the towering chimneys of Gravenhunger Manor a thin grey rain was falling.**[5]**
>
> Gravenhunger Manor isn't the only secret Phoenix's mother took with her to the grave. Something terrible happened at the home during her childhood, something**[6]** for which she never forgave herself. Phoenix is determined to uncover the truth, but as he begins to dig up the past, he finds himself in mortal danger…**[7]**

[1] What does the phrase 'award-winning author' make the reader expect about the reputation of the author and the quality of her work?

[3] What does this question suggest about the plot?

[5] How does this description add to the reader's impression of the house?

[6] What is the effect of the repetition of 'something'?

[7] The writer ends dramatically; why is this and how has it been achieved?

Putting it into practice: reading to access media texts

Below is the beginning of one student's response to this task:

Comment on how language has been used in the blurb to generate a sense of excitement about the book.

[1] Valid point supported by reference to the text.

[4] Appreciates how structural features enhance meaning.

[5] Valid explanation and grasps point about immediacy of the hook text.

> The blurb begins by making the reader aware of the 'award-winning' reputation of the author and referring to a previous book.[1] This has the effect of making the reader think positively about Gravenhunger as it has been written by someone who has received recognition for her work and knows how to please her audience.[2] This information will have particular appeal to fans who are already familiar with the author's work and they will be excited to read more.[3]
>
> The reader really begins to appreciate how exciting the book will be when they read the dramatic sentence, 'Phoenix gasped.'[4] This short sentence suggests the reader will be immediately immersed into a dramatic situation and the book will be a tense and gripping read. [5] The verb 'gasped' is dramatic and makes the reader think that this storyline will excite them and hold their attention.[6]

[2] Confidently explains the effect upon the reader by recognising how they react to what they read.

[3] Develops explanation by considering who will be most affected by this choice of language.

[6] Analyses specific use of language and its impact upon the reader.

Activity

Using your own responses to the blurb, complete the student response above by writing three more paragraphs, making sure you work your way through the blurb.

Now let's look at the front cover of *Gravenhunger*:

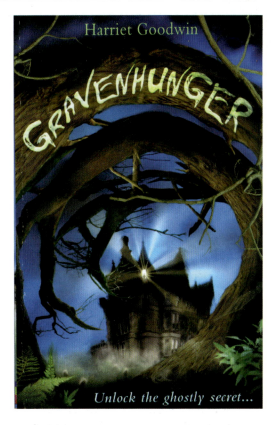

55

UNIT 1 SECTION B: READING TO ACCESS NON-FICTION AND MEDIA TEXTS

Below is the beginning of one student's analysis of how two presentational devices have been used in the *Gravenhunger* book cover:

First feature
Colour scheme

Explanation

The book cover favours a dark, muted colour scheme dominated by blue, brown and grey.**[1]** The combination of these colours suggest this is quite a serious book, with a mysterious plot,**[2]** which may have particular appeal to male readers as these are rather masculine colours and have connotations of mystery and darkness. Fans of the mystery genre of fiction will be attracted to this book.**[3]**

Second feature
Layout

Explanation

The cover relies heavily on image and colour to convey meaning with very little text, which confirms that it is targeting a young or teenage audience who would be put off by large amount of text.**[4]** The author's name is positioned prominently at the top of the cover to establish high expectations within the reader by implying she is a top-quality writer who is established within her industry.**[5]**

[1] Concisely identifies what colours have been used.

[2] Begins to analyse by explaining what the colours suggest about the book itself.

[3] Is able to appreciate target audience and specifically identify who will find the text appealing.

[4] Demonstrates an ability to analyse by stating what is observed and then offering detailed explanations.

[5] Makes a valid comment about layout and is able to offer a confident interpretation that considers the effect upon the reader.

Activity

The student response above has analysed the presentational devices of colour and layout. Write your own analysis of the front cover of *Gravenhunger* examining how the image and font reinforce the idea that this is an intriguing book.

Reading to access non-fiction and media texts: target success

UNIT 1

Matching grades to reading to access non-fiction and media texts

In Section B the essential qualities you need to show are highlighted at the important grade boundaries. Read these descriptions *carefully*; they tell you what your answer should be like.

Grade C work displays:

a In analysing language:
- ✔ Evidence of some evaluation of *how* language and structural devices have been used to achieve purpose.
- ✔ An explanation of *how* language and structural devices have been used to positively engage the target audience.
- ✔ A development of an appropriate interpretation that draws relevant supporting evidence.

b In analysing presentational devices:
- ✔ Evidence of an overall evaluation of *how* presentational devices have been used to achieve particular effects.
- ✔ A straightforward explanation of *how* presentational devices have been used to engage the intended audience.
- ✔ Some valid interpretations with relevant supporting evidence.

Grade A/A* work displays:

a In analysing language:
- ✔ An assured evaluation of *how* linguistic, grammatical and structural devices achieve their particular effects.
- ✔ A confident explanation of *how* these devices positively influence and generate positive engagement with the target audience.
- ✔ A perceptive interpretation based on precisely selected evidence.

b In analysing presentational devices:
- ✔ An assured evaluation of *how* presentational devices achieve their particular effects.
- ✔ A confident explanation of *how* presentational devices positively influence and aim to engage the target audience.
- ✔ A perceptive interpretation based on an insightful selection of consistently relevant supporting material.

UNIT 1 SECTION B: READING TO ACCESS NON-FICTION AND MEDIA TEXTS

Managing your time effectively

In Section B you have 50 minutes to complete four tasks based on reading two texts.

This means you will have 25 minutes to respond to the set non-fiction text and 25 minutes to respond to the set media text. When answering on non-fiction texts, spend 15 minutes on Task 2 and 10 minutes on Task 3. When answering on media texts, spend 17 minutes on Task 4 and 8 minutes on Task 5.

Practice question

Text A: Reading to access non-fiction texts

Read the article below and then answer the tasks.

Task 2

(Remember, Task 1 will be a writing task in Section A.)

Read the text below. Analyse how the writer depicts the hardships of living in Kibera Slum.

> Kibera slum is home to 1.2 million people and is one of the 29 slums that house 60 per cent of the population of Nairobi — Kenya's capital city. It was here I met Sarafina, who runs a feeding programme from her café. She is one of the 'Angels of the Slums' — men and women who are fighting the extremes of poverty in order to help children and the elderly and diseased in their communities.
>
> (*Daily Telegraph,* 18 November 2000)

Target success

Sample student response

[1] First point acknowledges an appropriate technique.

[2] Short relevant quotation embedded within the sentence.

> The writer depicts the hardships of life in the slum by using statistics[1] to inform the reader that it is home to '1.2 million people'.[2] This is a shocking statistic that forces the reader to appreciate the number of people who live in extreme poverty. The reader is encouraged to think of all the challenges that arise when so many people live so close together in a place like this.[3]
>
> The writer also alerts the reader to the hardships by informing us of projects such as this 'feeding programme'. The fact she refers to Sarafina as one of the 'Angels of the Slums' conveys the importance of her work,[4] and the phrase 'fighting the extremes of poverty' emphasises the scale of the poverty that exists here. The verb 'fighting' shows the reader how difficult Sarafina's task is by suggesting it is like a daily battle.[5]
>
> The writer also emphasises the hardships by showing that people of all ages are affected.[6] We read how Sarafina helps 'children and the elderly and diseased...'. The word 'diseased' makes us realise the unhygienic conditions these people are forced to live in and the effect this has on their health.[7]

[3] Developed explanation that considers the reader response.

[4] Valid interpretation of evidence from the text.

[5] Confident analysis of the writer's verb choice.

[6] Relevant point that demonstrates a secure understanding of the text.

[7] Continues to select relevant evidence and analyse the writer's language.

This response demonstrates an ability to:
- ✔ extract meaning
- ✔ support interpretation through relevant selection of quotation
- ✔ explain evidence in detail
- ✔ consider how specific words and phrases have an impact upon the reader.

Practice question

Task 3

Read the text below and answer this task:

In your own words, write down two reasons the writer gives to explain her strong emotions during her visit to the slum. Present supporting evidence.

> Trailed by hordes of squealing children, I arrive at Sarafina's café in the heart of the slum. It's a heartbreaking scene. The benches lining the walls of the corrugated iron shack are full of young mothers with their sickly, crying babies and skeletal old people with racking coughs. Homeless slum children flock in for their supper: 'This one with the little sister has no mother,' says Sarafina pointing to a child of eight carrying a malnourished baby with a swollen belly. 'Many of them are orphans but we can't afford medicine for those who are sick.' The stories make for difficult listening.
>
> (*Daily Telegraph,* 18 November 2000)

UNIT 1 SECTION B: READING TO ACCESS NON-FICTION AND MEDIA TEXTS

Sample student response

First reason

The writer accounts for her strong emotions during her visit because she herself has come to realise the many hardships faced by those who live in the slums.[1] She clearly has strong admiration for those like Sarafina who work hard to help those in need. She has witnessed first-hand the effects of poverty and disease on young and old people and seems overwhelmed by the number of people who need help.[2]

Supporting evidence

The word 'fighting' shows the writer recognises the challenges faced by workers like Sarafina. Words like 'hordes', 'full' and 'flock' confirm the large numbers needing help, which upsets the writer.[3]

Second reason

At the end of the extract, the writer accounts further for her strong feelings because her visit has made her realise how desperate the situation is in the slum as children are denied a childhood and people are dying of hunger. In the short sentence at the end we sense that she feels emotional but powerless.[4]

Supporting Evidence

The phrase 'a child of eight carrying a malnourished baby' emphasises how children are forced to undertake responsibilities. The word 'malnourished' confirms the extreme hunger that is killing people, even young babies who don't get a start in life. The writer states the stories she hears make for 'difficult listening', which confirms she feels she must listen as she doesn't know how else to help.

[1] Identifies and effectively summarises why the writer feels emotional during her visit.

[2] Develops an interpretation that shows confident understanding of the text.

[3] Offers supporting evidence and appreciates how word choices convey the writer's strong feelings.

[4] Gives an appreciation of how sentence structure enhances meaning.

This response demonstrates an ability to
- ✓ extract meaning
- ✓ support interpretation through consideration of language and structural features.

Practice question

Text B: Reading to access media texts

Study the text below and complete the tasks that follow.

Task 4

(Remember, in this section Tasks 2 and 3 will be based on non-fiction.)

How has language been used in the section opposite to make the reader feel concerned about animal welfare?

Garden centres are major retailers of pets

Selling in a garden centre environment encourages impulse purchases. If you have a pet-selling garden centre in your area, please urge the management to stop selling live animals. Their pet departments need not shut down; they can still sell food and accessories. Rather than contributing to the problem of animals being bred, bought and abandoned, garden centres should encourage people to adopt a companion animal from a local rescue centre.

Please Support Animal Aid

Target success

Sample student response

[1] Appreciates how punctuation enhances meaning and can select relevant evidence to support their point.

[4] Recognises specific language techniques and can support recognition with relevant quotation.

[6] Demonstrates how a range of language techniques are used within the text.

[8] Appreciates how the text has been structured for impact.

> The writer creates concern by beginning with an exclamatory sentence, 'Garden centres should sell plants, not pets!'**[1]** This is an opinion stated as fact and the exclamation mark emphasises the serious tone, which is meant to make the reader think that garden centres have been doing something wrong.**[2]**
>
> The writer also tells us that garden centres are 'major retailers' and that selling animals here promotes 'impulse purchases'. These phrases concern the reader by making them think that many animals are being bought by people who have not really thought about what is involved in caring for a pet and that this is unfair on the animals.**[3]**
>
> The writer increases the reader's concern by using direct address, 'If you have a pet-selling garden centre….'**[4]** This makes it seem like they are calling upon the reader personally to do something. The writer asks them to 'please urge the management' using an emotive tone through the word 'please' to suggest the reader should be doing something to stop this practice.**[5]**
>
> The writer uses a triple in 'contributing to the problem of animals being bred, bought and abandoned…'**[6]** This makes the reader confront how cruel it is to treat animals in this way, and the word 'contributing' makes us think that by selling pets, garden centres are actually making the situation worse.**[7]**
>
> The writer tries to actively engage the reader by using a pleading tone through the phrase, 'Please support Animal Aid.' By putting this at the end,**[8]** they are appealing to our emotions by making us feel we can put a stop to animal cruelty by donating to this not-for-profit organisation.**[9]**

[2] Explanation considers tone and reader response.

[3] Selects relevant evidence and offers a valid explanation with continued consideration of how language makes an impression upon the reader.

[5] Analyses by considering the impact of specific words.

[7] Continued appreciation of reader response.

[9] Valid analysis that considers how a reader feels.

This response demonstrates an ability to:
- ✔ analyse structural features
- ✔ analyse words and phrases
- ✔ analyse language techniques
- ✔ consider tone
- ✔ select relevant evidence from the text and confidently explain the intended effect upon a reader.

UNIT 1 SECTION B: READING TO ACCESS NON-FICTION AND MEDIA TEXTS

Practice question

Task 5

Using only this section of the Animal Aid leaflet, select two presentational features and explain how each reinforces the serious nature of this text.

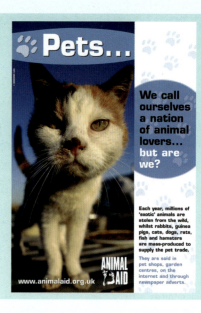

Sample student response

First feature
The image.

Explanation
The image dominates this part of the text as it is large and emotive.[1] It is a close-up image[2] of a cat that looks unhappy and it is intended to make the reader feel sympathetic to the animal.[3] The cat looks directly at the reader as though the not-for-profit organisation want us to notice it and stop our neglect. The cat has a serious expression and rather than generate the usual cute reaction from an audience, its expression makes it clear that something is wrong and so concerns the reader, who is encouraged to read on and find out the reason for this expression.[4]

Second feature
Layout.

Explanation
The title 'Pets...' is positioned at the top of the text to reinforce the message that we should be giving our pets greater priority.[5] Alongside the image there is a question contained in a coloured shape to draw our attention to it but also to make it seem like the cat in the image is asking us this question directly.[6] To direct the reader to think further about the issue there is more information placed towards the bottom of the leaflet with a web address to encourage them to find out more.[7]

[1] Concisely identifies *how* the image dominates and captures the reader's attention.

[2] Appreciates the arrangement of the image.

[3] Explains the effect upon the reader.

[4] Zooms in closely on the image and perceptively analyses its impact upon the reader.

[5] Is able to concisely identify positioning of title and consider effect.

[6] Perceptive appreciation of how image and layout combine to create meaning.

[7] Appreciates how less important information is positioned towards the bottom of the leaflet and its intended impact upon the reader.

This response demonstrates an ability to:
- ✓ analyse the use of images by considering their impact upon a reader
- ✓ analyse aspects of layout and their impact upon a reader
- ✓ recognise how image and layout work together for impact.

Reading to access non-fiction and media texts: key to success

POINTS TO REMEMBER

Begin by considering the two key issues:
  i What is the **purpose** of each of the texts? (What is being presented or promoted?)
  ii Who is the intended **audience** in each case?

Addressing these two questions about the texts will set you off on the correct path.

Use the following W, W, W, H questions to help you with your analysis:

1. **What?** Subject matter – what is the piece all about?
2. **Who?** Audience – exactly who is being targeted? Who is most likely to engage with each text?
3. **Why?** Purpose – what is the ultimate aim? To sell something, inform, entertain, persuade, amuse, be provocative?
4. **How?** Style, structure, language and presentational devices – the 'nuts and bolts' that are employed to successfully achieve the desired outcome.

Don't fall into the trap of judging a piece of writing aimed at a different kind of reader from yourself by seeing it purely through teenage eyes; instead, try to 'become the text's reader' when you judge its language, style and appropriateness.

Remember:

▶ You must demonstrate your understanding by using your own words.
▶ All points and interpretations must be supported by relevant quotation from the set text.
▶ All explanations should consider how the writer's use of language, structural features or presentational devices affect the reader.

Checklist for success: working towards Grade C	
Have you focused on the demands of the set task?	
Have you kept the focus on how the writer has achieved their effects?	
Have you developed an answer that considers the response of the reader?	
Have you clearly constructed your answer so that points are supported by evidence from the text?	
Have you tried to keep your focus on the writer's purpose and the techniques that they have used to accomplish their goals?	

Checklist for success: working towards Grade A/A*	
Does your analysis sustain its focus on the demands of the set task?	
Have you presented a range of relevant evidence that supports perceptive conclusions on how the writer has achieved their effects?	
Does your answer present a perceptive analysis of what the writer has achieved and how the reader responds?	
Have you focused your analysis throughout on the writer's purpose and the techniques that they have employed to accomplish their goals?	

UNIT 2
Speaking and listening

Introduction to speaking and listening
Unit 2 is tested under controlled assessment conditions and is built around three different **speaking and listening** contexts.

Target outcome: Conscious use of the various skills of oral communication in order to deal effectively with individual scenarios, as well as engaging appropriately in a range of group interactions.

Target skills
The target skills you will learn about in this unit are divided into three contexts:
- Individual presentation and interaction
- Discussion
- Role play.

In the **individual presentation and interaction** context, the target skills you will learn about will enable you to:
- communicate clearly and effectively
- present information and ideas
- use Standard English as appropriate
- structure and sustain talk
- choose and adapt language appropriate to audience
- respond appropriately to questions and the views of others.

In the **discussion** context, the target skills you will learn about will enable you to:
- interact with others
- make a range of effective contributions
- express ideas clearly, accurately and appropriately
- listen and respond to others' ideas and perspectives
- challenge what is heard where appropriate
- shape meaning through asking questions and making comments and suggestions
- use a variety of techniques as appropriate.

In the **role play** context, the target skills you will learn about will enable you to:
- create and sustain different roles from a range of real-life contexts
- experiment with language to engage the audience.

Assessment Objectives
Your Assessment Objectives in this unit are:
i Speak to communicate clearly and purposefully; structure and sustain talk, adapting it to different situations and audiences; use Standard English and a variety of techniques as appropriate.
ii Listen and respond to speakers' ideas and perspectives, and how they present meaning.
iii Interact with others, shaping meanings through suggestions, comments and questions, and drawing ideas together.
iv Create and sustain different roles.

UNIT 2: SPEAKING AND LISTENING

Controlled assessment tasks

You will be assessed under controlled assessment conditions in the context of an individual presentation and interaction, a discussion and a role-play activity. Speaking and Listening assessments account for 20 percent of your final GCSE grade.

The range of speaking and listening tasks you undertake will give you the opportunity to respond in a variety of formal and informal situations.

The types of activity you might be expected to undertake are:

- **Individual presentation and interaction** – e.g. deliver a five-minute presentation on a topic that interests you, followed by a question-and-answer session.
- **Discussion** – e.g. in a group of two or more, discuss the challenges facing young people today.
- **Individual role play** – e.g. you are a youth worker. Present your case at a monthly local council meeting for funding for your youth club.
- **Group role play** – e.g. you are members of the local council. Taking individual roles as councillors, discuss whether you should provide funding for a local youth club.

AO1 i 'I can speak and I can listen...'

> **Activity**
>
> In pairs, see how many different meanings you can create by saying each of these seemingly simple words and phrases using different facial expressions and tones, and by using your eyes, posture, volume and pace:
>
> ▶ Yes
> ▶ No
> ▶ I do
> ▶ Never
> ▶ Are you serious?
> ▶ I know

Wrong! We all secretly believe we have mastered speaking and listening, but these are subtle and sophisticated skills.

Two-thirds of all communication is non-verbal. This means words can have different meanings when non-verbal cues are added.

Most people have experience of listening to a boring speech or presentation. Too often the presenter fails to deliver in an engaging style. For this reason it is essential that you plan and carefully consider your content and your delivery.

Preparing to speak

Mark Twain, the famous American writer of *The Adventures of Huckleberry Finn*, once said: 'It takes more than three weeks to prepare a good impromptu speech.'

'Impromptu' means not prepared – made up on the spur of the moment. Twain was saying clearly that the only way to give a good speech is to prepare thoroughly – good speeches do not happen spontaneously; they are the product of careful groundwork.

Thorough preparation is the key to success not only in your individual presentation but in discussion and role-play tasks as well.

When speaking it is important that you:
- choose language that the audience will understand
- choose words and phrases that suit the situation
- use an appropriate tone
- control the speed and volume at which you talk
- are aware of the degree of formality you need to adopt
- control your body language
- make effective use of eye contact.

Preparing to listen

> The art of conversation is the art of hearing as well as of being heard.
>
> (William Hazlitt)

The three speaking and listening contexts are all interactive, so listening to what others say is very important. Listening is not the same as hearing! Listening demands focus and concentration.

You want to show that you are an attentive and sensitive listener. How many times have you heard a student ask a question that has already been answered by the teacher? Their contribution to the lesson is not constructive and highlights their poor listening skills. Your contributions to speaking and listening tasks not only demonstrate your speaking skills, they also indicate how well you have been listening to what others say.

When listening it is important that you:
- face the speaker and maintain natural eye contact – don't stare
- display open and relaxed body language – appear natural but attentive
- observe body language – study the speaker and any other members of the group
- don't rudely interrupt; wait until there is a natural pause and use non-verbal gestures to indicate your desire to respond or contribute
- show you are listening through non-verbal cues such as nodding, smiling or moving in closer
- think about what is being said and consider how you will respond.

The next three sections suggest a range of practical tasks you can use to help you learn and practise skills you will need for your speaking and listening controlled assessment.

AO1 i, ii, iii — Individual presentation and interaction

Many students find the individual presentation and interaction the most daunting of the three speaking and listening contexts. It is not easy to address an audience, even one that you know very well. The suggested duration for the individual presentation, before questions, is **five minutes**, but your teacher will assist and support you in working up to this if you are nervous. The key to delivering a successful presentation is to plan and practise! Some students find it helpful to record themselves, as they rehearse, so they can assess how they sound and get used to hearing their own voice.

Presenting

Here are some tips for preparing to deliver a presentation.

Do:

- Prepare thoroughly, bearing in mind **purpose** and **audience** – these will dictate the type of language you choose.
- Familiarise yourself with what you are actually going to say – where you intend to pause, where your tone and pace will alter.
- Write your speech using fluent spoken English that takes account of your audience.
- Practise aloud in front of your bedroom mirror – you may feel uncomfortable to begin with but that's better than being a quivering jelly of awkwardness in front of the class!
- Analyse your body language – plan your stance and remember that you can move your hands to help you present your speech in a measured way.
- Keep your head up – pick a point or two at the back of the room and address them – your audience will think that you are maintaining eye contact with them when you're not.

Don't:

- Don't write down all the words then read them out – your presentation must sound like a talk being delivered to an audience.
- Don't think that you're ready because you've read your speech twice; you won't be! Do at least six to ten slow readings or you will stumble.
- Don't write anything that is complex and hard to say aloud – change it.
- Don't rush through your speech, tripping over words. The larger the audience, the slower and louder your delivery needs to be.
- Don't fidget from foot to foot like someone who desperately needs the loo! Also, don't wave your arms around like a windmill – and don't scratch!
- Don't mumble. Most people feel shy and embarrassed so pretend that you feel comfortable making your presentation – that's what everyone else is doing!
- Don't read out what is on PowerPoint slides! The audience will focus on the on-screen content, so your talk should enlarge upon these points.

Individual presentation and interaction

Activity

Here are some possible topics for a presentation. You could use these to practise your skills:
- An individual interest or achievement.
- A current issue about which you feel strongly or on which you could focus to raise the audience's consciousness, e.g. homelessness or online safety.
- The history of… (much more interesting if it's something personal or somewhere local).
- A memorable experience.
- My hero/heroine.
- The person, place or thing I would put in Room 101.
- My hopes and dreams for the future.
- If I could go back in time, I'd visit…

Choose one of these topics and prepare a presentation to give to your class.

Activity

While each member of the class delivers their presentation, the audience should take notes under the following headings:
- The strengths of the presentations – which were the most enjoyable and why?
- The flaws that tended to spoil or detract from the presentations and how these could be overcome.

Feed back your constructive criticism in a whole-class discussion on making an effective presentation.

Interacting

Interaction means 'to respond appropriately to the questions and views of others'. After your presentation, you can expect members of your audience to ask questions or make comments on what you have said. You will be responding spontaneously, so do not get worried about hesitations or false starts, as these commonly occur in spontaneous speech. Your assessor is not expecting perfection here, so remain calm and confident.

Asking the right questions

Remember you will also have the opportunity to be part of an audience and to interact with others by asking questions or making comments on what you have heard. Support your classmates by asking questions that encourage them to offer a developed response, or to explain or expand upon something stated in their presentation.

Closed questions usually invite brief responses and may even be answered with a single 'yes' or 'no'. Beware of questions that begin 'Do you think…?' or 'Would you agree…?' and 'Are you…?' While you may be expecting a developed response with some explanation, with a closed question you will not put any pressure on the speaker to answer in any detail.

Open-ended questions require more thought and explanation, therefore they cannot be answered with a single word and so invite lengthier responses. Open-ended questions often begin with:

- How…?
- Why…?
- What would you say to those who…?

You can also promote interaction using **imperative statements** to encourage further expansion or development. For example, you might initiate interaction by beginning with one of these:

- Explain…
- Justify your claim…
- Tell me about…
- Clarify what you meant when you stated…
- Elaborate on your comment…

Activity

In groups of four, take on the following roles:
- One person interviews another about their weekend.
- One person is the interviewee.
- One person is the observer, who records the different types of questions asked and assesses their effectiveness.
- One person assesses the quality of the interviewee's responses, including their use of non-verbal communication.

Discussion

AO1 i, ii, iii

Discussion tasks will last between 20 and 30 minutes and will require interaction, so you will need to have a range of strategies to sustain conversation and be able to build upon the contributions of others. You should also be prepared to promote a point of view and to have your views challenged by others.

Chairing a discussion

You may be asked to chair a discussion. Not all discussion groups require a chairperson, but often it is a good idea to appoint someone to direct and control the discussion. The chairperson is responsible for:

- setting the context for the discussion and identifying the desired outcomes
- laying down any rules or guidelines about how the discussion should be conducted
- ensuring everyone has a chance to contribute
- moving the discussion forward, especially when others become fixed on a single point
- being aware of any individuals who are quiet and drawing them into the discussion
- keeping control of individuals who attempt to dominate the discussion
- summarising agreed decisions or outcomes
- keeping to the scheduled time.

Activity

Look again at each of the responsibilities of a chairperson listed opposite. With a partner, agree on the top four skills required to successfully chair each of these discussion topics:

- about the use of mobile phones in restaurants and on public transport
- at a school council meeting about proposed 'healthy' changes to the students' lunchtime menu.

You must be able to explain your choices to your classmates.

Not all chairpersons manage to fulfil all of these responsibilities and contribute to the discussion at the same time. Even if you are not appointed as chairperson you should still be aware of making sure that everyone has a chance to speak and trying to encourage involvement from anyone who is quiet or reserved. If you feel the discussion is drying up, try to offer a contribution that moves it in another direction.

Activity

Imagine you are participating in a group discussion. During the discussion you encounter several challenges, which are listed below. Identify how the group might address a member who is:

- constantly interrupting and attempting to dominate the discussion
- naturally reserved and reluctant to contribute to the discussion
- making irrelevant contributions and going off-topic.

UNIT 2: SPEAKING AND LISTENING

Participating in a discussion

Here are some tips for getting the best out of group discussions.

Do:
- Prepare a range of points on the topic under discussion.
- Present and respond to points in a measured way, e.g. 'That's interesting, Francis, but how would you see…?'
- **Listen** to what others are saying and be prepared to give your opinion.
- Make sure you get involved – try to make meaningful contributions.
- Move the discussion on to another issue within the topic if it seems to be flagging.
- Try to draw others who haven't made much of a contribution into the discussion, e.g. 'Another very real concern must be for the feelings of young people caught in this situation. What do you think, Peter?'

Don't:
- Don't think you just have to turn up and your natural brilliance will carry you through.
- Don't be abusive or dismiss points put forward by others, e.g. don't say: 'Don't talk rubbish!' or 'What would you know about it?'
- Don't monopolise the discussion, even if it is on a topic about which you feel strongly.
- Don't leave the discussion to others – make sure you take an active role.
- Don't talk over other group members.
- Don't get involved in one-to-one conversations at the expense of the group discussion.

Activity

Hold a two-minute debate on each of these points:
1. It is better to be a teacher than a student.
2. It is better to give than to receive.
3. Boys are better than girls!
4. Exams are a cruel form of assessment.

Below are some helpful phrases that can be used to indicate your intention when contributing to a discussion.

To promote a point of view:
- In my opinion…
- In my view…
- I think the main issue is…
- I believe…
- The way I see it is…

To interrupt:
- Excuse me, but can I just point out…
- Can I just say…
- If I could just come in here…
- If I may interject…

To build upon the contributions of others:
- To pick up on a point made earlier…
- I've been thinking about the point (name) made earlier and I'd like to add…
- Yes, I agree but I'd go as far as saying…
- If I could just develop that point…
- (Name) has raised a valid point there because…

Discussion

To agree with others:	To disagree with others:	To encourage participation:
• Yes, I agree… • Yes, that's right… • Yes, I think that's a good point… • That's a valid point you make… • I concur with (name)… • I think (name) puts forward a compelling argument…	• I disagree with that… • I am in complete disagreement with you… • I'm not sure that I agree with you about that… • Another way of looking at it is… • I oppose your claim that… • I reject your claim that… • I can't believe what I'm hearing…	Identify a person by name at the beginning so they are prepared to contribute: • (Name) I'm keen to hear your opinion on this… • (Name) how do you feel about…? • I know (name) has strong views on this… • I'll let you finish and then we'll hear from (name).

Activity

Evaluating performance in a discussion

A group of students is observed by the remainder of the class as they take part in a discussion.

Discussion group: Your school has secured £5,000 to improve facilities for students. As a group, discuss and agree on how this money should best be spent.

Observers: Adopt the role of 'critical friend' and make notes about how each member of the group performs in the discussion. Summarise:

▶ what each member did well – consider their verbal and non-verbal contributions
▶ what each member could do to improve their effectiveness in group discussions.

Feed back your comments in a whole-class discussion.

Activity

Student-based approach to bullying in school

Discuss how students can best tackle bullying in school. Consider:

▶ how bullying can be recognised
▶ what steps can be taken to stop or prevent it
▶ what help should be given to 're-educate' bullies and to support those being bullied.

Activity

Here are some more discussion topics you could use to practise your skills:
1. Is a university education still desirable? Discuss the advantages and disadvantages of pursing third-level education.
2. 'Educating boys and girls together is logical; it mirrors the world we live in!' Discuss the strengths and weaknesses of a co-educational approach to the education of young people.
3. 'Young people today have it so easy.' Discuss the advantages and challenges of being a young person growing up in the twenty-first century.
4. As a group, plan a suitable end-of-year trip for your class/year group. Discuss and agree on a suitable location and a programme of activities. Consider issues such as:
   • the timing of the trip
   • the location and activities on offer
   • the costs
   • staffing and safety issues
   • the benefits for the students and the school.

AO1 iv Role play

Activity

For one week, each student has the opportunity to address the class in role. You should agree on a set of rules and have fun introducing and concluding the class as another character. The rest of the class should be able to guess who you are.

The role play, which will last around 30 minutes, requires you to adopt a different persona. This may mean you having to take on a set of beliefs or opinions that differ from yours.

To get comfortable with participating in role-play tasks, begin by taking on the role of someone familiar to you. This could be a teacher, a principal, a parent, a coach or even a young person. Your school and family is full of individuals who can inspire you and help develop confidence in a role-play situation. Watch the people around you to get a sense of how they interact and how they behave in different situations.

Take every opportunity in class to develop your skills. Think about the voice of the character you are taking on. What do they sound like? Do they speak formally or informally? What kind of language do they use? You might then add some gestures to bring the character to life. To develop it further, you should consider the attitudes and values of the character. Consider the topic of the role play and what point of view your character will adopt, and why.

Remember you are still in role even when you are not speaking and this should be clear to anyone observing or assessing you.

Activity

Take on the role of a character who has been caught shoplifting from a local store. The police have been called and wish to discuss your actions. Consider:

- What has driven your character to shoplift?
- How does your character feel about getting caught?
- How will you react to the shop owner and to the police? How will your attitude be revealed through words, actions and mannerisms?
- How will your character speak? Why have you chosen this voice?

Observe your classmates as they take on this role. After each interview, one member of the class could summarise their observations about the character and how the role was developed.

Getting the best from role play

Here are some tips for how to get the best out of role play.

Do:

- Prepare a range of points on the topic from the viewpoint of your character. Consider how they would respond and **get in role**.
- Be prepared to move the scenario forward if it is becoming bogged down.
- Use the language patterns that you would expect from your character.
- In your preparation, it is sometimes useful to have a broadly agreed course for your role play to follow.

Don't:

- Don't think getting in role will be easy – sustaining a character is a difficult task to carry off convincingly.
- Don't keep repeating the same point.
- Don't 'entertain' the audience with colourful words and phrases.
- Don't allow the scenario to descend into a slanging match – that won't allow any of you to show your full potential.

Role play

Activity

Here are some role plays you could use to practise your skills:
1 Work in pairs. One of you is a customer and the other is a shop worker. The customer wishes to return a purchase but doesn't have their receipt. The shop's policy is not to issue refunds without proof of purchase. The customer should begin with, 'I'd like a refund...'
2 Work in pairs. One of you is an employee in a charitable organisation, who calls at the home of the other and tries to persuade them to sign up to give regular donations to support the charity. The homeowner is currently very busy and is sick of cold-callers.
3 Work in groups. You are attending a community meeting to discuss the increase in antisocial behaviour in the area and how to tackle this problem. Each group member should adopt one of the following roles:
- A community police officer, who will chair the discussion.
- A local senior citizen who has been a recent victim of antisocial behaviour.
- A parent whose child has been accused of antisocial behaviour.
- A 15-year-old boy who has got caught up in antisocial behaviour.
- A representative of the local Neighbourhood Watch Association.

Choose one of these role plays and prepare a presentation to your class.

While each pair or group performs their role play, the audience should take notes under the following headings:
▶ What were the strengths of the role plays – which were the most enjoyable and why?
▶ What were the flaws that tended to spoil or detract from the role plays, and how could these be overcome?

Feed back your constructive criticism in a whole-class discussion on making an effective role play. On page pages 72–3 there is a grid and a list of constructive comments that you may find helpful when evaluating performance in speaking and listening tasks.

Activity

Rent my house

This is a simple interview-style activity. Work in pairs, with one of you asking questions about a house for rent and the other answering as if they were renting out their family's home. Note details of the house and lease in a table like the one below to help give some structure to the interview.

Details
▶ Location – distance to city, school, shops, buses, type of neighbourhood
▶ Description – size, rooms, carpet, etc.
▶ Facilities – central heating, air conditioning, hot water
▶ Special features
▶ Lease – rent, deposit, time

UNIT 2

Speaking and listening: controlled assessment: target success

Matching grades to speaking and listening performances

In this unit the essential qualities you need are highlighted at the important grade boundaries. Read these descriptions *carefully*; they tell you what your performances should be like.

Grade C speaking and listening displays the ability to:

- ✔ adapt talk to the demands of different situations and contexts
- ✔ recognise when Standard English is required and use it confidently
- ✔ use different sentence structures and select vocabulary so that information, ideas and feelings are communicated clearly and the listener's interest is engaged
- ✔ listen carefully and, by developing own and others' ideas, make significant contributions to discussions and take part effectively in creative activities.

Grade A/A* speaking and listening displays the ability to:

- ✔ select suitable styles and registers of spoken English for a range of situations and contexts
- ✔ use Standard English in an assured manner
- ✔ confidently vary sentence structure and select from an extended vocabulary so as to express information, ideas and feelings in an engaging manner
- ✔ initiate conversations and demonstrate sensitive listening through contributions that sustain and develop discussions
- ✔ recognise and fulfil the demands of different roles, whether in formal settings or creative activities.

Assessing speaking and listening tasks

Below is an assessment grid that can be used when assessing the various contributions/presentations of your classmates.

Filling in this chart will ensure that you analyse the performances of others and, as a result, that you grow to understand the ingredients that make for successful speaking and listening performances.

Remember your role is that of a 'sympathetic friend' – don't forget that your own 'performance' will be open to assessment by others!

Name:
Task: presentation / discussion / role play
Content strengths (consider: structure and relevance; use of language; pace; intonation; emphasis and projection) 1. 2. 3. 4. 5.
Even better if… 1. 2. 3.
Non-verbal strengths (consider: eye contact; use of facial expression; gesture; posture and body language) 1. 2. 3. 4. 5.
Even better if… 1. 2. 3.
Level of performance:

Below are separate lists of comments that you might want to include or adapt when making your assessments.

Individual presentation and interaction

- Effectively communicated information and ideas.
- Adapted talk to situation and audience.
- Used a range of appropriate vocabulary.
- Made suitable use of Standard English.
- Briefly expressed points of view, ideas and feelings.
- Detail was occasionally used to aid development.
- Not always focused on target audience.

UNIT 2: SPEAKING AND LISTENING

- Straightforward vocabulary used.
- Displayed some awareness of Standard English and when to use it.
- Communicated complex and demanding subject matter, prioritising essential material.
- Used a sophisticated range of linguistic strategies.
- Displayed assured choice and flexible use of Standard English.
- Grammar and extended vocabulary used where appropriate to situation.

Discussion

- Listened closely and attentively, engaging and responding with understanding.
- Made significant contributions, moving the discussion forward.
- Analytically engaged with others' ideas and feelings.
- Responded to what was heard.
- Showed some interest.
- Occasionally made brief contributions.
- Followed the main ideas.
- Raised straightforward questions.
- Sustained focused listening, demonstrating an understanding of complex ideas by asking penetrating questions.
- Shaped and directed the content of the discussion, showing flexibility and challenging assumptions.
- Could initiate, develop and sustain the discussion by encouraging, participating and interacting with other group members.

Role play

- Developed and sustained role through appropriate use of language, gesture and movement.
- Made contributions to the development of situations and ideas.
- Showed insight into relationships and significant situations.
- Drew on obvious ideas to create a basic character.
- Related to situations in appropriate, if predictable, ways that showed some understanding.
- Created a complex character to fulfil the demands of a challenging role, using insightful and dramatic approaches.
- Explored and responded to complex ideas, issues and relationships.

The final row of the grid on page 77 is entitled 'Level of performance'. In order to complete this row, read the checklists for success below before deciding which of the statements in this table best describes the level of performance.

Working towards Grade C level	
Working at Grade C level	
Working between Grades A/A* and Grade C	
Working at Grade A/A* level	

Target success

Checklist for success: working towards Grade C	
Communicating and adapting language in individual presentations:	
Have you ensured that you communicated effectively to promote ideas and issues?	
Have you adapted your talk so that it matches the demands of different situations and audiences?	
Have you presented your ideas using a range of vocabulary, including Standard English where it is appropriate?	
Interacting and responding in discussion:	
Have you listened closely in order to engage with what you have heard?	
Have you tried to make significant contributions to move the talk forward?	
Have you made it possible for others to contribute, even if their views differ from your own?	
Creating and sustaining roles in role play:	
Have you developed a character and sustained it through use of appropriate language and stance?	
Have you made contributions that develop situations and ideas?	

Checklist for success: working towards Grade A/A*	
Communicating and adapting language in individual presentations:	
Have you communicated complex and demanding subject matter competently and with clarity?	
Have you made use of a range of strategies to meet challenging contexts and purposes?	
Have you presented your ideas using an assured and flexible choice of vocabulary and grammar, including Standard English, appropriately?	
Interacting and responding in discussion:	
Have you listened with concentration in order to critically question and manage complex ideas?	
Have you been flexible in order to challenge assumptions and to shape the direction and the content of the discussion?	
Have you initiated, developed and sustained discussion, encouraging participation and positive outcomes?	
Creating and sustaining roles in role play:	
Have you created complex characters that fulfil challenging roles by the use of insightful contributions?	
Have you explored and responded to complex ideas, issues and relationships in varied scenarios?	

UNIT 3

Task 1: The study of spoken language

Introduction to the study of spoken language

Unit 3 is tested under controlled assessment conditions and is made up of two tasks.
Task 1 assesses the study of spoken language. Your aim will be to write an analytical response based on two spoken language texts in terms of what is heard, in relation to context, purpose, technique, delivery and register.

Target skills
The target skills you will learn about in this task will enable you to:
- understand the characteristics of spoken language
- understand the influences on spoken language choices
- explore the impact of spoken language choices
- explore how language varies in different contexts

Assessment Objectives
Your Assessment Objectives in this task are:
i   Understand variations in spoken language, explaining why language changes in relation to contexts.
ii Evaluate the impact of spoken language choices in your own and others' use.

Controlled assessment tasks

This task is worth 10 per cent of your final GCSE grade. In one hour, under controlled assessment conditions, you will be expected to complete one written response in which you to investigate the characteristics of, and influences on, two pieces of spoken language.
You will be expected to focus your answer on the structure of the talk, choice of language, rhetorical devices, tone and pace. If watching a clip, you should *not* consider body language or appearance – **only what you hear!**

Preparing for controlled assessment
Before you write up your final assessment you will have opportunities in class to listen to the texts, study transcripts of what is heard and discuss the different factors influencing the spoken language. During this process you will begin to gain an understanding of the demands of the assessment task, but be sure to review your notes at home in preparation for the final write-up.
You will have one hour to write up your final response under formal supervision and with access to unannotated copies of both transcripts.

The skills of spoken language

AO2

Every day we rely on various forms of communication. Few of us will manage to get through a single day without engaging in spoken exchanges with different people. While we are familiar with analysing written language, we may not be so familiar with analysing our own spoken language or the spoken language of others.

Without even realising it, we adapt our spoken language depending on whom we are addressing and the purpose of our communication.

We use spoken language for different **purposes**:

- To express our ideas, opinions and feelings.
- To make sense of and confirm our understandings.
- To question and test our assumptions.
- To explore meaning.

Children develop their speaking and listening skills through contact with trusted adults and peers, and they learn to use language to develop their understanding of the world. They learn to interact with others for a variety of purposes and begin to develop understanding of registers (the types or groupings of words and phrases that are used depending upon the audience), tones and the use of expressive language.

In the study of spoken language you will look at many different kinds of spoken communication, from everyday conversation to formal public speeches. Along the way you will explore and discuss language issues, such as why and how language changes, and attitudes to regional accents.

This controlled assessment gives you the opportunity to explore **the way spoken language works** by looking at examples from:

- your own language
- the language of your own age group
- the language you hear around you
- the language you hear on the TV, the radio, the internet and other electronic sources, etc.

The characteristics of spoken language

AO2 ii

The best way to appreciate the characteristics of spoken language is to watch and listen.

Activity

Select one volunteer from your class who will try to persuade your teacher not to set homework at the end of the lesson.

As they are speaking the rest of the class should listen and record any observations about the characteristics of spoken language.

As a class, discuss what observations can be made about:

- the speaker's choice of language
- the structure of the speech
- the speaker's pace
- the interaction between the speaker and his/her audience.

How would this speech differ if it was written rather than spoken?

Activity

Select four volunteers to have a two-minute conversation about their favourite school subject. As they are speaking, the rest of the class should listen and record any observations about the characteristics of a spoken discussion.

As a class, discuss:

- how polite the other members of the group were when someone was speaking
- what observations can be made about the formality of the language used by the participants
- any evidence of non-verbal interaction between the participants, and whether this enhanced or detracted from the discussion taking place.

Each member of the group should make one suggestion about how their contribution would differ if they were writing it rather than speaking.

Activity

Now that you have had an opportunity to observe spoken language in action, work in a small group and agree a list of:

- five challenges for speakers in a discussion
- five challenges for listeners in a discussion
- five advantages that spoken language has over written language.

Share your comments with your class and summarise what they reveal about attitudes towards spoken language.

The characteristics of spoken language

As you observe spoken exchanges you will recognise some of the following characteristics:

- That the complexity and speed of most informal spoken language (such as a conversation or group discussion) makes it difficult to plan exactly what to say in advance.
- That the boundaries between sentences can be unclear and sentences can flow into each other or be joined with connectives such as 'and' and 'then'. This means sentences can be fairly lengthy, although intonation and pauses often separate speech into more manageable chunks for the listener.
- That the pressure to think while speaking encourages a looser structure than in written language, even in planned spoken language such as a presentation. This provides spoken language with opportunities for the speaker to go off on tangents, or to adapt their talk depending on the reaction of their audience.
- That in conversation or group discussion, the speaker can rely on instant feedback from others to ensure that they are understood or to see whether their points are agreed or disagreed with. Even when giving a speech or presentation, the speaker still gains feedback from the audience by reading their facial expressions or body language.
- That shortened expressions such as 'that one', 'in here' or 'over there' can be used, as body gestures can clarify meaning.
- That informal vocabulary can be used, such as 'whatchamacallit', as there is more opportunity to clarify meaning if the listener does not grasp it. If you are giving a formal speech or presentation, however, it is better to use to formal vocabulary.
- That interruptions and overlapping often occur in conversation or discussion.
- That spoken language frequently displays ellipsis – omission of words. For example: 'I'm going now, you coming?'
- That many expressions in informal spoken language do not really have any meaning or need to be included, e.g. 'You know what I mean' or '*Basically* I was *like* really angry.'

Spoken and written language

Both spoken and written language adapt depending on audience and purpose. These forms of communication have much in common but they also have unique features. When writing we are aware of spelling, punctuation and grammar rules that must be obeyed. We know that a newspaper report will not employ the same language features as a piece of prose fiction. Writers each have their own individual style. This is also true of our spoken language; we do not all express ourselves in the same way, nor do we all sound the same. Like written language, spoken language adapts and our language choices change depending on audience, purpose and context.

Use the tasks below to help you consider the main similarities and differences between spoken and written language. They will encourage you to understand how our language evolves due to changing modes of communication, such as mobile phones and social networking.

UNIT 3 TASK 1: THE STUDY OF SPOKEN LANGUAGE

Activity

Below is a list of statements. Copy this table and decide whether you think each statement applies to 'Spoken language', 'Written language' or 'Both'. Compare your results with a partner.

Spoken language	Written language	Both

- Is planned in advance.
- Can be formal or informal.
- Is rarely planned and often spontaneous.
- Tends to follow grammatical rules.
- May lack fluency due to hesitations and pauses.
- Has less consideration given to selected words and phrases.
- Allows for editing and redrafting.
- Shows evidence of a wide and varied vocabulary due to time available for consideration.
- Changes depending on audience and purpose.
- Tends to be permanent and can be read and reviewed later.
- Pace, tone and emphasis make an important contribution to the meaning.
- May have less varied vocabulary due to limited time for consideration.
- Often disregards grammatical rules.
- Words and phrases tend to be chosen for deliberate effect.
- The intended audience is not always present.
- Is more expressive due to gestures, facial expressions and body language.
- The intended audience is usually present.

Activity

Read the extracts below and decide whether each is a spoken text or a written text. You must be able to explain your decision-making.

Text A
OMG! Ya wanna see what yer woman was wearin' las' night. OMG! Seriously like she was workin' it. Absolutely stunnin'. Thon girl can put an outfit together, ya know what I mean like?

Text B
I was extremely impressed by the young lady's chosen attire. Her outfit confirmed her unique and sophisticated fashion sense. She was admired by many.

Text C
Hi babes u were gorg last nite

Factors affecting spoken language

Spoken language is affected by:
- **those involved (the participants):** their roles, status, expectations
- **the setting:** boardroom or coffee bar – though the topic may be the same

- **its purpose:** informative, persuasive, communicative, event (e.g. church service or meeting)
- **the audience:** the group of people you are speaking to
- **the form the message takes:** presentation, discussion, sermon, chat
- **long-term historic change:** words and language have changed and will continue to change over time – language and meaning are constantly evolving
- **short-term change or language fashions:** growing out of innovation, e.g. new words such as 'megabytes' or 'docudrama'.

It may have been challenging to categorise Text C in the Activity on the previous page because text language and online communication not only tend to combine features of written and spoken language, but also have unique features of their own, such as emojis. Some features that once were unique to texting have found their way into our spoken and written language.

Activity

Reread the three short extracts on page 84.

Using the above list as a guide, identify the different factors that may have influenced the language used in each of the three texts.

Can you think of any features, like emojis, that are unique to text language?

AO2 i — Spoken language terms

Over the next two pages you will encounter some terms that are related to the study of spoken language. The list below will help you understand what many of these terms mean and how they apply to your study of spoken language. You should begin to use these terms when analysing spoken language.

Term	Definition
Accent	How words are pronounced. Accents vary across regions and social classes.
Adverbials	Adverbs or phrases that tell how, where, why or when something is done, e.g. 'He played **beautifully**' or 'She spoke **aggressively at the end of the lesson**.'
Back-channels	Words, phrases or non-verbal utterances, such as **uh-huh**, **yeah** or nodding of the head, which are used by a listener to show they are following and understanding what is being said by the speaker.
Clipping	This occurs when a speaker drops off the beginning or end of a word, e.g. **goin'** instead of going. Clipping is an informal feature.
Colloquial language	Words or expressions that are used naturally in spoken exchanges but would not be used in written exchanges. Colloquial language is conversational. Slang language is colloquial.
Context	The situation or circumstances within which speech takes place.
Dialect	The distinctive language and grammar used by individuals from a particular geographical region or social group.
Discourse marker	Words that are used to signal the relationship between utterances, e.g. **Firstly**, **Moving on**, **Finally** and **On the other hand**.
Elision	The omission of sounds or syllables. A form of blending two words together, e.g. **wassup** (what's up), **dunno** (don't know), **gonna** (going to).
Elliptical expression	Missing out words from a sentence, e.g. '**Want a drink?**' The absence of 'Do you' makes this expression more informal.
Enunciation	Pronouncing words or parts of words clearly and distinctly so that you can be easily understood.
Euphemisms	Avoiding saying things directly, often to make the expression less unpleasant, e.g. **loss** for death.
False start	Where someone starts to speak then stops to re-express or self-correct.
Fillers	Utterances that do not carry meaning but are usually expressed to buy time, e.g. **um**, **ah**, **well**, **you know**, **like**, **I mean**.
Hedge phrase	Words or phrases that are inserted to soften the force of an utterance, e.g. **sort of**, **maybe**, **possibly**, **I think**.
Idiolect	An individual's unique way of speaking.
Imperative verbs	A commanding form of the verb that can be considered rude, assertive or aggressive, e.g. **go**, **take**, **buy**, **come here**. They might suggest that someone is used to getting their own way! Can be used by interviewers or other speakers to convey their power within an exchange.
Inclusive language	Language used to create a sense of group identity, e.g. **we** or **us**. Can also be used to slightly dodge individual responsibility, e.g. rather than say 'I cut spending' a politician may say '**we cut spending**' to imply collective responsibility.
Interruption	When one speaker takes control of an exchange by talking before another has concluded speaking.

Spoken language terms

Term	Definition
Intonation	The rise and fall in a speaker's voice.
Jargon	Technical or specialist vocabulary specific to a task or occupation.
Non-fluency features	Common characteristics of spoken language that break the 'flow' of talk, e.g. hesitations, false starts, filler phrases, repetitions and interruptions.
Overlapping	This occurs when more than one speaker speaks at the same time. It may occur when individuals disagree or when two people are on the same wavelength and one supports the other. Another reason it can occur is when one speaker is struggling to find a particular word or expression and another speaks it for them.
Pace	The speed at which words or ideas are spoken.
Phatic talk	Often referred to as 'small-talk' as it contributes little to the exchange other than to establish or maintain personal relationships or interaction between speakers, e.g. **'How are you?' 'Fine thanks.'** or **'Cold today, isn't it?' 'Yes, indeed.'**
Prosodic features	Features that influence how speech sounds, e.g. stress, pace, volume, pausing, rhythm, emphasis and intonation. When you read a transcript it is difficult to pick up on prosodic features. Capital letters, punctuation and emojis or emoticons can be used in text exchanges and online communication to indicate prosodic features.
Received Pronunciation (RP)	The English accent not associated with any specific geographical region. In the past newsreaders were expected to use RP as it indicated high social status.
Register	The style of language and grammar used in particular situations or contexts, e.g. informal register when conversing with friends.
Repetition	Words or phrases that are repeated by a speaker. You should be able to identify whether this is done deliberately or occurs because the speaker is struggling to maintain talk.
Rhetorical question	A question that is posed by a speaker to make their audience think, e.g. **'Are we prepared to sit back and do nothing?'**
Scripted talk	Talk that is prepared in advance, e.g. a business presentation to clients will require prior planning and practice.
Slang	Informal language and non-standard words and phrases used by particular groups.
Sociolect	The language used by a particular social group, e.g. individuals of the same age or with shared interests.
Spontaneous talk	Talk that is generated in the moment, as the ideas come to mind. There will be less time for the speaker to think about their choice of words and phrases.
Standard English	The form of English that is preferred in any formal context. It can be spoken in a regional accent.
Syntax	The way words are arranged in a sentence to change the emphasis or to create a formal or informal tone.
Tag-question	Words that are added on to a statement to turn it into a question, e.g. **'This is a nice part of the world, isn't it?'**
Transcript	A written record of spoken language.
Turn-taking	When participants in a spoken exchange converse in an orderly and courteous way without interruption or overlap.

AO2 i, ii

Idiolect

Each of us has a unique and distinctive way of speaking; this is known as our **idiolect**, which comes from the Greek words *idio* meaning 'personal' and *lect* meaning 'language'. When we study a person's idiolect we examine the words they use and how they sound.

Accent and dialect

Accent refers to our pronunciation of words and is largely influenced by where we live. It is the sound of our language. Our accent can indicate our regional identity, for example someone from Belfast will speak with a different accent to someone from Londonderry.

Dialect refers to the different words and phrases and grammatical features that are used by people within a specific region or social group. One of the most recognisable is the Cockney dialect. Teenagers also use a dialect that many adults find confusing.

> ### Activity
>
> As a class, compile a list of words that you might use to mean 'attractive'. Write these on the board and discuss:
> - Which of these words would you never use when speaking to an adult? Why not?
> - Which of these words are now outdated?
> - Which of these words are most relevant to young people today? Where did you first hear this word?

There are several factors discussed below that influence the way each of us speaks.

Context and register

When we study spoken language we must consider the **context**, that is, the situation in which the communication takes place. Your idiolect will be influenced by the different contexts within which you are required to communicate. For instance, do you or members of your family adopt a 'telephone voice' when you answer a call? This shows how context influences our spoken language.

Idiolect

Register refers to the kind of language we use in a particular context or setting. When we speak to our friends we may adopt an informal register, but we are more likely to use a formal register when speaking to an employer or the school principal.

Activity

Discuss these questions with a partner:
- What might cause someone to adopt a telephone voice?
- What changes do we observe when someone adopts a telephone voice? Think about how they sound and the register they use.

Your idiolect

Activity

Think about an occasion when you have spoken to the individuals listed below. Complete the table and think about how your language changed with each exchange.

Audience	What was the context?	What was the purpose?	How did I sound?	Observations about my register	Language features I avoided and reasons why
A parent					
A teacher					
A friend					

Activity

Read this student's observations about her idiolect:

> I live in Belfast, in a working-class area of the city, which might explain why my accent is pretty strong. Like most people from the city I speak quickly. When speaking I often add in words that are unnecessary, such as 'wee' or 'like'. So I might say, 'I'd love a wee cup of tea' or 'Do you know what I mean, like?' People from Belfast know I do not mean anything specific by using 'wee' or 'like'. It's simply a dialect feature.
>
> As a teenager I tend to think more about what I am saying and less about how I sound. When talking to family and friends, I use contractions such as 'I'm' and 'don't'. I also clip my words so that the '-ing' will be dropped so I will say, 'I'm goin' to school.' For the most part, no one passes any comment on this but my English teacher will always correct me and so when I speak to him I make sure not to clip my words. I will say, 'What page are we on, sir?' and definitely not, 'Wha' page?' I know he will not tolerate informal clipping and he likes to be addressed as 'sir', so my register tends to be more formal in the English classroom.

Using the response above as a model, write a short paragraph describing your own idiolect. Try to:
- assess the strength of your accent
- give examples of dialect features
- suggest reasons for the way you speak
- show awareness of when you adapt your register and why.

AO2 i, ii

Formal vs informal speech

The formality of spoken language varies depending upon the relationships, roles and statuses of all who participate in the exchange. Informal or **colloquial** language is often described as the language of everyday conversation. We tend to think of written language as formal and spoken language as informal, but even within spoken and written forms there are variations.

Standard English

The term **Standard English** refers to a dialect that has come to represent the English language. Standard English is used in both formal speech and formal writing, but here we are concerned only with its spoken form.

Standard English is the preferred form of language in any formal context, e.g. a job interview or delivering a presentation. The speaker will apply the accepted rules of grammar and pronunciation. Standard English can be spoken with a regional accent, but non-standard features such as dialect or slang are avoided.

Activity

Here is an informal comment made by one student to another:

1. Rewrite this exchange using Standard English.
2. Write how you think the student will relay the message when they find the Principal.

> 'Hey mate, have you seen the Head? Yer man, erm… the sub in Room 12, wants the old witch cuz some boys are goin' nuts and someone's touted that Dowdsy's mitching.'

Activity

Rank these exchanges in order of formality, from most formal to extremely informal. With a partner, explain your decision-making and discuss any differences in the rank order:

- A private conversation between you and your best friend
- A job interview
- A casual conversation with a parent or grandparent
- A meeting with your teacher to discuss progress
- A conversation between you and a friend on a public bus
- A phone conversation to order food
- A text exchange between you and a parent
- A text exchange between you and a friend
- Meeting a friend's parent for the first time
- Greeting a neighbour.

Formal vs informal speech

Below are some of the main differences between informal and formal spoken language.

Informal spoken language

- May relax rules of grammar or include instances of incorrect grammar.
- Usually accent is strong.
- Uses slang/colloquial language.
- Likely to clip syllables, e.g. 'I was doin' my work', or to use elision, e.g. 'I dunno' instead of 'I don't know'.
- Sounds less fluent due to hesitations, false starts and pauses.
- Less structured.
- Evidence of interruptions and overlapping.

Formal spoken language

- Usually observes grammatical rules.
- May soften or dilute accent.
- No slang; uses Standard English.
- Clear enunciation with no clipping or elision.
- Sounds fluent.
- Clear structure.
- Evidence of turn-taking between participants.

Activity

Look back at the list of scenarios on page 90. In pairs, select one formal and one informal scenario and write a short script using some of the features listed above. Be ready to read your script to the rest of the class to see how many features they can identify.

Spontaneous vs scripted speech

AO2 i, ii

When preparing to deliver a presentation, we will spend time thinking about the content, composing and reviewing the content, then practising the delivery. We have time to think about what we want to say and then to focus on how we want to sound. For this reason, **scripted speech** tends to sound formal and fluent – but it can also sound rehearsed.

In comparison, when engaging in a conversation, we are speaking spontaneously and therefore have little time to consider what we say. We are processing our thoughts while we are speaking, and therefore **spontaneous talk** can sound less fluent and less formal, but it does sound natural.

Prosodic features

As we listen to another person speaking we find clues in the content that indicate whether they are speaking spontaneously or are delivering scripted speech. **Prosodic features** are the aspects of speech that influence its sound: that is, volume, pace, tone, stress and rhythm are all prosodic features and change depending on whether or not a person is speaking spontaneously.

Many of the differences between formal and informal spoken language also apply to spontaneous and scripted, but below are some additional differences:

Scripted speech

- Evidence of a clear and deliberate structure.
- Grammatically accurate.
- Wide and varied vocabulary; words are used for effect.
- Deliberate use and control of prosodic features such as pace, intonation, emphasis and pausing.
- Evidence of a range of rhetorical devices.

Spontaneous speech

- Less structured – ideas will be verbalised as they come to mind.
- May contain grammatical inaccuracies.
- Less variation in vocabulary as the speaker tends to settle for the first word that comes to mind.
- Less controlled use of prosodic features. May be quick-paced if the speaker feels under pressure to contribute or keep the exchange going. Could be staccato with increased pausing and hesitation as the speaker thinks of what to say next.
- Fewer instances of rhetorical devices but increased use of filler phrases, e.g. 'erm…' as the speaker buys time. May contain off-the-cuff comments.

Spontaneous vs scripted speech

Activity

Below are extracts from the beginning and end of Barack Obama's farewell speech. You can search for this online and listen to it to gain a fuller understanding and an appreciation of how prosodic features are used to enhance meaning and delivery. As you read through it, find evidence that proves this is a scripted speech.

It's good to be home. My fellow Americans, Michelle and I have been so touched by all the well wishes we've received over the past few weeks. But tonight it's my turn to say thanks. Whether we've seen eye-to-eye or rarely agreed at all, my conversations with you, the American people – in living rooms and schools; at farms and on factory floors; at diners and on distant outposts – are what have kept me honest, kept me inspired, and kept me going. Every day, I learned from you. You made me a better President, and you made me a better man.

I first came to Chicago when I was in my early twenties, still trying to figure out whom I was; still searching for a purpose to my life. It was in neighbourhoods not far from here where I began working with church groups in the shadows of closed steel mills. It was on these streets where I witnessed the power of faith, and the quiet dignity of working people in the face of struggle and loss. This is where I learned that change only happens when ordinary people get involved, get engaged, and come together to demand it.

After eight years as your President, I still believe that. And it's not just my belief. It's the beating heart of our American idea – our bold experiment in self-government.

***

My fellow Americans, it has been the honour of my life to serve you. I won't stop; in fact, I will be right there with you, as a citizen, for all my days that remain. For now, whether you're young or young at heart, I do have one final ask of you as your President – the same thing I asked when you took a chance on me eight years ago.

I am asking you to believe. Not in my ability to bring about change – but in yours.

I am asking you to hold fast to that faith written into our founding documents; that idea whispered by slaves and abolitionists; that spirit sung by immigrants and homesteaders and those who marched for justice; that creed reaffirmed by those who planted flags, from foreign battlefields to the surface of the moon; a creed at the core of every American whose story is not yet written:

Yes We Can.

Yes We Did.

Yes We Can.

Thank you. God bless you. And may God continue to bless the United States of America.

(Barack Obama, 10 January 2017)

Contexts for spoken language

AO2 i, ii

Interviews

Being interviewed can be a daunting experience, but it can be made easier by a skilled interviewer. Some people make a living out of asking questions.

When analysing the language of interviews, it is important to look at the type of question being asked. **Closed questions** should be used to find out specific information, e.g. 'What is the capital of France?' This is a closed question because the answer is 'Paris' – there is nothing else to add. Closed questions are useful for obtaining simple answers and are often used to begin an interview as they can put the interviewee at ease. They can also be an effective way of wrapping up an interview.

To find out about something that has happened, what a person knows, or how they do something, **open questions** should be used. A chat show host will use open questions when they want someone to talk for a while – for example, 'Can you tell us a bit about your latest film?'

It is also important to look at who holds power within the exchange and to examine the interactions between interviewer and interviewee, for example is the exchange formal or more conversational? You should also examine what the interviewee has to say and how they speak, to determine how comfortable they are with being interviewed.

The transcript below is from an interview with a 17-year-old David Beckham at the very beginning of his career. You can find this media-training interview online and listen to it.

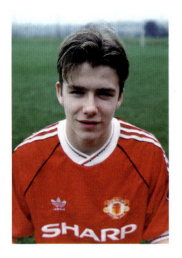

Interviewer: David, congratulations on a fantastic win.

Beckham: Yeah, it was a good win erm being away from home in the first leg it was was erm really difficult but that's the leg that we wanted so erm… we done well. The atmosphere was brilliant, the crowd was brilliant. United brought a lot of erm fans down and we was really pleased with the erm win.

Interviewer: Talk me through your goal.

Beckham: Well erm, it was nil–nil I think at the time and ah… I fink Ben Fornley erm got the ball off th' keepa and I fought he was gonna shoot but for once he passed it t' me and ah… and I just hit't wi' me… wi' me left foot an' s' just went in t'top corner and j'ss… unbelievable really.

Interviewer: A lot of footballers say, 'I just hit it and didn't know anything about it, it just went in', but when you hit a ball like that, as soon as it leaves your boot do you know where it's going to end up?

Beckham: Oh as soon as I 'it the ball I knew it was goin' in t'top corner 'cuz that's where I aimed it for really.

Interviewer: What about the goal you set up. What do you remember of that?

Contexts for spoken language

> **Beckham:** Amm… Well a… it was 2–1 and we was sor'of under pressur' and there was abou' five minutes t'go and erm someone played the ball down the wing fo' me an' I've just crossed it, I've seen Nicky Butt runnin' in an' he's just tapped it over the keepa (tuts) so… that was it really.
>
> **Interviewer:** So the first leg of the final over, the second leg to come. What's your prediction for the score in the second leg?
>
> **Beckham:** Ermm hopefully we'll win bu' it'll be hard again we'll hafta concentrate alot but… I fink we'll win
>
> **Interviewer:** 3–2?
>
> **Beckham:** Yeah, abou' 3–2'll do. (giggles)
>
> (www.youtube.com/watch?v=gIncXTp3ezU)

Activity

Re-read the interview transcript and discuss the following questions:
1 The interviewer does not begin with a question. Why do you think this is?
2 How does the interviewer change the type of questions asked as the interview develops?
3 Why does the interviewer ask '3–2?' at the end of the interview?
4 Look at David Beckham's responses. What informal features are evident? What explanations can we give for their inclusion in this interview?
5 Look again at Beckham's responses and listen to this interview if you can. What evidence is there that Beckham is speaking spontaneously?
6 Imagine you are a member of Beckham's media-training team. What advice would you give him ahead of his next interview?

Activity

Listen to a radio or television interview. Select a short extract and study it closely.
▶ What kind of strategies and skills does the interviewer use? Do they:
  • create an atmosphere that is formal or friendly, hostile or protective?
  • take an approach that is stand-offish or gushing, sneering or flattering?
  • use questions that are easy and undemanding or challenging and uncompromising?
  • use mainly closed or open questions?
▶ Which question in the interview generated the most interesting answer? Was it asked as a result of an earlier answer or was it, in your opinion, a question the interviewer had prepared in advance?

Commentaries

A commentary is a description of events by a commentator to a watching or listening audience. For live sports events and news feeds, the commentator must be skilled in communicating spontaneously for the audience to make sense of what is happening.

Sometimes commentaries take place after the event, but the commentator must not assume that the audience have witnessed the earlier events first hand.

UNIT 3 TASK 1: THE STUDY OF SPOKEN LANGUAGE

An effective commentary:
- creates or recreates the mood and atmosphere of the occasion
- uses precise language, especially when commentating on movements or actions occurring within a short period of time, e.g. a tackle in a football match
- makes use of appropriate senses, but mostly the visual and the aural.

Language features

Commentaries make use of the following language features:
- Jargon, e.g. a political commentator may use language such as 'opposition' and 'MP' whereas a football commentator is likely to refer to 'referee' and 'off-side'.
- Slang or clichéd phrases, e.g. 'Jones is playing on all cylinders.' Adverbials will be used to help the audience visualise, e.g. 'Hamilton takes the corner rashly.'
- Elliptical expressions communicate quickly what is occurring, e.g. 'To Hughes. Now with Grigg.'
- Fillers will be present, especially during quiet moments.
- Present tense if commentating live.

Prosodic features

Commentaries vary in tone, pace and emphasis, e.g. in sports commentary we may hear 'GOOOALLL!' as the voice of the commentator captures an unexpected and dramatic development. In other cases, a more composed and dispassionate delivery is required, e.g. 'The Prime Minister shakes the hand of the visiting ambassador.'

Formality

While most commentaries occur in real-time and are spontaneous, a formal register will dominate if they are being broadcast on television or radio. Informal features, however, including hesitations and even colloquial phrases or inaccurate grammar and syntax, may occur depending on the specific context.

Interactions

Commentators may interact with 'expert' guests, e.g. asking the perspective of a former professional player, or fellow commentators so that different views are represented. While there will be turn-taking there may also be interruptions.

Activity

Study the following transcript from a European Cup final. Two volunteers should take on the roles of the commentators and read aloud. The rest of the class should produce a short analysis of the language features, the prosodic features, and the formality and level of interaction between commentators if applicable. Identify specific examples and comment on their impact.

> **Clive Tyldesley:** Cross deflected, Effenberg, behind for a corner.
>
> Can Manchester United score? They always score.
>
> **Ron Atkinson:** The Big Goalie's coming up.
>
> **Clive:** Peter Schmeichel is coming forward.
>
> **Ron:** Can he score another in Europe? He's got one in Europe already.
>
> **Clive:** Beckham … In towards Schmeichel … It's come for Dwight Yorke. Cleared … Giggs with the shot … SHERINGHAM!
>
> (Sheringham scores)
>
> NAME. ON. THE. TROPHY!
>
> (www.youtube.com/watch?v=0xX570dVnOc)

Activity

Watch a television commentary and then listen to a radio commentary. Make a list of similarities and differences. You should be able to explain the differences.

Presentations

A presentation informs and explains. As it is intended to instruct, you can expect to hear:

▶ Imperative verbs, e.g. '**Get** 200 grams of sugar and **pour** into the mix.'
▶ Adverbials, e.g. '**Slowly** stir the mixture **over** a medium heat.'
▶ Discourse markers, e.g. '**Finally**, add in the salt and pepper.'
▶ Jargon, e.g. '**Sauté** the potatoes.'

Presentations are usually delivered using present tense, but the range of language techniques, the prosody and formality of the presentation will vary depending on the speaker, the audience and the context.

Occupational talk

Jargon is specialist language that is commonly used within the workplace. Some people hold a negative view of jargon as it can exclude and intimidate, but often it is necessary.

Activity

You have been asked to produce a guide to 'Teacher Talk'. In pairs, consider:
▶ the different spoken exchanges that take place within a school environment
▶ the language used by teachers – think about common terms and then pick three subjects and list examples of subject jargon
▶ how lessons are structured and what discourse markers are used
▶ the formality of teacher talk
▶ the prosodic features it uses.

Activity

Below is a transcript of a presentation by Jamie Oliver. You can access this online and listen to it, which will enhance your understanding and analysis. Read it carefully and write a detailed analysis, commenting on:
▶ features typical of a presentation
▶ the use of occupational language or jargon
▶ the register and formality
▶ the spontaneous nature of Jamie's spoken language.

I need 300 grams of nuts (.) it's called two nuts torte because it's got two nuts in it basically (.) got walnuts and almonds and I need 150 grams of each yeah? Which is pretty simple to remember and um and these are 100 gram packets (.) so there's a hundred grams of almonds (.) there's a hundred grams of almonds and then I'm not gonna get the scales out or nuthin' like that, just pour out the nuts and divide it into two, same with the walnuts (.) I think where at all possible do not use the scales okay (.) so just divide the old nuts in half again (.) what I'm gonna do (.) got the old Magimix (.) chuck the nuts in there okay and we're gonna whiz it up until it's a powder (.) 30 seconds 40 seconds (.) lovely (.)

(www.youtube.com/watch?v=2O05boE-tWA)

Analysing spoken language texts

AO2 i, ii

While there is no requirement to compare and contrast the two texts, many students do find a full analysis of spoken language texts naturally invites acknowledgement of key similarities and differences as well as a consideration of reasons for any differences.

You will need to source or produce transcripts of both texts. These will assist you in identifying the key features of each text. You will have access to unannotated transcripts when writing up your response.

Before commencing your written analysis, listen to both texts several times. Remember that you are analysing only what you hear. Try listening without any visuals so you are forced to concentrate on the language used and the prosodic features.

Before writing up, ensure you have an understanding of:

- the purpose, context and audience of each exchange
- the register used by each speaker and the formality or informality of their spoken language
- the variety of techniques used by each speaker and why
- the range of spoken language features used, e.g. fillers or hedge-phrases, and explanations as to why they are used by each speaker
- prosodic features and how they are used for effect
- whether each speaker is delivering scripted talk or is speaking spontaneously – be prepared to defend your decision-making
- any interactions that take place, e.g. is there evidence of turn-taking or overlapping?

It is best to avoid writing about one exchange and then the other. Using phrases like these will help you achieve a more evaluative analysis:

- **Language to compare:** Both speakers… Similarly… Like… Common to both is… In the same way…
- **Language to contrast:** Unlike… However… In contrast… On the other hand… Whereas…

On the next page is a partial student response analysing two interviews. As you read it you should appreciate the importance of **hearing** the texts in **order** to offer a full analysis of spoken language.

The transcript for interview 1 can be found on page pages 94–5. The relevant part of interview 2 follows here:

> **Parkinson:** Now at that time when you were dispossessed of the (.) of the captaincy (.) what was your reaction?
>
> **Beckham:** Erm well leading into the World Cup six (.) six months before that I'd decided that erm that I was gonna stand down as England Captain you know I'd had six years of being England Captain the biggest honour that (.) that any footballer could ever of… ah… hoped for. It was a big decision for me, no one knew about it apart from one of my best friends and obviously my wife(.)
>
> (www.youtube.com/watch?v=pvNo_5p_UUA)

Analysing spoken language texts

Interview 1 is a media-training interview involving 17-year-old David Beckham. It was intended for a select audience who would use it to train Beckham in interview skills. In contrast the second interview was an appearance on a talk show. By this stage in his career, Beckham had extensive interview experience. The television interview was watched by a global audience and Beckham was appearing through choice.[1]

The turn-taking approach adopted by both interviewers means Beckham is denied the security of interruptions, which can help direct spontaneous talk and establish informality.[2] Both interviewers favour closed questions[3] but in interview 2 the question is more personal and yet Beckham's response reveals improved composure. He replies initially with 'erm' to buy time before answering extensively. As the speech is spontaneous in both instances we expect hesitations, but in interview 1 these occur excessively because of nerves and inexperience.[4] In contrast, in interview 2 hesitations naturally occur as Beckham processes his thoughts without compromising fluency.[5]

Informal language features strongly in interview 1, such as the use of incorrect grammar, 'we done well',[6] and he does not self-correct implying that he thinks spoken language allows for some grammatical rule-breaking.[7] His informal expression is a consequence of his age and background.[8] Although interview 2 is not devoid of informal features, such as the elision 'gonna', there are no instances of clipping and his enunciation has clearly improved as we hear the '-ing' of 'leading'.[9]

[1] Shows understanding of purpose, audience and context.

[2] Analyses the interactions between interviewer and interviewee.

[3] Acknowledges the use of closed questions.

[4] Identifies features of spontaneous spoken language and their effect.

[5] Evaluates the impact of hesitations in interview 2.

[6] Selects relevant examples.

[7] Draws conclusions that consider attitudes towards spoken language.

[8] Understands factors that influence spoken language choices.

[9] Appreciates the effect of prosodic features.

UNIT 3 TASK 1: THE STUDY OF SPOKEN LANGUAGE

> **Activity**
>
> Below are two short transcripts. In the first, a teenager, Paul, is talking to his friend. In the second, he is speaking to a teacher. Hear the transcripts read aloud. Then write an analysis of each that shows how Paul's spoken language is shaped by the context in each case.
>
> ### Text A
>
> **Paul:** Right mate, whassup?
>
> **Joe:** Nuffin' you watch match las' night?
>
> **Paul:** Nah mate, busy. I had trainin'.
>
> **Joe:** Oh, I see. You didn't miss nuffin' to be fair. It was pretty lame like. Nil–nil, ref was brutal.
>
> **Paul:** Aye, my da watched it … erm I fink he turned it off actually. Anyway, erm, thingamajig will be here in a mo, you done your homework?
>
> **Joe:** Aye, ya wanna copy it?
>
> **Paul:** Oh yeah bro!
>
> ### Text B
>
> **Teacher:** Paul, bring me up your book, please?
>
> **Paul:** Yes miss, coming now.
>
> **Teacher:** Paul, this task is incomplete! If you continue to waste my time, I will put you in detention next week. What have you got to say for yourself?
>
> **Paul:** Erm… I ah… don't know miss, I'm sorry.
>
> **Teacher:** I am not interested in apologies, young man, I want an explanation for your repeated lack of effort. You do want a GCSE, don't you?
>
> **Paul:** I… I… yes miss, I forgot… I mean I didn't… erm I was gonna do it, I just forgot like.
>
> **Teacher:** Go sit down and *don't* forget again.
>
> **Paul:** Yes miss. Thanks.

The study of spoken language: controlled assessment: target success

UNIT 3

Matching grades to spoken language analysis

In this controlled assessment task the essential qualities you need are highlighted at the important grade boundaries. Read these descriptions *carefully*; they tell you what your responses should be like.

Grade C spoken language analysis displays the ability to explain and evaluate:
- ✔ different influences on language choices
- ✔ the effects of some regional variations in spoken language
- ✔ why spoken language shows variety and change over time
- ✔ how the student and others adapt spoken language for specific purposes.

Grade A/A* spoken language analysis displays the ability to explain and evaluate:
- ✔ subtle influences on language choices
- ✔ the significance of regional/non-standard variations in spoken language
- ✔ why various features of spoken language show variety and change over time, and in different places and contexts
- ✔ how the student and others use and adapt spoken language for specific purposes in different contexts.

The study of spoken language: key to success

POINTS TO REMEMBER

The writing-up period for this controlled assessment task is 60 minutes, so make sure you have pre-planned what you are going to do and that you are ready to use the time purposefully.

Efficient essay writing

- This assessment is a written one and so it is essential that you learn the rules of effective essay writing:
- The best writing results from the following process: **Think, Plan, Write**. You will have spent some weeks before the controlled assessment on the first two of these elements; even so, resist the temptation to start writing your answer immediately when you get in the room to start your write-up.
- Take the time to put your plan down on paper (this will be 10 or 15 minutes well spent) – this is essential if you are to produce your best work. Using your plan will ensure that your writing leads the reader through a clearly constructed analysis of your pieces of spoken language.
- You now have 45 minutes for the main writing of your task.
- A really strong introduction can give your answer its direction and set the tone for the remainder of your answer.
- A thoughtful and strong conclusion leaves the marker with a favourable impression.
- Allow sufficient time to review your finished work. You *must* review your work because when working quickly and under pressure *everyone* makes mistakes. Remember too that there are no marks for extreme neatness – it is much better that your work is accurate, even if it contains a few corrections.

Essay content

- Remember to keep the focus of your writing on what you have **heard** – the focus *must* be spoken language.
- Don't be tempted to over-prepare – trying to memorise whole essays is folly and will probably backfire on you, so don't contemplate it. Be content that you have prepared, that you know what you intend to write – so go in and do it!
- You may well have a transcript of the pieces you have studied as you do your controlled assessment write-up but use them purely for reference purposes.
- Any quotations you use should be quite brief – you will not get credit for copying out swathes of a text you have in front of you.

Checklist for success: working towards Grade C	
Have you shown understanding of what you have *heard* by **offering explanations** and **drawing conclusions** about the two pieces of spoken language?	
Have you **presented supporting evidence** from both texts to sustain your conclusions?	
Have you addressed all of the key terms of the question?	

Checklist for success: working towards Grade A/A*	
Have you sustained an **analysis** and **evaluation** of what has been *heard* in both pieces of spoken language?	
Have you presented a range of **appropriate** and **insightful supporting material** from both texts to sustain your analysis?	
Have you offered a **sustained and perceptive insight** into the distinctive qualities of both pieces of spoken language as required by the question?	
Have you constructed an answer that is fluent and assured in style and is competently structured, using accurate expression confidently?	
Have you employed vocabulary precisely to sustain focus on the subject matter?	

UNIT 3

Task 2: The study of written language

Introduction to the study of written language

Task 2 of Unit 3 assesses the study of written language. This task will be based upon your study of a poetry*, prose or drama text. (*A number of shorter texts is also allowed, e.g. poems.)

Your aim will be to present an informed and insightful consideration of how a writer or writers of literature have created/presented a perspective on a subject or theme.

Target skills

The target skills you will learn about in this task will enable you to:
- read and understand texts
- understand how meaning is constructed
- recognise the effect of language choices and patterns
- select material appropriate to purpose
- evaluate how texts may be interpreted differently depending on the reader's perspective
- explain how writers use linguistic features to sustain the reader's interest.

Assessment Objectives

Your Assessment Objectives in this task are:
i   Read and understand texts, selecting material appropriate to purpose, collating from different sources.
ii Develop and sustain interpretations of writers' ideas and perspectives.
iii Explain and evaluate how writers use linguistic, grammatical and structural features to achieve effects and to engage and influence the reader.

Controlled assessment tasks

This task is worth 10 per cent of your final GCSE grade. You will have one hour under controlled assessment conditions in which to write an essay on a set theme. For example:
Analyse how the theme of war has been presented in a text you have studied.
Or:
How are relationships presented in a text you have studied?
While you should have an overall understanding and appreciation of the entire text, you are not required to base your response on the whole text. For a more focused analytical study, your teacher will assist you in selecting relevant sections of your chosen text(s).

Preparing for controlled assessment

The controlled assessment task(s) will be based on texts chosen by your teacher. The theme(s) on which they focus are also specified. You will have several weeks in which to carry out planning and preparation. Your teacher will help you with your preparation in class, but you should also use your initiative to plan in your own time.

Writing up the response will be done in one hour and under formal supervision. Once this has begun it must be completed without the aid of any support materials other than plain copies of the text(s). If this controlled assessment is done over more than one session, your work will be held in school by your teacher.

The rest of this unit looks in turn at drama, prose and poetry and assesses the significant factors within each genre.

Drama

AO3 i, ii, iii

Drama is designed to be watched – it is in its natural environment on a stage. Take every opportunity to see the play you are studying (or for that matter *any* play) on stage. It is only then that you can really appreciate the combination of factors that lift dry, two-dimensional words off a page and give them life – the skills of the actors, the set, sound effects, lighting, make-up and costumes.

The key features of drama

A gripping play will use a mix of the following elements in order to hold an audience's attention:
- an interesting story or plot
- a story that contains dramatic tension before reaching a denouement
- characters that the audience can believe in
- situations that have to be faced up to and dealt with
- some sort of resolution – happy or tragic or somewhere in between.

Plot and structure

These are closely linked and you will have come across them before. Here's a reminder of their differences:
- **Plot:** how the storyline develops, with its twists, turns and unexpected incidents.
- **Structure:** how a playwright develops and divides up the storyline into different segments. In particular, you should consider the point at which certain scenes or acts open and close and how they build on what has gone before and prepare the audience for what lies ahead.

Structure is linked to changes in **mood** or **atmosphere**. These vary in order to keep the audience interested and to help direct the audience as to how to react to the characters and action. For example, Shakespeare's *Macbeth* (sometimes known 'the Scottish Play') opens with a short scene featuring witches. This sets the atmosphere for what will follow.

Often the mood will change as the story builds up to its dramatic **climax** – the play's most critical and dramatic moment (which is not always at the very end of the drama, as those of you studying *Macbeth* will know).

The **pace** or speed at which the action unfolds varies. The rate at which events occur will be controlled in order to create particular effects, such as an increase in tension or a sense of excitement. Often events happen in quick succession or there is a series of crises as the action builds towards the climax of the play.

Characters

We learn about the characters in a play mainly through the **dialogue** and **action**. Some playwrights also give detailed descriptions and background information about particular characters.

You need to focus carefully on individual characters within the play. What do they do? What types of relationships exist between them? Get to know the characters in your text and try to understand what motivates them to act as they do.

How writers set about presenting or revealing characters to the audience is called **characterisation**. This is also how the writer influences or controls our response to the characters and the situations they are in. As a result, we may share the anguish of one character while hoping another will get their comeuppance!

> **Activity**
>
> Hot seating is an effective way to gain an insight into a character.
>
> In groups, decide which character from your set text is to be the focus and to take the 'hot seat'. Take ten minutes to agree on four constructive questions to ask this character. Then take turns to role-play the character (take the hot seat) and answer these questions. Good questions will always try to find the reasons behind the character's attitudes and behaviour.

UNIT 3 TASK 2: THE STUDY OF WRITTEN LANGUAGE

Activity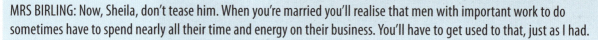

The extract below is from Act 1 of *An Inspector Calls* by J.B. Priestley. The Birling family have gathered to celebrate the engagement of Sheila Birling to Gerald Croft and to welcome Gerald into the family. Arthur Birling is the head of the family, Sybil is his wife, and Sheila and Eric, both in their twenties, are the Birling children. Read through the extract, stopping to complete the set tasks. For each task, identify evidence from the extract to support your points.

GERALD: ...I insist upon being one of the family now. I've been trying long enough, haven't I? (*as she [Sheila] does not reply, with more insistence*) Haven't I? You know I have.

MRS BIRLING: (*smiling*) Of course she does.

SHEILA: (*half serious, half playful*) Yes – except for all last summer, when you never came near me, and I wondered what had happened to you.

GERALD: And I've told you – I was awfully busy at the works all that time.

SHEILA: (*same tone as before*) Yes, that's what you say.

MRS BIRLING: Now, Sheila, don't tease him. When you're married you'll realise that men with important work to do sometimes have to spend nearly all their time and energy on their business. You'll have to get used to that, just as I had.

SHEILA: I don't believe I will. (*half playful, half serious, to Gerald*) So you be careful.

(J.B. Priestley, *An Inspector Calls*)

Based on what you have read so far:
▶ What social class do these characters belong to?
▶ What different attitudes can you detect towards Sheila and Gerald's relationship?
▶ Are there any clues of possible tension within this relationship?

Activity

Eric suddenly guffaws. His parents look at him.

SHEILA: (*severely*) Now – what's the joke?

ERIC: I don't know – really. Suddenly I felt I just had to laugh.

SHEILA: You're squiffy.

ERIC: I'm not.

MRS BIRLING: What an expression, Sheila! Really the things you girls pick up these days!

ERIC: If you think that's the best she can do—

SHEILA: Don't be an ass, Eric.

MRS BIRLING: Now stop it, you two. Arthur, what about this famous toast of yours?

(J.B. Priestley, *An Inspector Calls*)

Sheila and Eric Birling are in their twenties.
▶ What do you notice about their relationship?
▶ How does their mother treat them?

Drama

Activity

> BIRLING: Yes, of course. (*clears his throat*) Well, Gerald, I know you agreed that we should only have this quiet little family party. It's a pity Sir George and – er – Lady Croft can't be with us, but they're abroad and so it can't be helped. As I told you, they sent me a very nice cable – couldn't be nicer. I'm not sorry that we're celebrating quietly like this–
>
> MRS BIRLING: Much nicer really.
>
> GERALD: I agree.
>
> BIRLING: So do I, but it makes speech-making more difficult–
>
> ERIC: (*not too rudely*) Well. Don't do any. We'll drink their health and have done with it.
>
> BIRLING: No, we won't. It's one of the happiest nights of my life. And one day, I hope, Eric, when you've a daughter of your own, you'll understand why. Gerald, I'm going to tell you frankly, without any pretences, that your engagement to Sheila means a tremendous lot to me. She'll make you happy, and I'm sure you'll make her happy. You're just the kind of son-in-law I always wanted. Your father and I have been friendly rivals in business for some time now – though Crofts Limited are both older and bigger than Birling and Company – and now you've brought us together, and perhaps we may look forward to the time when Crofts and Birlings are no longer competing but are working together – for lower costs and higher prices.
>
> (J.B. Priestley, *An Inspector Calls*)

Based on these extracts from the play:
- What impression have you formed of Eric and his position within the Birling family?
- Why might Gerald Croft's parents not have attended the engagement celebration?
- Why is Mr Birling in favour of this engagement? What does this tell us about him:
  - as a father?
  - as a businessman?

Analysing a character

Here are some aspects you need to consider when you are analysing a character in a play. Use this checklist to help you gain a sound and detailed grasp of individual characters:

UNIT 3 TASK 2: THE STUDY OF WRITTEN LANGUAGE

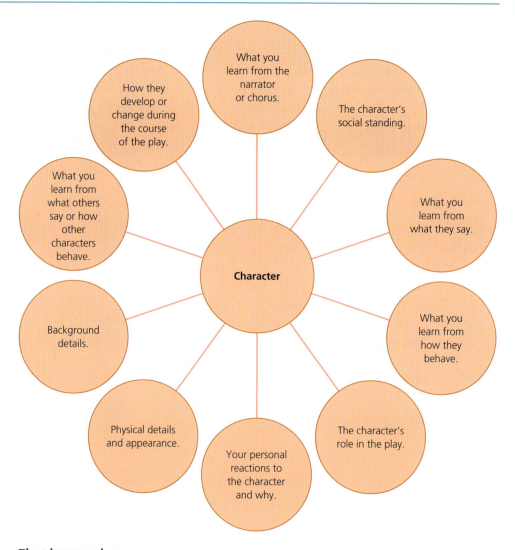

First impressions:
- How the character is introduced to the audience, if this is their first appearance on stage.
- Background information supplied by other characters.
- Details regarding physical appearance or personal facts.

Dialogue:
- What the character says to others.
- How others reply to them.
- Voice tones, e.g. anger, concern, sarcasm.
- What the character says in asides or soliloquies – a strategy Shakespeare used extensively.
- What a narrator or chorus says about them.

Drama

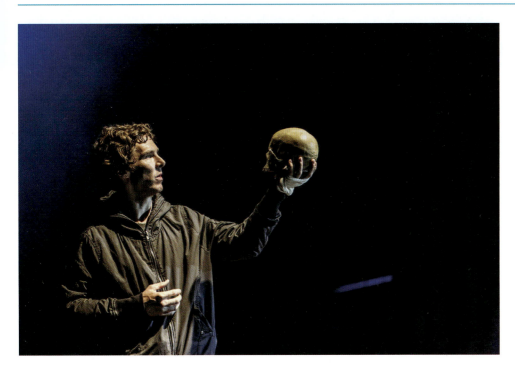

Actions:
- What the character does to others.
- How others behave or react in response.
- Any unexpected actions or responses.
- How the character enters and exits the stage.
- The pace of the action.

Language or particular words and phrases:
- How this reflects the character's mood and the moods of others.
- The power of particular speeches.
- How the character's choice of language reveals their personality.
- Use of humour.
- Use of colloquial or formal speech.

Setting:
- The importance of location to the character.
- The relevance of descriptions of place in the stage directions.
- How the historical setting helps the audience understand the character.
- The significance of social setting to the character.
- Use of flashbacks (or flash-forwards) to another time or place.
- How the general mood or atmosphere affects how the audience feels towards the character.

Activity

Pick a character from your set play and produce a detailed set of notes using the five headings (above and on the previous page). Concentrating on a specific scene or part of a scene will ensure your analysis is focused.

AO3 i, ii, iii Prose

The best way to begin studying a prose text is to enjoy the story. The study of a prose text for controlled assessment is not just a matter of knowing the story well, however.

You will need to be aware of the **themes** or **issues** that the writer wants to explore. You will also need to be able to analyse the **writer's craft**: the techniques employed to make the story interesting, such as use of language, structure and plot, narrative stance, and character development. You will be expected to show a thorough understanding of the **writer's purpose**.

The key features of prose texts

Gaining a thorough, detailed knowledge and understanding of the text is your first objective. You will develop this as a result of work in the classroom, as well as through your own personal study, which could include internet research. If you are going to discuss and evaluate a novel thoroughly, the most important aspects to consider are:

- **Setting:** the backdrop to the story.
- **Plot:** the sequence of events that shapes the storyline.
- **Characters:** including their relationships with each other.
- **Language and style:** use of description, dialogue, imagery (e.g. similes and metaphors), dialect, etc.
- **Themes:** the significant, frequently underlying issues that the author is drawing to the attention of the reader.

Setting

Stories always have a specific location or are set against a certain background. For example, in John Steinbeck's novel *Of Mice and Men*, the backdrop is the Great Depression in America in the 1930s and the story is set amid the tough life on a ranch outside the town of Soledad. This allows Steinbeck to portray the harsh existence that itinerant labourers endured at this time.

> **Activity**
>
> In pairs, identify the **main features** of the setting in a prose text you have read. Note your findings in a bulletpoint list.
>
> Outline the main **reasons why** you think the writer chose this setting.

Plot

In a prose text the linked sequence of events provides the basic storyline or plot. The plot is the skeleton of the text, around which the writer develops the flesh of their creation.

A plot can take a fairly straightforward form and be based on a time sequence. For example, *Lord of the Flies* is a chronological account; it is a frightening description of how life on the island deteriorates over a period of time. A plot may not be so straightforward and may involve flashbacks, or techniques similar to those Jennifer Johnston uses in *How Many Miles to Babylon?*

Writers often increase the suspense or add to the mystery of the story by developing unusual twists and turns in the plot in order to sustain the reader's interest. You need to be aware of the reason for and the outcome of these devices.

The critical stage of the plot is the finale, the climax of the account, when the writer makes their point and leaves a final impression upon the reader. For example, in *Animal Farm*, the climax happens when Benjamin and Clover are looking through the window at the special feast in the farmhouse. As they look from pig to man and from man to pig, they realise that they can no longer tell the difference: pigs and men are impossible to differentiate. Both are equally corrupt.

> **Activity**
>
> Consider the ending of your prose text, was it expected or unexpected? Bullet point the reasons for your answer.
>
> Identify what point the writer is making at the end of your text and what impression the ending leaves upon you as a reader.
>
> Share your responses with the class and discuss possible alternate endings.

Characters

When you are studying a novel or short story it is important to pay close attention to the characters. When you first read the text you will gain a general understanding of whom the characters are and what they do, but you will need to reflect on the characters in more depth.

Main characters will be three-dimensional, believable individuals who change as a result of what happens to them. By the end of the text they may have gained a deeper understanding of themselves.

You can identify changes within a character by focusing on:

- **Thoughts and feelings:** Consider the thoughts and feelings of the character. Look for thoughts that are repeated throughout the story. What are the goals, ambitions and values of the character, and how do they change? If the thoughts and feelings of the character change, it will generally be because they have learnt something about themselves and life, which will help inform you of the theme of the text.
- **Conversations and interactions:** What does the character say and do? Writers put words in their characters' mouths for good reasons.
- **Learning outcomes:** What does the character learn and therefore what do you learn?

Conflict

Writers frequently put their characters in a conflict situation, so you may want to focus on the conflicts that are evident within the text:

- Is there a conflict between two or more people?
- Is the main character in conflict with the world?
- Is the character in conflict with society?
- Is the character in conflict with himself or herself?

The outcome of such conflicts is usually determined by what the writer wants the reader to learn, so the outcome emphasises the theme.

UNIT 3 TASK 2: THE STUDY OF WRITTEN LANGUAGE

Activity

Read the extract from *Of Mice and Men* by John Steinbeck and answer these questions:
1. Whom is the conflict between?
2. What themes or issues are hinted at in this short extract?
3. What do the highlighted words and phrases tell us about the character of Curley?

'You the new guys the old man was waitin' for?'

'We just come in,' said George.

'Let the big guy talk.'

Lennie twisted with embarrassment. George said, 'S'pose he don't want to talk?' Curley lashed his body around. 'By Christ, he's gotta talk when he's spoke to. What the hell are you gettin' into it for?'

'We travel together,' said George coldly.

'Oh, so it's that way.'

George was tense, and motionless. 'Yeah, it's that way.'

Lennie was looking helplessly to George for instruction.

'An' you won't let the big guy talk, is that it?'

'He can talk if he wants to tell you anything.' He nodded slightly to Lennie.

'We jus' come in,' said Lennie softly.

Curley stared levelly at him. 'Well, nex' time you answer when you're spoke to.' He turned toward the door and walked out, and his elbows were still bent out a little.

(John Steinbeck, *Of Mice and Men*)

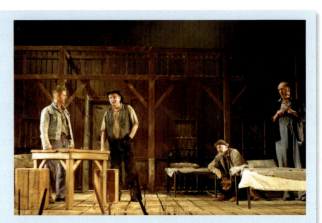

Point. Evidence. Explain.

You may already be familiar with P.E.E, which can be a useful technique for writing about texts:

P Make a **point** about the text.

E Select relevant **evidence** from the text to support your point.

E **Explain** what the reader thinks/feels/understands from the selected quotation.

When we are writing about characters we must infer rather than simply rely on what the writer tells us. 'To infer' means to deduct and form our own reasoned conclusion based on the evidence contained within the text or extract.

In the above extract we infer that Lennie is feeling uneasy in the presence of Curley. Although Steinbeck does not state this explicitly, he does imply it by having Lennie say very little. When he does speak his words are delivered 'softly', as though he does not want to upset or offend Curley.

A student produced this PEE paragraph:

[1] Makes an accurate point that shows an ability to infer.

[2] Selects short, relevant evidence from the text to support the point made about Lennie.

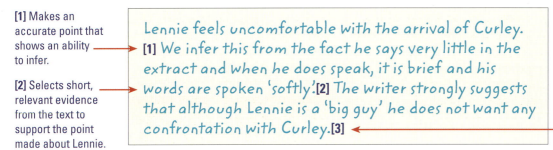

Lennie feels uncomfortable with the arrival of Curley. [1] We infer this from the fact he says very little in the extract and when he does speak, it is brief and his words are spoken 'softly'. [2] The writer strongly suggests that although Lennie is a 'big guy' he does not want any confrontation with Curley. [3]

[3] Explanation outlines the reader's understanding of the writer's intentions.

Insight into characters

Characters do not invent themselves; they are deliberately created, shaped and perfected by the writer.

You need to understand how writers create and develop characters and how they control our feelings about those characters.

You can develop an insight into characters by assessing:

- what they look like
- what they do
- what they say – and how they say it!
- what they think and feel
- what other characters say about them
- how other characters treat them or react to them.

Activity

Select relevant evidence from the *Of Mice and Men* extract and write two P.E.E paragraphs on the character of Curley.

Language and style

Every writer selects a distinctive **style** of writing to suit:

- the setting they have chosen
- the characters they are creating
- the sort of story they are presenting
- what is happening in the story at a particular point.

One of the first features to note is the narrative style – the point of view from which the story is told. *To Kill a Mockingbird*, for example, is presented in the **first person**, through the eyes of one of the characters in the novel. The writer has **adopted the persona** of a character and the effect of this is to draw the reader more intimately into the events of the story, to make it somehow more personal and immediate.

By contrast, *Lord of the Flies* is presented in the **third person**, through the eyes of an outside observer. The writer therefore seems more detached and objective in their presentation of the story.

The language and style of a prose text can include a wide range of features. For example:

- **Vivid adjectives or descriptive phrases** – e.g. in the description of the tropical island in *Lord of the Flies*: 'Here and there, **little breezes** crept over the **polished waters** beneath the **haze of heat**. When these breezes reached the platform the **palm-fronds would whisper**, so that **spots of blurred sunlight** slid over their bodies or **moved like bright, winged things** in the shade.'

- **Metaphors** and **similes** – e.g. in *Of Mice and Men*, Slim's '**hatchet face** was ageless'; in *The Woodlanders*, '**the bleared white visage** of a sunless winter day emerged **like a dead-born child**.'
- **Dialogue** – e.g. the tense dialogue between the signalman and the narrator in Dickens' *The Signal-man*.
- **Symbols** – e.g. the **conch** or the **pig's head** in *Lord of the Flies*.

- **Verbs of action or violence** – e.g. in *To Kill a Mockingbird*, the description of the shooting of the mad dog: 'Atticus' hand **yanked** a ball-tipped lever as he brought the gun to his shoulder. The rifle **cracked**. Tim Johnson **leaped**, **flopped over** and **crumpled** on the sidewalk in a brown and white heap.'
- **Dialect** or **colloquial expressions** – e.g. in *Of Mice and Men*, Candy 'said excitedly, "We **oughtta let 'im** get away. Curly **go'n'ta wanta get 'im** lynched."'
- **Building of tension** – especially towards the end of a chapter or an important event, e.g. in *Lord of the Flies* (end of Chapter 11), the writer hints at the violence that Sam and Eric are about to endure: 'Roger edged past the Chief, only just avoiding pushing him with his shoulder. The **yelling ceased**, and Samneric lay looking up in **quiet terror**. Roger advanced upon them as one wielding a **nameless authority**.'

Themes

In many cases the theme(s) will be the writer's starting point. The writer may want to illustrate their views on a particular issue, or even to manipulate readers' attitudes towards that issue. For example, in *Animal Farm* Orwell is exposing the problems arising from totalitarian government.

A theme may also be expressed through key events in the novel. For example, in *To Kill a Mockingbird* Harper Lee portrays, through the trial of a black man accused of the rape of a white woman, how racial prejudice prevents justice from being done.

Writers may explore more than one theme in their story, and they often present a range of views on the way people live their lives or on society and its values.

You can judge the writer's success in illustrating their theme(s) by the impact that you feel when you have studied and reflected upon the work. You should be aware that writers also explore themes through their characters, so even when you are answering a theme-based task you will be required to consider how certain characters are used to bring the different themes to life. For example, in *Of Mice and Men*, Steinbeck uses the character of Crooks to explore the theme of racial prejudice.

> **Activity**
>
> Make a list of the key themes that are explored in your prose text. Select one main theme and produce a spider diagram. Begin by identifying the characters and events that are connected to it. Next, select key quotations. Finally, at the bottom of your diagram summarise what message the writer is communicating through his/her exploration of your chosen theme.

Poetry

AO3 i, ii, iii

Poetry has always been written to be heard. So, if you are given some poems to read, keep this in mind. It is also worth remembering that not only have the poem's form and language been carefully selected, so too has the punctuation. If you are trying to get to the heart of a poem, read it according to the punctuation rather than line by line.

The aim for your study of poetry is that you can:

- demonstrate a clear and confident understanding of the nature of the poetry and its implications
- illustrate this through a perceptive analysis of the use of poetic and linguistic devices
- show that you are aware of how poets deliberately exploit language to impact upon the reader.

This sounds tough – and it will be if you don't make sure that you have a thorough understanding of the poems that you are going to explore in your controlled assessment. Your teacher will take you through these but it is essential that you also put in time at home to enable you to build up a confident understanding of the poems.

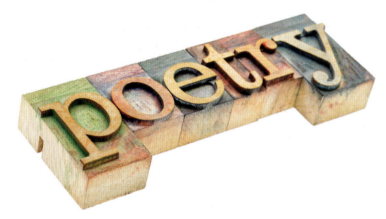

Poetic language and structure

Poets use many structural and linguistic techniques in their work. Remember, however, that simply recognising linguistic or structural features within a poem – such as simile, metaphor, quatrain, sonnet – is not your primary objective as you study poetry. You need to analyse the effect the poet is trying to achieve by using particular devices. Normally these devices are not used in isolation but are very carefully combined to create both an aural effect on the reader (what you hear) and an emotional impact.

Activity

Read 'Who's for the Game?' by Jessie Pope. It is a piece of propaganda poetry.
1. What does the title lead us to expect?
2. This poem is arranged in verses or stanzas. Do we associate war with order? Why might the poet have used stanza division?
3. Do you notice any patterns across the stanzas? What is the effect?
4. Which stanza do you think is most persuasive and why?

UNIT 3 TASK 2: THE STUDY OF WRITTEN LANGUAGE

Who's for the Game?

Who's for the game, the biggest that's played,
The red crashing game of a fight?
Who'll grip and tackle the job unafraid?
And who thinks he'd rather sit tight?

Who'll toe the line for the signal to 'Go!'?
Who'll give his country a hand?
Who wants a turn to himself in the show?
And who wants a seat in the stand?

Who knows it won't be a picnic – not much –
Yet eagerly shoulders a gun?
Who would much rather come back with a crutch
Than lie low and be out of the fun?

Come along, lads –
But you'll come on all right –
For there's only one course to pursue,
Your country is up to her neck in a fight,
And she's looking and calling for you.

(Jessie Pope)

Activity

Sometimes with poetry it can be useful to have visual stimuli to help arrive at an understanding of the images and ideas contained within the poem. Work with a partner to create or source a series of images to accompany one stanza. Make any important words or phrases stand out. Be ready to present your work to the class and be prepared to explain your choice of images.

Analysing a poem

Your analysis of a poem can be broken down into smaller tasks, looking at the major elements of a writer's craft:

1 Begin by looking at the **subject matter** of the poem: what event, situation or experience does the poem feature?
2 Does the poet have a **purpose** or a **theme** or a **message**? What was the poet's purpose in writing this? What is being conveyed?
3 What is the **mood** or **feeling** of the poem? Is there a key emotion or mood? Does that mood change through the course of the poem? What response does the poem conjure up in the reader?
4 What are the poem's **key features**? What **techniques** has the poet used, what specific skills have been employed in creating this poem? This should be a major element within your analysis.
5 Finish off with a **summary**. You have analysed the poem, now pull together the significant information. What impact has the poem had upon you? How successful is it? Do you think that it succeeds in its purpose; if not, why has it failed?

Key features of poetic techniques

Identifying the key features of a poem and explaining **how** the poet achieves particular effects is an important part of your analysis. Use this checklist to help you tackle this:

- **Structure:** How is the poem structured? Does it have a conventional structure such as a sonnet or an ode? Does it have stanzas with a regular number of lines, or any other features in its structure? What is the effect of this structure?
- **Language:** How would you describe the poet's use of words – are they vivid, striking, effective, drab, predictable or unusual? Is the language in keeping with the subject and/or theme? What part does the language play in the poem's impact?
- **Imagery:** Are there any striking examples of similes, metaphors, personification or symbols? What is their effect and what do they achieve?
- **Rhythm:** Does the poem have a regular (slow or fast) or fragmented rhythm? What is the effect of its rhythm?
- **Sounds:** Does the poem have any significant sound features, e.g. onomatopoeia, alliteration or assonance? Does the poem rhyme? How do these features influence the impact of the poem on the reader?

> **Activity**
>
> Go back and re-read 'Who's for the Game?' With a partner, make a set of bulletpoint notes on the poem using the prompts above.

> **Activity**
>
> Using 'Who's for the Game?' or another poem of your choosing, write a detailed analysis using the above scaffold to shape your response.
> Remember to think carefully about the effect of any identified techniques or features.

AO3 i, ii, iii Writing about literary texts

Planning is important but do not get anxious about the prospect of writing a detailed analytical response; think of it as a collection of P.E.E paragraphs!

Remember **P.E.E – Point, Evidence, Explain** – but vary the way in which you construct your points, evidence and explanation so that there is not an increasingly mechanical or formulaic feel to your writing. Use the lists of words and phrases below to help you.

Point:
- firstly
- initially
- furthermore
- to begin with
- in addition
- moreover
- finally

Evidence:
- for example
- as revealed by
- this is shown when
- demonstrated by
- for instance
- to show that
- such as

Explain:
- it appears that
- perhaps the reader can infer
- it is possible that
- this suggests
- this makes it seem
- which makes us think
- we can conclude that

It is important to bear in mind that there are two basics to be balanced here:
- what you say
- how you say it.

As you complete each paragraph, look back at its content and ask yourself if you have answered the question; this will ensure you are not straying from the main point.

Below is a partial student response produced under controlled conditions. The practice task set was as follows: 'Examine how Shakespeare makes Act I Scene 1 of *Macbeth* intriguing and dramatic.'

Writing about literary texts

[1] Acknowledges Shakespeare as the creator of this text.

[3] Evaluates the overall effect.

[5] Considers structure of the selected scene.

[6] Provides a valid personal interpretation.

[8] Appreciates that the text is intended to be performed.

Shakespeare creates interest in this first scene by having the witches mention Macbeth and an upcoming meeting with him.[1] Macbeth is the central protagonist and yet immediately the audience are encouraged to question his character.[2] Shakespeare's contemporary audience would enquire whether Macbeth was aware of this meeting or if he has associated with these evil characters in the past. The overall effect here is to engage the audience's interest in the character of Macbeth and his potential relationship with the witches.[3]

Shakespeare also makes the opening scene dramatic by suggesting that a strong bond exists between the witches. They operate as a unit and are therefore a force to be reckoned with. The fact the witches are unnamed and instead identified as 'First Witch', 'Second Witch' and 'Third Witch' makes them seem less human and more sinister.[4] Shakespeare's conclusion to the scene,[5] with the witches speaking in unison, creates a highly dramatic effect as the final lines are spoken by the characters without introduction or prompt, implying they have spoken these many times before and that, like their voices, their minds and intentions are synchronised.[6] The lines 'Fair is foul and foul is fair / Hover through fog and filthy air' have a rhythmic, chanting quality[7] that would grab the attention of the theatre audience.[8] The words themselves seem paradoxical and their meaning is not quite clear. Shakespeare has the witches use equivocal language[9] to stress their difference and shroud these characters in uncertainty.

[2] Considers audience response.

[4] Offers appropriate explanation that is relevant to the set task.

[7] Offers a relevant quotation and appropriate explanation.

[9] Gives a confident appreciation of the writer's crafting of language.

Activity

Re-read the student response and the comments. Then summarise three strengths of this response.

UNIT 3

The study of written language: controlled assessment: target success

Matching grades to the study of written language

In this controlled assessment task the essential qualities you need are highlighted at the important grade boundaries. Read these descriptions *carefully*; they tell you what your responses should be like:

Grade C writing:

- ✔ shows an engaged, personal and critical response to literary texts
- ✔ refers to relevant aspects: language, main ideas, themes and characters
- ✔ shows some understanding of the intended impact upon the reader
- ✔ makes references from texts to support valid ideas and interpretations.

Grade A/A* writing:

- ✔ demonstrates a discriminating analysis that offers critical and perceptive interpretations of literary texts
- ✔ explores and evaluates key aspects of use of language, structure and presentation
- ✔ explores and evaluates how these key aspects engage and affect the reader
- ✔ makes aptly selected textual references that illuminate the purpose and meanings of texts.

The study of written language: key to success

POINTS TO REMEMBER

Efficient essay writing

- Keep your essay focused. Always link what you have to say back to the question – but vary how you do this. Think of synonyms for words that occur frequently in your essay, such as:
    - **shows:** reveals, implies, conveys, portrays or suggests
    - **discuss:** consider, explore or evaluate.
- Try to use an extensive range of words, which will enable you to say exactly what you want to say. Reading helps expand your vocabulary.
- Generally, try to avoid abbreviations: etc., e.g., i.e., TV.
- Write out numbers unless they are awkwardly long: write 1 as one, but leave 123,476 as digits.
- Check your spelling and grammar.
- Use signpost words and phrases:
    - **for development:** in addition…, furthermore…, also…, similarly…
    - **for emphasis:** in particular…, especially…
- Use a new paragraph for each area being explored. Avoid too many short paragraphs as they give a disjointed feel to your work. Equally, avoid very long paragraphs as the reader's concentration will be tested. This is good practice and will help make your essay easier to read, but will not be awarded marks in the exam.
- You will be credited for using brief quotations to back up points that you make. If you are quoting more than one line of a play or poem, then use the line spacing and layout as it appears in the text. Individual words and phrases can simply be put in inverted commas and presented in the body of your answer without any formatting.
- When you are referring to the title of a text it should be put in inverted commas – this will clarify whether you are writing about 'Macbeth' (the play itself) or writing about Macbeth as a character in the play of the same name.

Essay content

- Maintain focus on the purpose of the task – the question!
- Show a sustained awareness of the intended audience and use language that is appropriate to that audience.
- Content coverage needs to deal with all aspects of the question and be well judged and detailed.
- Interpretations/arguments need to be convincingly developed and supported by relevant detail from the text(s).
- Ideas should be carefully selected and prioritised to construct a coherent discussion – so make sure that you plan and prioritise.
- Paragraphs should have a topic sentence – this will help you stay on task.

During the course of your preparations for the controlled assessment tasks you may well be given the opportunity to write an essay (not on the actual controlled assessment question that you will be answering) to get used to the write-up process. If you are also studying English Literature you will certainly have experience of writing about literary texts.

Below are checklists for success that may prove useful both before and after you have attempted any such 'practice writing'.

UNIT 3 TASK 2: THE STUDY OF WRITTEN LANGUAGE

Checklist for success: working towards Grade C	
Have you shown a straightforward understanding of the **writer's purpose**?	
Have you shown recognition of the **central theme(s)**?	
Have you demonstrated an understanding of some of the use that has been made of **literary devices**?	
Have you addressed all of the key terms of the question?	
Have you presented your interpretations in an **organised and fluent** essay?	
Have you used words and phrases that help **clarify meaning**?	

Checklist for success: working towards Grade A/A*	
Have you demonstrated a clear and confident understanding of the text and its implications?	
Have you presented a perceptive analysis which evaluates literary techniques and devices?	
Have you shown a clear awareness of how writers exploit literary techniques and language to impact upon the reader/audience?	
Have you constructed an assured answer that competently sustains a perceptive discussion?	
Have you employed an appropriate, extended vocabulary precisely to sustain focus on the issues under discussion?	

UNIT 4

Section A: Personal or Creative Writing

Introduction to Personal or Creative Writing

Unit 4 is externally examined and consists of two sections. Section A is an assessment of writing and you will choose to complete *either* the Personal Writing task *or* the Creative Writing task.

Personal Writing: The task will require you to write from your own experience.

Creative Writing: The task will require you to write imaginatively. You will be provided with an image to stimulate your thinking and help you create a narrative.

Target skills

The target skills you will learn about in this section will enable you to:
- ✔ write clearly, fluently and imaginatively
- ✔ organise ideas to support coherence
- ✔ use an appropriate writing form
- ✔ select vocabulary appropriate to task to engage the reader
- ✔ use a range of sentence structures for effect
- ✔ use accurate grammar, spelling and punctuation.

Assessment Objectives

Your Assessment Objectives for Personal or Creative Writing are:

i   Write to communicate clearly, effectively and imaginatively using and adapting forms and selecting vocabulary appropriate to task and purpose in ways that engage the reader.

ii Organise information and ideas logically into structured and sequenced sentences, paragraphs and whole texts, using a variety of linguistic and structural features to support cohesion and overall coherence.

iii Use a range of sentence structures for clarity, purpose and effect, with accurate spelling, punctuation and grammar.

Exam question ❓

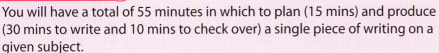

You will have a total of 55 minutes in which to plan (15 mins) and produce (30 mins to write and 10 mins to check over) a single piece of writing on a given subject.

AO4 ii Planning for writing

The three Ws

Before committing anything to paper you must be clear about:

▶ *Why* you are writing. What is your **purpose**?

▶ *What* the specific demands of your task are. What is the context for your writing – Personal or Creative?

▶ *Whom* your **audience** is. Your writing should show an attempt to use language and tone that are appropriate for the audience and purpose.

Sample Personal Writing task

[1] Your *audience* will be the people in your local area. As you are writing an article your writing should be formal and your language choices appropriate.

> Write an article for your local newspaper**[1]** entitled 'Things I like about where I live.'**[2]**

[2] The *context* is Personal Writing as you are required to select the things that *you* like most about your area. Your *purpose* is to inform your reader about where you live, to describe the things you like best and to explain why you like them.

Sample Creative Writing task

[1] Your context is Creative Writing as you are required to make up a short fictional story. Your purpose is to entertain your reader by producing an imaginative and interesting narrative that holds their attention.

[2] This task does not state a specific audience but you should avoid being too informal. Once you have selected your task and are confident that you have an understanding of *why* you are writing, *what* you are expected to write and *whom* you are writing for, it is time to plan the content of your writing.

> Use the image above to write a creative story**[1]** involving this character.**[2]**

Why plan?

To write well, you must plan effectively. It is important that you spend time planning your response. It is natural to want to start writing straight away, but by investing time planning your ideas you will feel more confident when it comes to putting your response down on paper.

The time allocated for this section is 55 minutes, which includes 15 minutes planning time so you should make best use of this valuable time.

▶ By generating and organising your ideas in advance you will know exactly what you want to say and where your story will go.
▶ Once you have the ideas you can organise them so that your writing is clear and coherent.
▶ You will feel more confident that you are focusing on the question throughout.
▶ Planning ensures you are mindful of demonstrating your ability to employ a variety of writing techniques, rather than relying on a few.
▶ Well planned responses are nearly always stronger, for the reasons above.

How to plan effectively

Once you have decided upon an idea for your writing, you should consider *what exactly* your reader will want to know. After spending up to 15 minutes planning you will have 30 minutes to write your response, so be realistic about what you can communicate in this time. The remaining 10 minutes should be spent reading over and editing your work. Remember: you are writing a short story, not a novel!

There is no single planning method that suits everyone. Below are a few suggestions and you should experiment with each of them to determine which approach you prefer.

The story tree

This is similar to a spider diagram but is more comprehensive as it encourages you to think about each paragraph or section of your writing. You should be confident about developing and expanding your paragraphs so that they are all relevant to the set title. This planning approach also encourages you to consider the different techniques you will employ to add interest. Below is one student's planning for the question, 'Write an essay about a time you were faced with a challenge.' The detailed nature of the plan means this student will feel confident writing up their response.

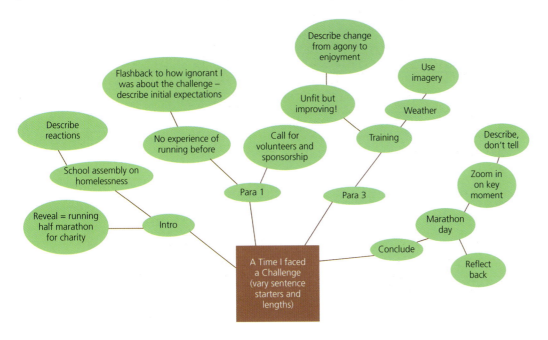

UNIT 4 SECTION A: PERSONAL OR CREATIVE WRITING

> **Activity**
>
> Produce a story tree for the task, 'Write an essay about a memorable holiday.' After you have recorded all your thoughts, number the paragraphs in the order you would write them. Share your plan with a partner and discuss why you settled on a particular order.

The bulletpoint list

Others prefer simply to list their ideas and then number them to indicate the order in which they will appear in the writing. In the planning list below the student decided to write about their talent for dancing:

- Dancing since I was a baby. (1)
- First place in recent European Dance Championships. (5)
- Fear that I might never dance again following broken leg. (3)
- Support from family who travel with me to competitions and pay for training.
- Aged five when I attended my first dance class. (2)
- Balancing schoolwork with training and competing. (4)
- Currently training to retain title. (6)
- Future plans for my own dance school. (7)

You can see that one of the points above does not have a number as the student has decided not to include this in the final piece. They are confident that they can develop each of the numbered points into detailed and interesting paragraphs.

The flow chart

Another suggestion is to record your initial ideas in a flow chart, which will also encourage you to think about the development and structure of your response.

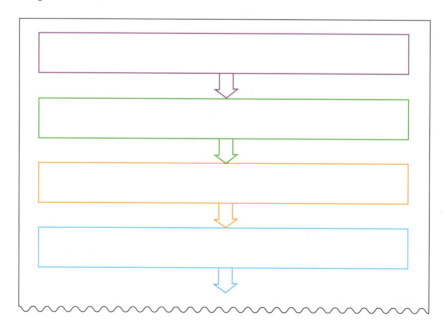

Using an appropriate form of writing

AO4 i, ii

As well as planning, you will also need to consider what form is appropriate for your writing. To do this, think about the **purpose** of your writing.
▶ Are you being invited to inform the reader?
▶ Are you being asked to explain something?
▶ Does the task require you to describe a place or perhaps a situation?

When you have sorted out the purpose, decide what **form** your writing will take. Will it be:

▶ **a letter?** There is no need to include an address as the content and quality of your writing is the most important aspect. Think carefully about how a letter should begin and avoid, 'I am writing to…'
▶ **a magazine article?** There is no need to write in columns or include images, though you may include a headline or sub-headings. You should ensure that you maintain an appropriate tone and engage your audience.
▶ **an online blog?** Ensure you focus on getting the content right rather than spending time trying to achieve the appearance of an online document. Again, your priority is to engage your audience through your content and to maintain an appropriate tone.
▶ **a speech?** All successful speeches begin in written form. From the beginning you should demonstrate an awareness of audience and attempt to sustain engagement with them throughout your writing. Remember you are writing to be heard!
▶ **a diary?** Diary entries are usually written in the past tense and reflect on significant events. Many people who write diaries write as though they are sharing their innermost thoughts and feelings with a confidante, so they often have a very conversational tone.
▶ **a story or account?** Sometimes an essay may be the most suitable form if you are writing a story or an account of an experience.

You will see that while it is important to demonstrate an appreciation of form, you can usually achieve this by thinking carefully about how you begin your writing.

Activity

Identify the purpose, form and audience for each of the writing tasks below.
1. Write an online blog about an interesting place you have visited. Describe your experience there and explain why you found it interesting.
2. Write an article for your school magazine, entitled 'Things I love about growing up in the twenty-first century.'
3. You have been asked to deliver a speech to your classmates, informing them about your hopes and dreams for the future.
4. Write an essay entitled 'My favourite time of year.' Inform your reader of your favourite season or celebration, describe your experiences of your chosen time of year and explain why it is your favourite.

UNIT 4 SECTION A: PERSONAL OR CREATIVE WRITING

Structuring your writing

Depending on the form of your Personal or Creative Writing, you will most likely use a chronological structure or a flashback structure.

Chronological structure

Using a chronological structure means organising your writing by relating events in the order in which they happened. You might use this structure if you are writing about:

- an important aspect of your life or important events and people that have shaped you
- several events – tracing how you were involved or how events unfolded
- a single event or person – recounting an event hour by hour, or the life events of the person being described.

When writing chronologically, make sure you:

- make the order of events clear and keep the story moving forward – gloss over the dull bits and don't tell more of the story than helps you make your point
- start and end with action and have events take place within the context of the story
- describe events, people and places in specific, colourful terms
- make sure that you use a range of linguistic devices.

To the left is an example of chronological writing.

> After a restless night I dragged my weary body downstairs in search of one of Mum's delicious home-cooked breakfasts. Much to the delight of my mother I devoured every morsel, it was just the fuel I needed to feel human again. After breakfast I headed upstairs ready to tackle the bombsite that my bedroom had become…

Flashback structure

You can use flashback in different ways to structure your writing. You could start with the present and cut to the past before ending with the present again. Jennifer Johnston uses this approach in her book *How Many Miles to Babylon?*

It opens:

> Because I am an officer and a gentleman they have given me my notebooks, pen, ink and paper.
>
> (Jennifer Johnston, *How Many Miles to Babylon?*)

and finishes:

> Because I am an officer and a gentleman they have not taken away my bootlaces or my pen, so I sit and wait and write.
>
> (Jennifer Johnston, *How Many Miles to Babylon?*)

You could also begin and end your writing with two halves of the same event. The middle might give an interpretation of or background to the event. Suppose, for example, you are writing about passing an important exam, and you decide to describe the moment when you opened the envelope and read the result. You could:

- begin your piece with the words, 'My hard work clearly paid off.'
- cut to the day of the exam, when you opened the paper and felt like you were totally unprepared
- describe your panic and regret at having failed to do the necessary revision
- describe spending the last few days trying to avoid your parents and all talk of results day
- describe results morning, anticipating the arrival of your statement of results
- describe the opening of the envelope
- end with your parent's/teacher's words, 'Congratulations, your hard work clearly paid off', as you stand by stunned.

Once you have settled on an idea and are confident about the organisation and structure of your writing, you must turn your attention to adding interest and engaging your reader.

Personal Writing

AO4 i, ii, iii

Introducing your Personal Writing essay

The introductory paragraph is an important one as it forms first impressions and establishes expectations about what is to follow. Begin with a strong introduction that hooks the attention of your audience and encourages them to continue reading. To achieve this, you could begin with:

- a question, e.g. 'Have you ever had one of those days when you just knew, from the moment you woke up, that everything would go wrong?'
- an anecdote, e.g. 'Let me tell you about last Thursday, my day from hell…'
- direct address, e.g. 'If you're anything like me then you will struggle with nerves, especially when it comes to exam season…'
- a descriptive opening, e.g. 'The fireworks squeal as they soar into the black night sky before exploding into a kaleidoscope of colour…'

- sharing your response to a task, e.g. 'A time I coped under pressure? Well, initially I felt inclined to tell you about my first time babysitting my brother, but to be honest that's an occasion I'd rather forget. Instead allow me to share with you the story of my audition for the lead role in the school show…'

> **Activity**
>
> Write three introductions to the task 'Write about a vivid childhood memory.' Decide which of your three is the most effective and share it with your classmates.

Developing your Personal Writing and adding interest

Once you have hooked the attention of your reader with your lively introduction, your challenge is to maintain their interest. Strong responses will show evidence of conscious crafting and an ability to add interest through using a variety of techniques, well-chosen vocabulary and varied sentence lengths and punctuation. Above all you want your writing to be credible and authentic; this is achieved when you write from your own experiences.

Techniques to add interest

One of the most common ways to start a sentence is with subject followed by verb and so it is not unusual for students to rely on 'I', 'He', 'The' and 'It' to begin sentences, but this gets boring and predictable. By varying your sentence openers and adding sentence variety, you will make your writing more interesting. You can:

- use an adverb, e.g. 'Stealthily, the cunning thief crept into the house.'
- open with a phrase indicating location (a prepositional phrase), e.g. 'Inside the house, the cunning thief located the precious jewels.'
- begin with an '-ing' form of the verb, e.g. 'Creeping around the house, the cunning thief finally located the precious jewels.'
- use a drop-in clause, e.g. 'The cunning thief, who was not working alone, knew he had to get out quickly and quietly.'
- use 'Although' or 'Despite', e.g. 'Despite his age, the thief was still nimble and quick.'
- use the '-ed' form of the verb, e.g. 'Terrified, Mrs Brown tiptoed out of bed, certain there was someone downstairs.'
- use a triad/rule of three for impact, e.g. 'She took a deep breath, reached for her gun, and took aim.'
- use speech, followed by action and an '-ing' clause, e.g. '"Don't do it!" cried the thief, dropping his bag to the floor.'

UNIT 4 SECTION A: PERSONAL OR CREATIVE WRITING

As well as considering sentence structures, successful writers employ a variety of techniques to add interest in order to ensure their audience are engaged and want to keep reading. Common techniques used to add interest are:

- **Alliteration** – commonly used to make writing catchy and interesting, e.g. 'Beautiful Belfast will take your breath away.'
- **Direct address** – engages your reader by giving the impression you are talking directly to them. It can be used to establish a conversational tone if your task demands it. You may wish to address your reader by asking a question, for example, 'Can you imagine how embarrassing it was to have fallen in front of all those people?' Another method is to use imperatives to command your reader, for example, 'I know what you're expecting here, but stick with me…'. You can also involve yourself with the reader by using inclusive language, for example, 'We all know what it's like to experience success…'.
- **Imagery** plants pictures in the mind of the reader, but you should avoid relying on clichés and instead show your own originality when using **similes**, **metaphors** and **personification**. For example:
  - 'His face was wrinkled like a little child's sketch.' (simile)
  - 'Mr Clarke's classroom was a torture chamber.' (metaphor)
  - 'Turning the key in the ignition, the car coughed and wheezed. I made my way on to the main road with only the radio for company.' (personification)
- **Vivid verbs and adjectives** – try to select verbs that give clues about feelings and that add drama, e.g. instead of writing, 'I walked through the crowds, holding my bag tightly, fearful that someone might take it.' You could write, 'I **snaked** through the crowds, **gripping** my bag tightly, fearful that someone might **snatch** it.'

Like verbs, a well-chosen adjective can add interest to your writing, for example, 'In front of me stood a **majestic** horse with a **glossy**, **raven black** coat.' Aim to be ambitious and precise with your vocabulary choices and to avoid using general descriptions such as 'small', 'tall', 'pretty', 'beautiful', 'horrible' or 'ugly', because your reader will struggle to conjure up a vivid mental image; after all, what does pretty or beautiful or ugly look like?

- **Sensory details** – too many students over-focus in their writing on what can be seen and heard, but what about smells and tastes? This student response demonstrates how these other senses help us memorise experiences:

> I inhale deeply and allow the scent of pine to spiral up my nostrils. Tentatively I move forwards; with each step the crisp dry leaves crunch beneath my boots but the terrain is uneven and every once in a while I am forced to seek the support of a coarse tree trunk to prevent me falling ungracefully to the forest floor. Pausing, I reach for my flask and gulp in a most uncivilised fashion as the cool water gushes down my throat, quenching my thirst.

Making the ordinary extraordinary

As well as using techniques, there are other ways to add interest to your writing.

Do not fall into the trap of simply informing your reader. Although this is Personal Writing, your audience does not need to know every detail and you must be selective about what you share. Many students feel under pressure to tell exciting stories and don't realise that their everyday experiences can inspire great writing.

One of the best ways to improve your writing is to read widely to develop an appreciation of how professional writers communicate ideas and craft descriptions. Read the extract below from Bill Bryson, in which he is recalling looking out of an aeroplane window. This does not sound particularly significant or exciting, but note how the writer makes this simple act seem dramatic and conveys his personal excitement:

[1] Makes us aware of his anticipation.

[2] Short sentence emphasises how memorable this occasion was.

[4] Long sentence used to capture his eagerness to soak up the sight of the landscape below.

[6] Short sentence to emphasise his dissatisfaction with the American landscape.

[8] Ellipsis gives the impression he was so excited he was struggling for words.

> I was secretly watching**[1]** out of the window for Europe. I still remember my first sight.**[2]** The plane dropped out of the clouds and there below me was this sudden magical tableau**[3]** of small green fields and steepled villages spread across an undulating landscape, like a shaken-out quilt just settling back on to a bed.**[4]** I had flown a lot in America and had never seen much of anything from an aeroplane window but endless golden fields on farms the size of Belgium, meandering rivers and pencil lines of black highway as straight as taut wire.**[5]** It always looked vast and mostly empty.**[6]** You felt that if you squinted hard enough you could see all the way to Los Angeles, even when you were over Kansas. But here the landscape had the ordered perfection of a model-railway layout. It was so green and minutely cultivated, so compact, so tidy, so**[7]** fetching, so…**[8]** European. I was smitten. I still am.**[9]**
>
> (Bill Bryson, *Neither Here Nor There: Travels in Europe*)

[3] Makes the eventual sighting of Europe seem enchanting.

[5] Reader appreciates why this view was special – it was so different to what he was used to seeing in America.

[7] Repetition of 'so' to convey indulgence in this first encounter.

[9] Two short sentences to make his excitement clear. The shift to present tense lets us know he has not lost any of his initial admiration.

Below is an introductory paragraph to the task, 'Write an article for your school magazine entitled "My favourite song".'

> My favourite song is 'Mr Brightside' by The Killers. I like this song because it is catchy and gets stuck in your head. I was travelling with my family to Donegal when I first heard 'Mr Brightside' and within seconds I was hooked; I knew it was a song I'd never tire of hearing.

UNIT 4 SECTION A: PERSONAL OR CREATIVE WRITING

You can see in the example on the previous page that this student has attempted to respond to the task, but overall its tone is informative and it relies on sharing straightforward information in an uncomplicated style, which means it is not particularly interesting to read. After studying how Bryson added interest, the student redrafted their piece.

> ### Activity
>
> Read the redrafted response below and identify how the student has improved it. Make a list of what they have done in each paragraph to add interest. Compare your list with a partner.
>
> > Have you ever found yourself falling in love with a song you just can't get enough of? You know the sort of song that, even hours after you've heard it, the tune still swims around inside your head? For many of us, it would be impossible to select a single favourite song of all time, but not me; when it comes to music I have very definite tastes and when it comes to songs, I have a firm favourite.
> >
> > I'm sure most of you have heard 'Mr Brightside' by The Killers. A few years ago it was the song you just couldn't avoid; it was on every radio station, booming out of every car and on every video music channel. It was EVERYWHERE! If you are unfamiliar with the song, let me tell you what to expect… 'Mr Brightside' was the debut single by Las Vegas band The Killers, fronted by the amazingly gorgeous and ultra-cool Brandon Flowers. Apparently the song was inspired by an unfaithful ex-girlfriend of frontman Flowers (was she insane?). Be warned, the opening chords are amazingly addictive, in fact I challenge you to hear them and stand still! If you're not yet convinced, then it may interest you to know that 'Mr Brightside' was voted Song of the Decade in 2010. Totally deserved!
> >
> > I can still vividly recall the day I was introduced to 'Mr Brightside' and The Killers. Of course in that initial meeting I had no idea just how breathtakingly beautiful Mr Flowers was, but his voice, the music, those lyrics, what can I say? It was a recipe for greatness! I was actually enduring a long, boring car journey to rainy Donegal. We abandoned our usual radio station due to the loss of frequency and my dad was doing a quick search for some tunes to occupy us. Suddenly the car rang out with that catchy opening guitar riff. I was hooked!

In the re-draft above the student adds interest by:
- ▶ adopting a conversational tone and addressing their reader directly
- ▶ varying sentence lengths and including a range of punctuation
- ▶ adding descriptive detail to create an interesting narrative, making the overall piece more engaging and convincing
- ▶ taking an everyday occurrence and making the event seem memorable and interesting.

Personal Writing

Describe, don't tell

Many students make the mistake of stating things rather than describing. This commonly occurs when it comes to sharing feelings and emotions. Many students will state, 'I was terrified', but it is more effective to think about how emotions such as fear manifest themselves in our appearance and behaviour, for example, 'Instantly I could feel an eruption of goose bumps break out all over my body. A clammy sweat gathered in the hollow of my back and I found it hard to swallow.'

Slow the action down and zoom in

Don't assume your Personal Writing must be based on something extraordinary or that you need to cover a lot of time and/or space. Remember that you are writing a short story. You should develop the skill of slowing the action down, and zooming in on small details. As you are writing from your own experience you should be able to identify those moments or details that are worth developing. For example, if writing about your favourite holiday, you would not need to include everything from the moment you arrived at the airport to the moment you departed. Instead, it would be more effective to share a specific memory, a particular day, or a particular moment of a particular day? Someone who has not mastered the art of slowing the action down may write:

> We arrived at the airport and joined the check-in queue, where we waited for forty minutes before making our way through security and then into the boarding gate.

Activity

Write about encountering something for the first time. Try to capture the moment by offering vivid description and your immediate reactions. Remember to vary your sentence length and try to use punctuation to enhance meaning.

Whereas a more confident student may write:

> The glass doors of the airport hissed and glided open to reveal a colony of holidaymakers. It was chaos; red-faced men lugged bulging suitcases while stressed-out mothers clutched the hands of petulant toddlers desperate for release. From where we stood the check-in desk seemed nothing more than a faint speck in the distance. I fought my frustration as I calculated that approximately eight hundred people stood between me and that check-in assistant with the plastic smile and ruby red lips. We spent the next forty minutes shuffling forward, tugging our suitcases a few inches further each time. Occasionally we'd exchange sympathetic looks with a fellow holidaymaker-in-waiting. You know the look: tight lips, roll of eyes and shake of head, quickly followed by a craning of the neck to assess just how far away one actually is from the destination. It's a look known to anyone who has found themselves stuck in an endless queue.
>
> After a four-hour flight…

Essentially this student is writing about entering the airport and joining a queue, but they are able to focus on small details and inject description by zooming in to allow the reader to fully imagine the scene. The result is that they can retell the event in a detailed and convincing style. Note how the student feels confident to skip the boring details of an uneventful plane journey, preferring to get on with telling their story by beginning their next paragraph with details of their arrival.

Balance action with reaction

Students who succeed will not simply rely on telling their reader what happened, they will also give details about how they reacted (using describe, don't tell!). Actions on their own can be good, but in Personal Writing the reader is keen to know about the impact this event had upon you and how you thought and felt at key moments. A student responding to the task 'Write about an embarrassing experience' decided to write about fainting in Biology class:

> I knew as soon as the teacher produced that pulpy purple bag that this wasn't going to end well. Scanning the room, I observed the composed faces of my classmates; not one bead of sweat or trembling hand among them. Were they normal? Was I destined to become the class coward? That was not a label any student desired so I tried to expel my fear in long breaths as my inner voice screamed, 'You can do it! You CAN do it!' With a loud slap the teacher launched the heart on to the tray in front of me. I gagged. 'Lift your scalpels and make a small incision,' she ordered coldly, completely unaware of my panic. Slowly I lifted the scalpel. Everything went fuzzy. Suddenly I felt as though I was standing in a furnace. I could hear my partner speak, 'David, are you okay mate?' but his voice sounded distant. I knew I was drifting, sliding to the floor, but I was powerless to stop it.

You can see how the student shifts between telling us **what** was happening and **how** he was reacting by giving descriptions of thoughts and feelings. It is this combination that helps make this an interesting piece of writing.

> **Activity**
>
> Write a short passage about a time you felt nervous. Remember to balance action with reaction and try to capture how the emotion affected your actions and behaviour. Share with your reader the events taking place and describe your inner thoughts and feelings.

Concluding your Personal Writing

Earlier you were made aware of the importance of having a strong introduction, but your conclusion is equally important as it leaves a lasting impression upon your reader. You want to demonstrate your skill in purposefully bringing your piece of writing to a close and should avoid just ending abruptly as this gives the impression that you simply ran out of time or, even worse, ran out of things to say.

> **Activity**
>
> Write a descriptive paragraph about the moments that follow the sound of the bell at the end of the school day. Remember to slow the action down and zoom in on details that will add interest.

Do:
- Keep it concise.
- Try to make it engaging.

Don't:
- Don't begin with the predictable 'In conclusion…'
- Don't introduce any new ideas.

Practise using the following strategies to help you craft an effective conclusion.

Reflect

You could reflect back on an event or situation and share your thoughts on how you have changed or grown as a consequence. The concluding paragraph to a piece of writing on 'A time I coped under pressure' could read:

> Looking back on this event I now realise how significant it was in shaping me as a person. I now know not to give in to pressure, I now know that challenges are to be confronted and, I am pleased to say, I am now someone who believes I will emerge victorious from whatever life throws my way.

Predict

Rather than looking back it may be more appropriate to end your piece by looking forward with a prediction. Below is an example of how one student concluded on the topic 'My hopes and dreams for the future':

> Clearly I have a lot of intensive study ahead of me if I am to realise my dream of becoming a doctor but I know that along the way I'll also make new memories and discover fascinating facts. Maybe sometime in the not-too-distant future I'll be revolutionising the medical world by discovering a cure for cancer. I certainly hope so!

Question

You may decide to end by addressing your reader and asking a question to get them thinking about what they have read:

> We all have that one person who makes us laugh when we feel down, who picks us up when we stumble and who inspires us to chase our dreams. Who is the one person you look up to?

Compel

You may wish to compel your reader to take action at the end by using imperatives:

> Don't sit back and quietly hope that your dreams will come true; get out there and make it happen!

UNIT 4 SECTION A: PERSONAL OR CREATIVE WRITING

The cyclical conclusion

Another approach is to return to a scenario or location that you described at the beginning of your piece of writing. Read the first and final paragraphs of a piece entitled 'My proudest moment' to see how one student adopted this approach:

> 12 May 2015 will be a date forever etched in my memory. Only now can I admit to having serious doubts as my team lined up silently on the football pitch that afternoon. We had experienced something of an injury crisis and it was doubtful whether two of our key players would last the full ninety minutes. On the side line our coach was doing his best to appear confident but every few minutes he'd gnaw at his fingernails and restlessly scan the field. He was tortured by the very same question that swam through my own mind, 'Could we do it?'...
>
> ***
>
> ...The doubts were gone, the fingernails of our coach were red raw but his eyes shone with pride. We had done it! The victorious chants of my teammates and our jubilant fans flooded the stadium. With our hard-fought victory we were leaving the field as champions.

Activity

Write two conclusions for a piece of writing entitled, 'A memorable journey'.

Decide which is most effective and share it with your classmates.

Creative Writing

Much of the advice for succeeding in Personal Writing can be applied to Creative Writing. For example, you will begin by identifying the specific audience and purpose and deciding on an appropriate form. You will then plan your ideas and organise them before beginning to write the story itself.

In this task you will have an image to help inspire your writing and you should spend your first 15 minutes generating ideas. As with Personal Writing, you should be realistic about what you can achieve in the 30 minutes you have to write your response and again remember you are producing a short story.

Selecting an appropriate form

AO4

Selecting an appropriate form for your creative writing is an important decision as you need to select a form that will allow you to **showcase your skills**, **show imagination** and **effectively engage** your reader.

1 If you are inspired to create a character you may decide to write a diary entry that allows the reader to understand the primary concerns of the character, and gives access to their private thoughts and feelings about certain situations and people.

Below is an extract from *The Martian* by Andy Weir, which is a science-fiction story about an American astronaut who is presumed dead and left behind on Mars. Sections of the book take the form of log or diary entries.

> 'Six days into what should have been the greatest two months of my life, and it's turned into a nightmare.
>
> I don't even know who'll read this. I guess someone will find it eventually. Maybe a hundred years from now.
>
> For the record… I didn't die on Sol. Certainly the rest of the crew thought I did, and I can't blame them. Maybe there'll be a day of national mourning for me, and my Wikipedia page will say, "Mark Watney is the only human being to have died on Mars."
>
> And it'll be right, probably. 'Cause I'll surely die here. Just not on Sol 6 when everyone thinks I did.
>
> Let's see… where do I begin?
>
> The Ares Program. Mankind reaching out to Mars to send people to another planet for the very first time and expand the horizons of humanity blah, blah, blah. The Ares 1 crew did their thing and came back heroes. They got the parades and fame and love of the world. Ares 2 did the same thing, in a different location on Mars. They got a firm handshake and a hot cup of coffee when they got home.
>
> Ares 3. Well, that was my mission. Okay, not *mine* per se. Commander Lewis was in charge. I was just one of her crew. I would only be "in command" of the mission if I were the only remaining person.
>
> What do you know? I'm in command.
>
> I wonder if this log will be recovered before the rest of the crew die of old age. I presume they got back to Earth all right. Guys, if you're reading this: It wasn't your fault. You did what you had to do. In your position I would have done the same thing. I don't blame you, and I'm glad you survived.'
>
> (Andy Weir, *The Martian*)

UNIT 4 SECTION A: PERSONAL OR CREATIVE WRITING

2 You might write a letter from a given character. Bram Stoker's *Dracula* is written in the form of letters and journals. Below is an extract from a letter that appears in Chapter 5 and is sent from Miss Mina Murray to Lucy Westenra.

> 9 May.
>
> My dearest Lucy,
>
> Forgive my long delay in writing, but I have been simply overwhelmed with work…
>
> …I will tell you of my little plans when we meet. I have just had a few hurried lines from Jonathan from Transylvania. He is well, and will be returning in about a week. I am longing to hear all his news. It must be nice to see strange countries. I wonder if we, I mean Jonathan and I, shall ever see them together. There is the ten o'clock bell ringing. Goodbye.
>
> Your loving
>
> Mina
>
> Tell me all the news when you write. You have not told me anything for a long time. I hear rumours, and especially of a tall, handsome, curly-haired man.???
>
> (Bram Stoker, *Dracula*)

3 You might decide to write a monologue, from a character at a specific moment in time. Below is the opening to *Stone Cold* written by Robert Swindells. Read it and see how the central character Link, who is sixteen years old and homeless, seems to speak directly to the reader, immersing us into his situation:

> You can call me Link. It's not my name, but it's what I say when anybody asks, which isn't often. I'm invisible, see? One of the invisible people. Right now I'm sitting in a doorway watching the passers-by. They avoid looking at me. They're afraid I want something they've got, and they're right. Also, they don't want to think about me. They don't like reminding I exist. Me, and those like me. We're living proof that everything's not all right and we make the place untidy.
>
> Hang about and I'll tell you the story of my fascinating life.
>
> (Robert Swindells, *Stone Cold*)

Activity

With a partner, re-read the extracts above and discuss your impressions of each of the characters. What makes us want to know more about them?

Selecting an appropriate perspective

AO4 i, ii

All of the previous three examples are written from a **first person perspective**, that is, the author writes as the central character. An alternative is to write using an omniscient **third person perspective**, which involves writing in an observational style, as though the 'voice' telling the story is detached from the events taking place.

Below is an example from *Of Mice and Men* by John Steinbeck which is told using a third person omniscient perspective, allowing the reader to judge the various characters and situations for themselves:

> The thick-bodied Carlson came in out of the darkening yard. He walked to the other end of the bunk house and turned on the second shaded light. 'Darker'n hell in here,' he said ... He stopped and sniffed the air, and still sniffing, looked down at the old dog. 'God awmighty, that dog stinks. Get him outta here, Candy! I don't know nothing that stinks as bad as an old dog. You gotta get him out.'
>
> Candy rolled to the edge of his bunk. He reached over and patted the ancient dog, and he apologised, 'I been around him so much I never notice how he stinks.'
>
> 'Well, I can't stand him in here,' said Carlson. 'That stink hangs around even after he's gone.' He walked over with his heavy-legged stride and looked down at the dog. 'Got no teeth,' he said. 'He's all stiff with rheumatism. He ain't no good to you, Candy. An' he ain't no good to himself. Why'n't you shoot him, Candy?'
>
> (John Steinbeck, *Of Mice and Men*)

Activity

Using the image on the right, write four different paragraphs:
1. Write a paragraph from a diary entry written by this character.
2. Write a paragraph from a letter sent by this character to a close friend revealing dramatic news.
3. Write the opening paragraph to a monologue where the character speaks to the reader and immerses us into his situation.
4. Write the opening paragraph to a story that introduces this character using a detached, third person perspective.

Share your examples with your class.

Agree on the best and discuss how the piece would continue.

Beginnings and endings

AO4 ii

The challenge with Creative Writing is to write something you would like to read – to produce a piece of writing that will hook the attention of your reader and successfully hold their interest. It is sometimes best to have an idea of how and where you want your story to end, then work backwards making decisions about the events that will unfold to arrive at that point. For example, you may wish to end with the words, 'You're fired' and think about the actions taken by the character that resulted in their dismissal.

Beginnings

There are many techniques that can be used to begin a piece of Creative Writing and you should experiment with different approaches to develop your skills. Here are some ideas for getting started:

▶ Begin with an exchange of dialogue between two characters that will intrigue the reader:

'Didn't I tell you never to come here?'

'Yes, but I had to let you know, he's discovered your secret and he's coming for answers. Now.'

▶ Begin with a dramatic moment:

Gill woke up in a cold sweat. There was a light on in the hallway and she could hear the sound of footsteps climbing the stairs. Shadows danced up the walls outside the bedroom. She was paralysed with fear.

▶ Begin with a discovery or revelation:

Tentatively he opened the letter, removed the thick white page and carefully opened it up to reveal his fate. His eyes quickly scanned the page and his face broke into a wide grin as he read, 'Dear Mr Giles, congratulations, you have successfully passed our recruitment process. Welcome to S.E.P.A.' He was officially a secret agent.

▶ Begin with an intriguing situation:

Jess had arrived on time as instructed. Without wasting another second, she knocked loudly on the door of number 29. She had no idea what or who was waiting for her on the other side...

▶ Begin with a description of character:

Mr Crane patrolled the school corridors like a prison warden, swinging both arms and looking left and right in search of a fresh victim, usually some poor kid engaging in petty rule-breaking like having a tie out or the wrong haircut. As soon as he believed he'd spied some act of indiscipline he'd stop suddenly, rise up on tip-toes, twitch his head and blink incessantly like he could hardly believe

Activity

What makes the situation opposite intriguing? With a partner discuss how this opening could be developed. Share your ideas with your class.

what he was seeing. Everyone sympathised with the poor kid summoned to stand in front of Mr Crane, for the man was incapable of speaking without showering the listener in his saliva. Up close you could see the patchwork of stains over his suit jacket and when he swooped down to get right into your face, his nose hairs danced as he delivered his monologue. He was disgusting!

▶ Begin with a description of setting:

The moon was disappearing behind solemn grey clouds as Emily made her way home through the park. Only hours before crowds had thronged the green fields, but now it was eerily empty, except for Emily and whatever creatures were rustling in the bushes that framed the pathway. Gravel cracked beneath her feet, causing her to jump and then laugh at her own foolishness. Just ahead she could make out the silhouette of the old gate…

▶ Begin with a compelling flashback:

It had been almost six years since I had last encountered Jonathan Quaker. As I observed him now celebrating his success, I felt sure he held no memory of that day, but I would never forget, nor would I forgive…

Activity

1. Re-read the sample opening paragraphs above and on the previous page. Select your three favourites and rank them in order. Be prepared to explain your decision making.
   Then select one of the sample paragraphs that you feel could be improved. Re-write it and share with a partner. You **should** be able to explain how you improved upon the original.
2. Find an image that you think would inspire an interesting piece of creative writing. Select three of the suggestions for writing an interesting beginning and write the opening paragraphs. Share your writing with a **partner**.

Activity

Select a sentence that you think is an effective opening to a story from a novel in your English classroom or school library (it may not necessarily be found at the beginning of a chapter!). Share it with your class and explain why you think it is a successful introduction.
Swap your suggestion with a peer and have a go at continuing the story.

Endings

It is important to end your story in an appropriate and convincing way. Below are some suggestions on how you could end your piece of Creative Writing.

▶ End with an unexpected twist that takes the reader by surprise:

At that moment Harry realised he had got it all wrong: it was not Sam who had betrayed him, it was Ben, his own brother and the one person he had shared all his suspicions with right from that first discovery in the garden. How had he been so blind?

▶ Resolve all conflict and end with a 'feel good' conclusion:

Leaving school that afternoon Anna felt content for the first time in weeks. The torture was over and the true culprits had been discovered. She was now free to put the whole horrible episode behind her.

UNIT 4 SECTION A: PERSONAL OR CREATIVE WRITING

> **Activity**
>
> How does leaving the ending unresolved make this an effective conclusion? With a partner, discuss what might have happened in the lead up to this moment.

▶ Leave the ending unresolved. A question can be an effective way of prompting the reader to speculate:

After weeks of meticulous planning Logan Bailey was in position. Would he make it out alive?

▶ End on a cliffhanger. If you think of your writing as the first chapter of a larger story, you should be able to decide the right moment to end so that your ending is dramatic and your reader is encouraged to want to know what happens next:

At that moment the candle was extinguished, plunging the place into darkness. Ross could feel a presence behind him. He turned slowly. 'Who's there?' he whispered. The reply was faint but it sent spasms of fear snaking up his spine, 'I've been waiting for you... Ross.'

▶ End with an epiphany. This is when your character achieves an awakening or a moment of striking realisation that alters their view of themselves and the world around them:

It all made sense now. Tessa had to leave. If she stayed she would achieve nothing. All of her dreams would fade to nothing. She would become like every other girl on the estate, a devoted wife and selfless mother. That might be enough for them, but it wasn't the life she wanted. She dared to dream big and only she could turn her dream into a reality. The prospect of leaving frightened and excited her all at once, but she knew she must say goodbye to the security of family and routine that had held her back for so long.

Creating narrative

AO4 i, ii, iii

A great story is something everyone enjoys but there are a number of key elements you need to consider to make your story enjoyable:

- **Plot**: This is the basic storyline. It can be relatively straightforward and uncomplicated or it can contain unexpected twists and turns.
- **Structure**: How your story begins; how events unfold and develop, perhaps to a dramatic climax; how your story ends; how you use different sentence structures for maximum effect.
- **Narrative stance**: The viewpoint from which the story is told – most writers use first- or third-person narrators.
- **Characters**: You will have time to develop only one main character and perhaps two or three others. The storyline should revolve around these characters and how they interact.
- **Setting**: Where the events of the story take place. This is an important factor in generating mood and atmosphere as well as pulling the reader into the narrative.
- **Language**: The words and phrases and linguistic techniques selected are at the heart of creating a story that will absorb the reader.

Plot and structure

In any narrative, plot and structure are closely connected:

- A story is often structured as a series of **key moments**, each of which move the narrative forward. Some of these key moments may surprise or shock the reader.
- The **time sequence** in which events are presented is a crucial feature of the structure. A common structural device is the use of **flashback**. Letting the reader glimpse the past in this way can add dramatic impact. It can also provide insight into what motivates characters, so helping the reader understand their behaviour. For example, a plot can unfold in a **chronological** manner or **time shifts** can be used such as starting in the present, going back to past events and concluding by coming back full circle to the present.
- Structure is also linked to changes in **mood** or **atmosphere**. This should be varied in order to keep the audience interested. For example, the opening could be light-hearted, with the mood gradually darkening as the story builds up to a dramatic **climax**. **Tonal shifts** can be introduced through description, the use of setting and how characters are presented.
- **Foreshadowing** is a more complex device used to good effect in Steinbeck's *Of Mice and Men*. The shooting of Candy's dog foreshadows the tragic end to this famous novel.
- The **pace** or speed at which the action is revealed should vary in order to create effects such as an increase in tension or a sense of excitement. Events can happen in quick succession or there could be a series of crises as the action builds up to an exciting conclusion.

In Unit 4A: Personal Writing you will find more about how you can use these structural features to create an interesting narrative. You can also learn about the importance of varying sentence openers and sentence structures to keep your reader interested and enhance meaning.

UNIT 4 SECTION A: PERSONAL OR CREATIVE WRITING

Activity

Find and read a short story.

(You might choose *The Signal-Man* by Charles Dickens or *The Fib* by George Layton.)

Using the bullet list on plot and structure on the previous page, identify how the writer develops the narrative for maximum impact on the reader. Note your findings in a grid like the one below.

Key or significant moments	Time sequence	Mood and atmosphere	Pace of action
Opening sequence			
First key moment			
Second key moment			
Next key moment			
Next key moment (and so on as required)			
Climax			
Ending			

You can also use a grid like the one above to help you plan your narrative writing. It will help you think through how the key moments in your story can connect to changes in time, mood and pace.

Remember: The climax of your story does not have to occur at the end.

Creating characters

AO4 i, ii, iii

As you are writing a short story it is probably best to focus on creating one or two central characters that your reader will get to know well. Your reader will be interested in the relationships and interactions between the characters. When creating characters there is a lot to consider:

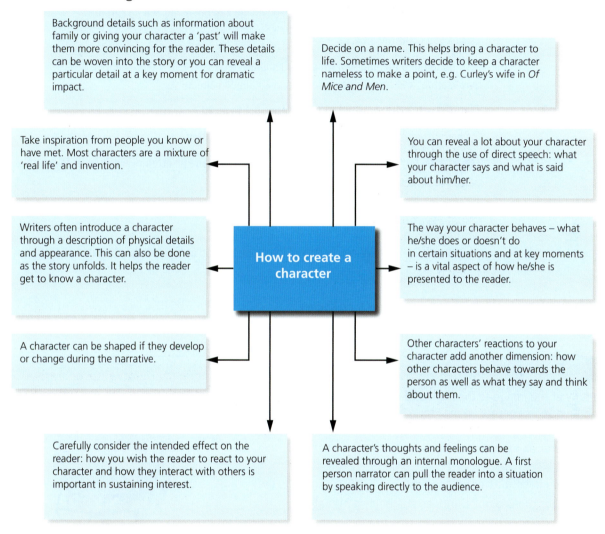

Memorable characters ignite a reaction within the reader. For example, your character may have a villainous streak which creates conflict, and causes the reader to dislike them. On the other hand, your character may carry a secret that makes them mysterious and intriguing. Alternatively, your character may overcome hardship or adversity, allowing the reader to admire them and feel an emotional connection. As the creator of your character you will shape the reader's response.

Read the extract on the next page from *A Kestrel for a Knave* by Barry Hines. The central character Billy Casper comes from a difficult home and in this episode Mr Sugden, the PE teacher, embarrasses Billy for forgetting his PE kit. As you read it consider how the author makes us dislike the character of Mr Sugden:

UNIT 4 SECTION A: PERSONAL OR CREATIVE WRITING

> 'Well get changed lad, you're two weeks late already!'
>
> He lifted the elastic webbing of one cuff and rotated his fist to look at his watch on the underside of his wrist.
>
> 'Some of us want a game even if you don't.'
>
> 'I've no kit, Sir.'
>
> Mr Sugden stepped back and slowly looked Billy up and down, his top lip curling.
>
> 'Casper, you make me SICK.'
>
> 'SICK' penetrated the hubhub, which immediately decreased as the boys stopped their own conversations and turned their attention to Mr Sugden and Billy.
>
> 'Every lesson it's the same old story, "Please, Sir, I've no kit."'
>
> The boys tittered at his whipped-dog whining impersonation.
>
> 'Every lesson for four years! And in all that time you've made no attempt whatsoever to get any kit, you've skyved and scrounged and borrowed and…'
>
> He tried this lot on one breath, and his ruddy complexion heightened and glowed like a red balloon as he held his breath and fought for another verb.
>
> '…and…BEG…' The balloon burst and the pronunciation of the verb disintegrated.
>
> 'Why is it that everyone else can get some but you can't?'
>
> (Barry Hines, *A Kestrel for a Knave*)

Activity

Look carefully at the image to the right and consider the prompts to help you generate an idea for a story involving this character.

Give this character an appropriate name and consider what it suggests about her.

- How would you describe her personality?
- What was/is her profession? Did/does she enjoy it? What did/do her co-workers think of her?
- Note how she wears her glasses on the end of her nose – why is this?
- Look at how she is dressed. What do her clothes suggest about her?
- Look at her lips – what do they suggest about her feelings? Why does she feel this way?
- Who is she staring at? Describe her eyes and eyebrows.
- When she speaks how does she sound?
- What common gestures accompany her speech?

On the next page is an introduction written by a GCSE student based on this image. Read it and note the comments which indicate how they have crafted this passage in a way that shapes the reader's response to the central characters.

Creating characters

[1] Abrupt opening sentence provides a clue to the narrator's dislike for the character of Mrs Kissinglot. The choice of character name prompts the reader to make predictions and quickly proves humorously inappropriate once the story develops and we get the narrator's perspective.

[4] Some brief details on Mrs Kissinglot's past help the reader understand more about the character and her behaviour.

[6] Inclusion of direct speech brings the character of Mrs Kissinglot to life. The writer's choice of the verb 'shrieking' is deliberately used as it suggests to the reader that even the voice of the character is shrill and unpleasant. The fact she labels the children 'brutes' confirms her lack of compassion.

[8] Specific zoom-in on a feature – the eyes – helps to make Mrs Kissinglot seem villainous which influences the reader's response to her character.

Mrs Kissinglot. **[1]** You hear a name like that and you imagine someone kind and friendly, someone with a face that oozes compassion. I don't think Crazy Kissinglot **[2]** had a compassionate bone in her dumpy body. She lived next door in number twenty-seven and never in my life had I met someone more inappropriately named – the woman was a demon. **[3]** Apparently she'd spent years working as a dinner lady and prided herself on being able to make young kids cry with just a look. She rarely smiled but it seemed her bitterness had got worse since her husband had died just over a year ago. **[4]** To pass her days old Kissinglot gawked out her front window watching us kids, seizing any opportunity to come bounding out into the garden and create a scene. **[5]** Crazy Kissinglot should have been an actress; she was a master of melodrama. She'd storm half way down the garden path, waving a fist and shrieking, 'You brutes. I'll not tolerate you any longer!' **[6]** Then she'd stop, tuck her chin in tightly to her chest so her glasses would slide down her nose, raise an overly-plucked eyebrow and stare at us with her dark judgemental eyes before shooing us away like we were stray animals. **[7]** Her eyes were unnaturally dark, almost black like they no longer knew what happiness was. **[8]** I swear that woman lived to destroy our childhood. **[9]** For the next half hour or so she'd busy herself knocking on our front doors telling our parents <u>we</u> were harassing <u>her</u> and spewing out other lies in a pathetic effort to win their pity. **[10]** I had been thrilled when mum announced that she'd got a new job but delight quickly turned to despair when she revealed who would be looking after me during the summer holidays, none other than Crazy Kissinglot! **[11]**

---

[2] Use of nickname and harsh alliteration of 'Crazy Kissinglot' emphasises the unpleasant nature of the character.

[3] Exaggeration emphasises the narrator's deep dislike of Mrs Kissinglot. The use of impersonal language 'the woman' and the metaphor comparing her to 'a demon' makes the reader side with the narrator and begin to share their dislike of Mrs Kissinglot.

[5] Well-chosen verbs force the reader to form a negative impression of Mrs Kissinglot's behaviour and make her seem like an angry and unpleasant character.

[7] Vivid description of the character's actions and gestures force the reader to dislike her. The simile 'like we were stray animals' is used to make the reader side with the narrator and dislike the old woman and how she interacts with the children.

[9] Varied sentence length – longer sentences followed by short sentences to vary the pace of the narrative and allow the narrator to influence the reader. The use of the verb 'destroy' makes Mrs Kissinglot seem like a formidable enemy in the eyes of the children.

[11] Contrast creates drama as the narrator's 'delight' turns to 'despair'. The vocabulary choices help increase the dramatic quality at this point as 'despair' is stronger than 'sadness.' Exclamatory sentence to end this paragraph emphasises the shock and helplessness of the narrator which earns them our sympathy.

[10] Underlining for the words 'we' and 'her' emphasises the narrator's disbelief. Verb choices such as 'spewing' along with the adjective 'pathetic' increase the reader's dislike of Mrs Kissinglot due to her dishonesty and her manipulative nature.

147

AO4 i, ii, iii — Creating dialogue

Dialogue is a conversation between people. To make characters convincing and reveal more about them, writers will include interactions and direct speech that helps bring characters to life and gives them a 'voice.' Dialogue can also be used to push the plot forward and, when used effectively, it can break up the action.

When we are relating something that has happened to us, without even thinking about it we usually quote what was said to us. This is because we instinctively know that using direct speech will make the anecdote more interesting for our listener.

The opening (below) to Alan Gibbons' novel *The Edge* shows this in action. What actually happens is that a mother wakes up her son and tells him to get out of bed. It's not very exciting when expressed like that! Gibbons, however, has added dialogue and internal monologue to bring the scene to life, so creating an opening full of tension.

Note how the dialogue in this extract is set out and punctuated. (You may need to revise how to do this.) Observe also the effect of using a variety of 'saying' verbs such as 'hisses' and 'whispers'.

He awakes with a start. Somebody is shaking him. Roughly.

'What ...?'

A hand covers his mouth, choking off the question. For a moment he gives in to a surge of panic, then he makes out a face in the darkness. His mother. She is crouching by his bed, one hand on the headboard, one clamped to the lower half of his face. He can see her properly now, her features slightly illuminated by the streetlamp a couple of doors away. It's her eyes he notices first, the frightened, pleading expression. Oh no, don't tell me it's happening again. He has learned to read his mother's face. Interpreting her looks, her mouthed warnings, has been essential to his survival. But this he can't read. It is too sudden, too unexpected. He gives a questioning frown.

'We've got to go,' Mum hisses. 'Now.'

'Go? Go where?'

Her hands are waving, palms down, reinforcing the pleading look in her eyes. 'Keep your voice down, Danny,' she whispers. 'Please!'

He does as he is told. His next words are barely audible, 'What's going on?'

'Can't explain. But we have to go. Right now.'

(Alan Gibbons, *The Edge*)

Activity

Write a story involving an interaction between these two characters. Include some dialogue, thinking carefully about what each character says and how they speak. Swap your writing with a partner and ask them to share their impressions of your characters and the relationship between them.

Get the balance right

It is important to achieve the right balance of action and dialogue. Too much dialogue can get boring and it can even become difficult for the reader to keep track of who is talking at any given time. In real life we rarely stand motionless while we speak. Instead, our dialogue is accompanied by actions and gestures so you should give careful consideration to what your characters are doing as they speak.

> ### Activity
>
> Write a short passage involving these two characters. Include convincing dialogue that is correctly laid out on the page. Choose verbs that give your reader an indication of how the words are spoken and provide details of convincing actions or gestures that accompany the words.

Create a convincing voice

How your characters speak can also provide clues about their age or where they are from, for example. You want to make your characters believable and convincing so on occasions you should feel comfortable in abandoning Standard English, if it adds to your characterisation.

In *Of Mice and Men* the character of Carlson is a ranch worker:

> Carlson was not to be put off. 'Look, Candy. This ol' dog jus' suffers hisself all the time. If you was to take him out and shoot him right in the back of the head –' he leaned over and pointed, '– right there, why he'd never know what hit him.'
>
> (John Steinbeck, *Of Mice and Men*)

Steinbeck makes this exchange convincing by bringing the character to life through what he says and how he says it. His request to kill the dog suggests that he is unsentimental but his way of speaking confirms his lowly social status as the final letters of words are omitted. Steinbeck also uses idiomatic expressions such as 'hisself' to make the character's voice and dialect seem authentic. It is important not to overdo this as a lot of omissions and informal vernacular can be off-putting for the reader – it's all about getting the balance right!

When giving your characters individual identity take care that they do not all sound the same. For example, a school principal may speak with authority when questioning a school student. The responses of the student may be brief and hesitant. An exchange between two strangers will be very different from that which occurs between friends. Similarly, if you were writing dialogue between an elderly character and a teenager there would be some notable differences in the voices of the characters.

AO4 i Creating empathy

We have already identified the importance of creating convincing characters and how dialogue can be an effective way of bringing characters to life so that your reader can connect with them. Successful writers are able to create characters their readers will empathise with. Empathy is the skill of being able to put yourself in the position of another person. To get a reader to empathise means that they will be able to relate to a character and have an interest in their situation.

In this short extract from *Whispers in the Graveyard*, the author Theresa Breslin makes us empathise with the character of Solomon. Solomon has dyslexia and finds school challenging but he has been benefiting from support offered by Ms Talmur.

> I look at the words on the page, at my crabbed writing carefully spaced out on alternate lines, and I know I should remember what they mean. I reach around inside my head and it's not there.
>
> Then she tells me. Smiling patiently. And I recall that she told me that word yesterday, and the day before, and the day before that...
>
> Embarrassment and humiliation are on my face, a sour taste in my mouth.
>
> 'It's no good,' I say.
>
> 'Yes, it is,' she says firmly.
>
> The words tremble on the page. I shake my head. The ragged black hole of despair widening in and around me. Rage rushing in fast to fill up the void.
>
> 'No,' I shout.
>
> 'Did Sir Edmund Hillary give up on the slopes of Everest?' she demands. 'Did Captain Scott turn back? Did Columbus? Did Ezekial McGribbons?'
>
> I fall for it.
>
> 'Who's Ezekial McGribbons?'
>
> 'I don't know. I made him up, didn't I?'
>
> I laugh and we start again.
>
> And again.
>
> And again.
>
> 'Will it ever come right?' I ask.
>
> She meets my eyes and doesn't look away. 'Not completely,' she says. 'When you're rich and famous, don't ever write out a cheque without having someone make sure that your numbers are correct.' She laughs. 'You'd be just as likely to put down 3,000 pounds as 300.' She puts her hand on my arm. 'But you CAN cope with it. Enough to get by. Remember it's a difficulty, not a disability. You must move past it and get on with your life. Do what you want to do.' Her nails are through the wool of my jumper. 'You control it, not the other way around.'
>
> (Teresa Breslin, *Whispers in the Graveyard*)

Creating empathy

You do not need to have dyslexia to empathise with Solomon as we are all able to relate to his feelings of insecurity and his need for reassurance. The use of first person narration helps us empathise with the character as he shares his private thoughts and feelings. The reader is able to relate to the emotions experienced by the character, therefore they are able to empathise.

It is also possible to get your reader to empathise with a character's situation. In the following extract Stanley Yelnats has been sent to Camp Green Lake. The author writes using an omniscient third person perspective. The character of Stanley says very little but you can imagine how he must be feeling as he arrives at the prison camp:

> He stepped on to the hard, dry dirt. There was a band of sweat around his wrist where the handcuff had been.
>
> The land was barren and desolate. He could see a few rundown buildings and some tents. Farther away there was a cabin beneath two tall trees. Those two trees were the only plant life he could see. There weren't even weeds.
>
> The guard led Stanley to a small building. A sign on the front said, YOU ARE ENTERING CAMP GREEN LAKE JUVENILE CORRECTIONAL FACILITY.
>
> The guard led Stanley into the building, where he felt the welcome relief of air-conditioning.
>
> A man was sitting with his feet up on a desk. He turned his head when Stanley and the guard entered, but otherwise didn't move. Even though he was inside, he wore sunglasses and a cowboy hat. He also held a can of soda, and the sight of it made Stanley even more aware of his own thirst.
>
> He waited while the bus guard gave the man some papers to sign. He had a tattoo of a rattlesnake on his arm, and as he signed his name, the snake's rattle seemed to wiggle … Then the man in the cowboy hat walked around the desk to Stanley. 'My name is Mr Sir,' he said. Whenever you speak to me you must call me by that name, is that clear?'
>
> Stanley hesitated. 'Uh, yes, Mr Sir,' he said, though he couldn't imagine that was really the man's name.
>
> 'You're not in the Girl Scouts anymore,' Mr Sir said.
>
> Stanley had to remove his clothes in front of Mr Sir, who made sure he wasn't hiding anything. He was then given two sets of clothes and a towel. Each set consisted of a long-sleeve orange jumpsuit, an orange T-shirt, and yellow socks …
>
> Stanley got dressed.
>
> (Louis Sachar, *Holes*)

Activity

Write a story involving this character. If you decide to use a first person narration you may wish to write a diary entry, a letter, a speech or stream of consciousness. Alternatively, you may decide to write using an omniscient third person perspective.

AO4 i, ii, iii — Creating setting

As well as characters and plot, setting is another important feature of narrative writing. Short stories tend to contain their action within a specific setting, which can be an effective way of engaging the reader as the setting can enhance our understanding of the characters and contribute to an interesting plot.

The contribution of setting in involving the reader is clearly demonstrated in the following extract. Here, the main character, Ian, is being pursued by McClean, a villain also known as wolfman. He has taken refuge in an empty flat in a tower block but McClean is closing in on him. At this point in the story Ian feels his only choice and chance of escape is to climb out on to a ledge that is eleven floors up.

> **Activity**
>
> Make a list of features that make this extract dramatic and interesting for the reader. You may wish to use the 'LADDERS' mnemonic on page 156 to help you think critically about what the writer has achieved.

> Cold as it is up there on his precarious eleventh-floor perch, Ian is sweating. His palms are slimy against the wall. Ever so slowly he moves his right hand from the wall and wipes it on his shirt. Then, returning his right hand to the wall and easing his left off, he repeats the operation. Finally, realising he has no choice but to go on, he makes his first move since McClean's head appeared at the window.
>
> Trying not to look down the dizzying precipice of the building, Ian takes the weight on his toes and on the balls of his feet and starts to inch forward. A few more steps and those aching muscles will be shrieking with pain.
>
> You can do this, he tells himself.
>
> He barks insults at himself under his breath. Coward! Idiot! It doesn't matter how much noise he makes, not in this howling wind.
>
> *Come on! You can do it.*
>
> But, as he feels the tendons in his legs starting to shudder again, as he feels the wind trying to suck him off the wall, he isn't sure he can ...
>
> He knows that the keenness of his mind is all that is standing between him and fatal impact with the ground below. So, heels over the drop, toes clinging to the ledge, he edges forward, sliding his feet. And it is left foot, right foot, palms flattened against the bricks, fingernails clawing at the narrow crevice.
>
> *Not far now.*
>
> He continues to shuffle along the ledge. His movements are slow and deliberate, all the more so because of the rain that is trickling down the brickwork, sluicing over the ledge and puddling round his feet.
>
> *A few more steps.*
>
> (Alan Gibbons, *The Defender*)

You can see that in this extract the pursuit adds excitement. Ian's desperation allows the reader to empathise with him but the setting injects an added element of danger and complicates the plot. We are now keen to read on and see if Ian avoids wolfman, and if he survives. This extract would not have the same power if the action took place on the ground floor.

Location! Location! Location!

We have seen how setting can enhance the reader's interest in character and plot, but many writers prioritise setting and a description of a location can be an effective way of beginning your story. In *Of Mice and Men*, John Steinbeck begins each of his six chapters with a description of the setting, which prepares the reader for the events to follow.

In the exam, the image may inspire you to write a description of a character's movements through a particular setting. Your challenge will be to bring the place to life so that the reader can imagine it in their mind's eye. Read the extract below from *The Woman in Black* by Susan Hill. There is very little in the way of action but it still succeeds in holding the interest of the reader due to the vivid description of the setting and the ominous atmosphere:

> …I emerged into a small burial ground. It was enclosed by the remains of a wall, and I stopped in astonishment at the sight. There were perhaps fifty old gravestones, most of them leaning over or completely fallen, covered in patches of greenish yellow lichen and moss, scoured pale by the salt wind, and stained by years of driven rain. The mounds were grassy, and weed-covered, or else they had disappeared altogether, sunken and slipped down. No names or dates were now decipherable, and the whole place had a decayed and abandoned air.
>
> Ahead, where the wall ended in a heap of dust and rubble, lay the grey water of the estuary. As I stood, wondering, the last light went from the sun, and the wind rose in a gust, and rustled through the grass. Above my head, that unpleasant, snake-necked bird came gliding back towards the ruins, and I saw that its beak was hooked around a fish that writhed and struggled helplessly. I watched the creature alight and, as it did so, it disturbed some of the stones, which toppled and fell out of sight somewhere.
>
> Suddenly conscious of the cold and the extreme bleakness and eeriness of the spot and of the gathering dusk of the November afternoon, and not wanting my spirits to become so depressed that I might begin to be affected by all sorts of morbid fancies, I was about to leave, and walk briskly back to the house, where I intended to switch on a good many lights and even light a small fire if it were possible, before beginning my preliminary work on Mrs Drablow's papers. But, as I turned away, I glanced once again round the burial ground and then I saw again the woman with the wasted face, who had been at Mrs Drablow's funeral. She was at the far end of the plot, close to one of the few upright headstones, and she wore the same black clothing and bonnet, but it seemed to have slipped back so that I could make out her face a little more clearly. In the greyness of the fading light, it had the sheen and pallor not of flesh so much as of bone itself.
>
> (Susan Hill, *The Woman in Black*)

In this passage the writer slowly reveals the setting to the reader, taking us through it a footstep at a time and detailing the narrator's observations and reactions to the place. The writer begins by **immersing** the reader into the setting of the graveyard. Then we are **introduced** to the character's thoughts on the location but the situation is **complicated** as the daylight fades and the wind increases. The passage **concludes** with the sighting of the mysterious figure.

This structure is one way to begin developing your skills:

UNIT 4 SECTION A: PERSONAL OR CREATIVE WRITING

Immerse	Begin by immersing your reader in a location with a detailed description of the setting. The reader should know where the action is taking place, what time of day/year it is and what the weather conditions are. Use the method of zooming in, which you were introduced to in the Personal Writing section.
Introduce	Introduce your character or characters so that your reader is made aware of the circumstances by which they find themselves in this place. The reader will be keen to know how the character(s) feel about being in this setting.
Complicate	Try to develop your plot by introducing some complication; this could be something as simple as deteriorating weather conditions or it could be a more dramatic turn of events, such as a fall or an unexpected sighting.
Conclude	Select an appropriate conclusion for your story. There could be a resolution or an inconclusive cliffhanger. The choice is yours!

Using this **mnemonic** can help you remember the key features to bring your setting to life.

L **Location:** Establish a sense of where different scenes take place.

Language: Select words and phrases that will influence your reader's reactions and emotions. Dialogue or direct speech can play an important role in creating setting.

A **Atmosphere:** This is the mood or tone you wish to convey to the reader. You can use setting to bring about tonal shifts and contrasts to add interest, e.g. start a story with a happy mood but build up a growing sense of tension. **Pathetic fallacy** (using the weather or landscape to reflect mood) can be used to reinforce a particular atmosphere or reflect a character's feelings.

D **Descriptive:** Descriptive or visual details bring a scene to life by adding convincing touches.

D **Details:** A well-placed detail can have real impact.

E **Effect on the reader:** Aim to create interest through appealing to emotions such as fear, anger, joy or shock. Encouraging a sense of empathy with a character will also engage the reader.

R **Reactions of the characters:** The physical and emotional reactions of the characters within a setting also pull the reader into what is happening. Thoughts and feelings can be revealed through internal monologue.

S **Senses:** As well as creating imagery, appeal to other senses – smell, taste or touch – to make your writing more vivid.

Structure: Sustain the reader's participation through a variety of sentence structures.

Activity

Use this image to write a story that takes place in this setting. You may wish to practise using the immerse, introduce, complicate and conclude approach suggested at the top of the page. Remember to try to bring the setting to life and allow your reader to conjure up a vivid mental image.

Creating atmosphere

AO4 i, ii, iii

As you write your story, you will be making decisions about the mood or atmosphere you want to create. The first step in creating a suitable atmosphere is to select an appropriate setting for the events to take place. To achieve a romantic atmosphere, for example, you may decide to tell the story of a proposal that takes place on a candle-lit balcony at sunset. The same event in a dark, litter-strewn alleyway would simply not have the same effect!

Imagine you were tasked to write a suspense story. Answer these questions:

1 What season or time of year will you set your story?
2 What time of day will you have the action take place?
3 What will the weather be like?
4 Where will you set your story?
5 What action might take place?
6 What is the time frame for the events taking place?

The most common answers to these questions include:

1 Autum or winter.
2 Late at night.
3 Adverse weather such as torrential rain, a storm or dense fog.
4 An isolated setting such as a graveyard or forest. Other common suggestions include a derelict setting such as an abandoned house.
5 A pursuit, a sinister discovery or unexplained happenings, perhaps even the suggestion of supernatural activity.
6 To escalate the tension you will probably have a very short time frame, with the situation developing minute by minute.

These are some of the conventions of suspense writing and if you want to create a sinister atmosphere you are likely to include most of these in your writing. When we watch a horror film or a thriller, the lighting effects, the camera angles and the music all contribute to the atmosphere and provide clues that something menacing is about to occur. Writers must rely upon words, techniques and sentence structures to achieve the same effect. Descriptions of setting, time, weather and sensory details all contribute to creating atmosphere but to be successful you will need to think about your writing style as well as your content.

Style

The style of our writing is shaped by the *choices* we make about our use of words and phrases, our inclusion of linguistic devices, our sentence structures and our use of punctuation for effect. As writers we are fortunate to have many choices when it comes to telling a story but we must do our best to make the right choices!

Read the following short extract from *And the Mountains Echoed* by Khaled Hosseini and see how every sentence is contributing to the tense atmosphere and working to convey the panic of the young boy Abdullah:

UNIT 4 SECTION A: PERSONAL OR CREATIVE WRITING

[1] The dramatic opening creates intrigue and suspense. It also lets us understand the reason for Abdullah's panic.

[3] The description of the fire adds to the character's feelings of abandonment – there is no source of warmth or comfort. An ominous atmosphere is unfolding.

[5] Another short sentence confirms the child's intense fear and increases the tension.

[7] One word is spoken and it is 'whispered.' Here the writer is escalating the tension as both Abdullah and the reader are hopeful of a reply from his father.

> Abdullah woke later and found Father gone.**[1]** He sat up in a fright.**[2]** The fire was all but dead, nothing left of it now but a few crimson specks of ember.**[3]** Abdullah's gaze darted left, then right but his eyes could penetrate nothing in the dark, at once vast and smothering.**[4]** He felt his face going white.**[5]** Heart sprinting, he cocked his ear, held his breath.**[6]**
>
> 'Father?' he whispered.**[7]**
>
> Silence.**[8]**
>
> Panic began to mushroom deep in his chest. He sat perfectly still, his body erect and tense, and listened for a long time.**[9]** He heard nothing.**[10]**
>
> (Khaled Hosseini, *And the Mountains Echoed*)

[2] The use of a short sentence emphasises the child's sudden and intense fear.

[4] The longer sentence reflects the desperate movements of Abdullah to try to understand his situation. The darkness is described as 'vast' and 'smothering' which makes Abdullah seem more vulnerable as his panic increases.

[6] Abdullah's actions confirm his growing anxiety. The reader can appreciate how the darkness and the silence combine to create a fearful atmosphere for the child.

[8] This one-word sentence is positioned in a paragraph of its own to emphasise the significance of the silence, allowing us to appreciate the terror it induces within Abdullah.

[9] The description of Abdullah's internal and external reaction to the silence and the reality of his abandonment escalate the atmosphere of fear and tension.

[10] A short sentence ends the extract and emphasises the atmosphere of isolation and the despondency felt by Abdullah.

In the section on Personal Writing (p.129) you encountered a list of techniques that could be used to add interest. You were also made aware of the importance of choosing dramatic verbs and vivid adjectives. Review this advice and make sure you feel ready to put it into practice.

Activity

Write a short descriptive passage based on this image. Remember to think carefully about your choice of words and phrases, your use of techniques and your sentence structures to create your desired atmosphere.

Now change the season and/or the time of day and write a second description creating a different atmosphere.

Writing a theme-based narrative

AO4 i, ii

We all carry memories of enjoyable stories which leave a lasting impression upon us. This can be due to the characters and the events that unfold, but writers also use their work to examine themes.

A theme is an idea that runs throughout a piece of work and most stories explore various themes. In *Lord of the Flies,* for example, William Golding does more than simply tell a great story about schoolboys stranded on a desert island. As we read this novel, we are encouraged to reflect upon the themes of relationships, leadership, conflict, society and civilisation to name but a few.

In the same way that many words have more than one meaning, images can also communicate more than one meaning. As you study the image provided in the examination, you may feel inspired to base your writing on what you see, which will involve writing a description of the scene or adopting the persona of the character. You may also be asked to write a story based on the themes or emotions conveyed by the image shown.

Did the photographer of this picture want to simply capture an image of a hurricane or does this picture convey other messages?

When presented with this image one student may write a story about experiencing a hurricane and will offer a description of what is shown in the photograph. Another student may interpret this as an image of destruction or power and decide to write a story on these themes.

> ### Activity
> Look at each of the images below and consider the different options they offer you as inspiration for your writing. Select one and write a short story based on your chosen image.
>
>

157

AO4 iii — Editing tips

The last 10 minutes spent reviewing and editing your writing could make that all-important difference to your final grade. Reviewing and revising your writing is one of the best ways to maximise your performance.

Don't be afraid to cross things out and make changes: it shows you are a thoughtful writer.

Make sure you keep changes readable and make your corrections clear.

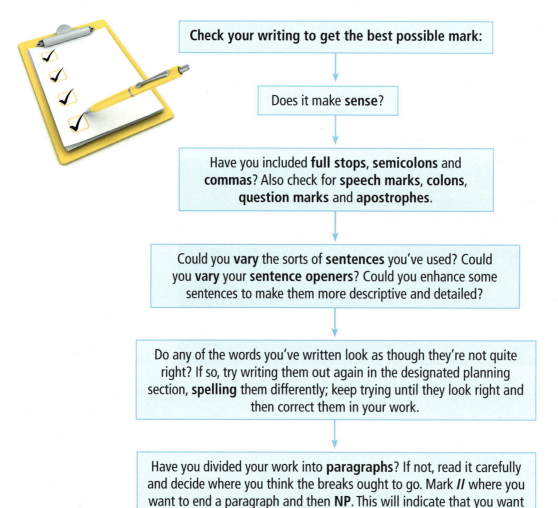

Check your writing to get the best possible mark:

Does it make **sense**?

Have you included **full stops**, **semicolons** and **commas**? Also check for **speech marks**, **colons**, **question marks** and **apostrophes**.

Could you **vary** the sorts of **sentences** you've used? Could you **vary** your **sentence openers**? Could you enhance some sentences to make them more descriptive and detailed?

Do any of the words you've written look as though they're not quite right? If so, try writing them out again in the designated planning section, **spelling** them differently; keep trying until they look right and then correct them in your work.

Have you divided your work into **paragraphs**? If not, read it carefully and decide where you think the breaks ought to go. Mark **//** where you want to end a paragraph and then **NP**. This will indicate that you want to begin a new paragraph.

Have you **included all that you wanted to say**? If not, mark the place where you want to add something with an asterisk *, make the same mark at the end of your piece, where you have some space, and then write the points or ideas you wish to add by the second mark. If you want to add extra points or ideas somewhere else use a different mark, such as **. Avoid excessive additions by planning effectively before you commence writing.

Personal and Creative Writing: target success

UNIT 4

Matching grades to Personal and Creative Writing

In Section A the essential qualities you need to show are highlighted at the important grade boundaries. Read these descriptions *carefully*; they tell you what your answer should be like.

Grade C writing displays:
- ✔ development that holds the reader's attention
- ✔ an appropriate sense of audience and purpose
- ✔ clearly structured and increasingly fluent expression
- ✔ a series of sentence structures, competently handled
- ✔ accurate use of basic punctuation that makes the meaning clear
- ✔ generally accurate spelling and the use of a widening range of language.

Grade A/A* writing displays:
- ✔ development that is sophisticated and commands the reader's attention
- ✔ a sense of a positive relationship with the audience
- ✔ an assured use of structure and a confident style
- ✔ sentence structuring that enhances the overall effect
- ✔ a range of punctuation, confidently employed to enhance fluency
- ✔ accurate spelling and use of an extended vocabulary – errors tend to be one-off mistakes.

Practice question
Personal Writing
Write a speech to be delivered to your classmates, in which you tell them about your proudest moment.

Practice question
Creative Writing
Write a suspense story based on this image.
Response time: 55 minutes
15 minutes thinking and planning
30 minutes writing
10 minutes checking your writing

Sample student response for Personal Writing

Good morning classmates, allow me to begin by asking you, if you had a chance to live one moment of your life over again, what would it be?**[1]** For the past few days I have tortured myself with this very same question. My predicament has not been helped by the fact that as a talented footballer I have been fortunate enough to win many awards and hold aloft several impressive trophies.**[2]** After a period of indulgent reminiscence, I have decided that my standout moment was playing in the final of the Schools' Cup.**[3]**

Our journey to the final was challenging;**[4]** on more than one occasion we snatched victory from the jaws of defeat! However, all that mattered was that we had indeed made it to the final. Now those of you**[5]** who know Mr Jackson well will appreciate that he is not a coach who subscribes to gentle persuasion and encouragement; no, our own Mr Jackson stepped right out of the 'Alex Ferguson School of Coaching' and if you're not playing like your life depends upon it, you're going to hear about it. (The unfortunate thing is, so too will anyone else within a five-hundred-mile radius of the pitch!)**[6]**

As the Cup final beckoned, it seemed that our training sessions became more gruelling. There were days where it felt like we barely got our feet near the ball but instead spent our time squatting and lunging before running laps of the pitch, but it was paying off and we were feeling like finely honed athletes.**[7]**

On the day of the match**[8]** we walked out of the changing room to a sea of supporters.**[9]** Lining up we each cast an eye over our opponents and felt certain this would be an easy ninety minutes... Looking back I can admit we were arrogant and cocky, but isn't that essential for a winning mentality?**[10]**

The first half was... brutal!**[11]** We lost our shape and our heads were dropping with each passing minute. Frustration was growing and we were snapping at each other rather than getting on with doing the job. On the side line Coach Jackson was gesticulating

[1] Effective use of questions to engage the audience from the start.

[2] Demonstrates clear appreciation of audience, purpose and form.

[3] Reveals the specific topic they have chosen by the end of the introduction.

[4] Accurate use of semi-colon to link ideas.

[5] Establishes a conversational tone to sustain a rapport with the audience.

[6] Adds a humorous aside to engage the audience.

[7] Well-chosen precise vocabulary – 'gruelling' and 'finely honed'.

[8] Effective structuring of ideas – moves the story on, sharing essential details with the reader.

[9] Use of imagery – 'sea of supporters' – to exaggerate the numbers in attendance and to conjure up a vivid image.

[10] Further use of rhetorical question to engage the audience.

[11] Short, exclamatory sentence and punctuation used for impact.

Target success

wildly like a man possessed. The squeal of the whistle signalled the end of the first half and like a convoy of war-wounded soldiers[12] we wearily trudged off the field, anticipating an almighty telling off from our coach… but we were wrong! The man who had spent the last forty-five minutes hollering and jumping around in a frenzied state, walked calmly into the changing room, stood still and looked each of us in the eye as he nodded his head. We were unnerved. We were puzzled.[13] Finally, he cleared his throat and spoke, more quietly than we had ever heard him speak before, 'I believe in you boys. You've worked hard and have never let me down yet. We may be behind, but this game is not over. Go out and be the footballer I know each of you can be. It's a good side you're facing out there but you must believe you are better and you will be better.' We were stunned.

In the second half we played like a different team; we kept our formation, we kept possession and we were on target with our shots so that with four minutes to go the score was 3–3. Coach Jackson had also undergone something of a transformation, as he stood tall and proud, arms folded across his chest, only occasionally giving a thumbs up or applauding our play.

[14]When the ball found my feet, I knew time was of the essence. I spotted our striker, who had created space and was signalling for the pass, but instead I took aim and my laces connected with the ball, sending it soaring beyond the reach of the tall gangly goal-keeper.[15] He leapt like a salmon but his fingertips missed the ball, which found its home comfortably in the back of the net. Involuntarily, I let out a shrill squeal and raised my arms aloft.[16] I vividly remember my teammates bounding towards me as I found myself face first in the grass under a mountain of elated[17] players. We were champions!

[18]Looking back, my sense of pride comes not so much from the fact that I scored the winning goal (though I can't deny it remains a personal highlight!), but that I learned not to underestimate any opponent, to be resilient, to dig deeper when things aren't going to plan, but most of all I learned about the power of belief.

[12] Further use of imagery – similes evoke the scene. Alliteration of 'w' has also been used here to emphasise their tiredness and feeling of defeat.

[13] Long complex sentence, followed by two short sentences to emphasise a sudden shock.

[14] Zooms in on one very specific moment of the match and retells it in detail.

[15] Long complex sentence emphasises the intensity of this moment.

[16] Follows action with reaction and uses sibilance in 'shrill squeal' to emphasise delight.

[17] Exaggeration of 'mountain' creates strong image, and precisely selected vocabulary – 'elated' – conveys the extent of their emotion.

[18] Concludes appropriately with a reflection.

UNIT 4 SECTION A: PERSONAL OR CREATIVE WRITING

> This strong response demonstrates:
> - ✓ confident awareness of purpose and audience, with an ability to sustain an engaging style
> - ✓ a confident style
> - ✓ confident organisation of ideas
> - ✓ deliberate manipulation of a range of sentence structures
> - ✓ evidence of punctuation used for effect
> - ✓ evidence of linguistic devices to enhance the reader's engagement.

Sample student response for Creative Writing

[1] The student immerses the reader into the character's situation and establishes an uneasy atmosphere through the description of the weather and the choice of the adjective 'harsh.'

[4] Use of long sentence to capture the sudden flurry of movement and activity around the house which adds to the character's uneasiness and the reader's intrigue.

[6] Maintains a sense of danger and tension by providing the character with limited options.

[8] Details allow the reader to empathise with the character. Also the student has varied their sentence opening here by beginning with the '–ing' form of the verb.

The harsh snow pelted against my face as I walked tentatively further and further down the icy pathway. **[1]** Each step was becoming more difficult as the storm gathered strength. Every few seconds I was temporarily blinded and my toes ached with the pinch of cold but I was reassured by the knowledge that the old decaying mansion stood three or four hundred yards up ahead. **[2]** It looked far from welcoming but I had no choice, out here I would freeze to death.

Approaching my dilapidated sanctuary, I remained cautious as the branches beneath my feet cracked like brittle bones **[3]** and in an instant the whole place seemed to come alive; in the bare trees birds fluttered in alarm, in the bushes I could hear the scuttling of wild animals and even the gate gave a moan to mark my arrival. **[4]** The mansion itself was suffocating **[5]** under a tangle of moss and ivy. A thick blanket of snow served to intensify the blackness of the building and in truth I was looking for any excuse not to enter but a cold icy wind seemed to push me forward, as if reminding me I was quickly running out of options. **[6]**

Once inside I became aware of the heaviness and discomfort of my sodden clothes. **[7]** Shivering and vulnerable I stood dwarfed by the vast hallway. **[8]** The scuttling of spiders and the creaking of floorboards made me feel like the entire house objected to my intrusion…or was warning someone or something of my presence. **[9]**

---

[2] Long sentence to emphasise the character's struggle against the snow storm. The reader has an understanding of where the action is taking place and the mention of the old mansion injects an ominous atmosphere.

[3] Use of this simile is foreboding and adds to the creepy atmosphere of the house.

[5] Personification and use of the verb 'suffocating' adds suggestions of death while allowing the reader to conjure up an image of the house.

[7] Good use of vocabulary and convincing details.

[9] In this sentence the student demonstrates their ability to use alliteration and the inclusion of ellipsis heightens the tension, compelling us to read on.

Target success

> As my eyes adjusted to the darkness I moved down the hallway and pushed on a large door which opened abruptly, catapulting me into a large living room. Coughing and spluttering, I picked myself up off the dust strewn floor and took a good look around.
>
> The moon shone in brightly illuminating the room. I felt comforted by its company[10] and moved closer to the beam of light which revealed a canopy of cobwebs above my head. Normally, I would be shrieking at the mere possibility of a nearby spider, but I knew on this occasion that I was the invader[11] and so I remained silent.
>
> Outside the snow scene looked beautiful, almost idyllic. For a few minutes I stood hypnotised by the spectacle. Soft downy flakes pirouetted in the night sky before gently cascading to the ground.[12] An unexpected noise ruptured my reverie and brought me back to my horrifying reality.[13] It was a low guttural growling sound and at once it sent my heart pummelling against my chest. I froze.[14]

[10] The student follows up action with reaction. The personification of the moon as a companion momentarily eases the tension.

[11] The student has the character identify themselves as an 'invader', which is a word we associate with hostility and conflict. The student makes clear that the character feels like an outsider in this setting.

[12] The student makes impressive use of vocabulary and description here to control the atmosphere. The controlled sentence lengths contribute to the feeling of calmness.

[13] The student introduces a complication with the sudden unpleasant noise that changes the atmosphere. The vocabulary is again impressive with the choice of the word 'reverie'.

[14] Action is balanced with reaction – the character's racing heart contrasts with their outward stillness. The short sentence to conclude this paragraph is dramatic and again the student escalates the tension.

This answer demonstrates:
- ✔ confident awareness of purpose and audience
- ✔ a developing, confident style
- ✔ deliberate manipulation of a range of sentence structures
- ✔ some extended use of vocabulary
- ✔ some effective use of linguistic devices.

Personal and Creative Writing: key to success

POINTS TO REMEMBER

Read these key pointers to help you prepare:

▶ Remember that the skills for Personal and Creative Writing are transferable.

▶ The best writing results from the following process: **Think, Plan, Write**. Resist the temptation to start immediately; taking the time to think and plan is essential to produce your best work.

▶ Make your writing lively and engaging. Let your personality come through in the writing – the last thing anyone wants is to read something dull!

▶ Remember you have only 55 minutes in which to complete the writing process.

▶ There are no prizes for finishing first so use all of the time wisely – the only reward for finishing early could be a low grade if you do not make the most of the time available.

▶ Review your finished work – you must review your work to get the most out of your answer because everyone makes mistakes when they are working quickly and under pressure. Remember too that there are no marks for extreme neatness – it is much better that your work is accurate even if it contains a few corrections. As you check your work, consider the following questions and correct any mistakes that you find:

 i) Have you used paragraphs?
 ii) Did you use a range of sentence lengths?
 iii) Did you vary the sentence openings?
 iv) Have you used a varied vocabulary?
 v) Have you left out any words or are there any sentences where the meaning is less than clear?

Personal and Creative Writing: key to success

Checklist for success: working towards Grade C	
Have you shown understanding of the purpose and structure of the task?	
Have you shown and maintained awareness of the reader/intended audience?	
Does the content fit the purpose?	
Is the piece paragraphed and does each paragraph have a topic sentence?	
Have you used some language devices (rhetorical questions, emotive language, etc.) that are in keeping with the purpose and audience?	
Is there a range of appropriate vocabulary used to create effect?	
Is there appropriate variety in the sentence structures?	
Is there clear punctuation and is it used to vary pace and clarify meaning?	
Have you checked your spelling?	

Checklist for success: working towards Grade A/A*	
Does your writing show an understanding of the purpose, and is your writing structured appropriately?	
Have you shown an ongoing awareness of the reader/intended audience?	
Is the content coverage detailed and fitting for the purpose?	
Have you made sure the paragraphs have a topic sentence?	
Have you used a range of language devices (rhetorical questions, emotive language, etc.) adapted to purpose and audience?	
Is there a wide range of precise, extended vocabulary and is it used to create effect or convey precise meaning?	
Is there confident and effective variation of sentence structures, and use of simple, compound and complex sentences to achieve particular effects?	
Is there accurate punctuation used to vary pace, clarify meaning, avoid ambiguity and create deliberate effects?	
Is virtually all spelling, including that of complex irregular words, correct?	

UNIT 4
Section B: Reading literary and non-fiction texts

Introduction to reading literary and non-fiction texts

Unit 4 is externally assessed and comprises two sections. Section B is the second section and it assesses reading literary and non-fiction texts. There are three tasks in this section (Tasks 2 to 4 on the examination paper), which examine your understanding of how writers employ a variety of linguistic devices, words and phrases, sentence structures and punctuation to create fiction and non-fiction writing that engages the reader.

Target skills
The target skills you will learn about in this section will enable you to:
- read and understand texts
- understand how meaning is constructed
- recognise the effects of language choices and patterns
- select material appropriate to purpose
- evaluate how texts may be interpreted differently depending on the reader's perspective
- explain and evaluate how writers use linguistic, grammatical and structural features to sustain the reader's interest.

Assessment Objectives
Your Assessment Objectives in this section are:
i Read with insight and select material appropriate to purpose.
ii Develop and sustain interpretations of writers' ideas and perspectives.
iii Explain and evaluate how writers use linguistic, grammatical and structural features to achieve effects and influence the reader.

The exam questions
You will have 50 minutes to answer three short tasks based upon your reading of three texts. Task 2 will require you to compare and contrast two literary texts. Tasks 3 and 4 will be based upon your reading of two shorter non-fiction texts. You should pay attention to the timing advice stated at the beginning of each question as this will help you manage your time more effectively. You will answer in the spaces provided in the exam booklet.
The set tasks will focus on the ways in which writers craft their texts to convey meaning and to influence the reader.

Literary and non-fiction texts

AO3 i, ii, iii

Fiction and non-fiction are two types of writing that you will be familiar with. This section of Unit 4 is concerned with reading literary (fiction) and non-fiction texts. There are overlaps between fiction and non-fiction as you will come to appreciate as you work through this chapter.

The key thing to remember about **fiction texts** is that they are made up. They are imaginary. They are based on an imagined world and contain imaginary characters in imaginary situations. What makes fiction successful is that while reading you believe it to be real. For this to work, the writer needs to make careful decisions about plot, setting and characterisation.

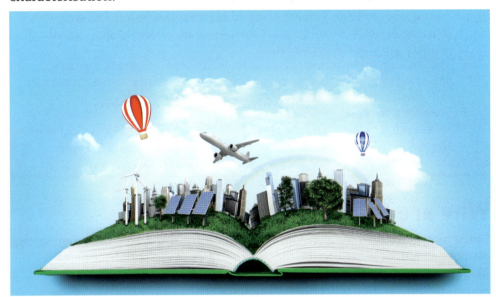

Non-fiction texts are about reality and facts; the material can be authenticated. They are based on the real world – on real people, real things and real events. Non-fiction texts are all around us and are an important part of everyone's lives.

It is important to bear in mind that although non-fiction is based on the real world, it is not always factual or true. Non-fiction is an account or representation of a subject that is presented as fact. This presentation may be accurate or it may not be; that is, it can give either a true or a false account. It is generally assumed, however, that authors believe their accounts to be truthful when they write them.

Activity

In pairs or groups:
1 Think about a piece of fictional writing that you have read that was completely believable and realistic to you. (It could be a book that you have studied at school or one that you read in your own time.) What made it so realistic?
2 Think about a piece of fictional writing that you did *not* find believable or realistic. Try to work out why it was unsuccessful as a work of fiction.

UNIT 4 SECTION B: READING LITERARY AND NON-FICTION TEXTS

3 The extracts below are different types of texts. Identify which are literary fiction and which are non-fiction. Be prepared to explain your decisions.

A 'Eliza lay motionless and surrounded by the darkness. Her heart was racing and her throat was dry. Petrified, she reached for the light switch but the power was out.
"Mama," she cried out, but her cry was drowned out by the roar of the storm.'

B 'Knackered again. This camp has been really tough. It was the first foreign training camp of the Olympic run-up, a chance for the group to blow away the cobwebs that three weeks of holiday had gathered.'

C 'Cassius Clay entered the ring in Miami Beach wearing a short white robe, "The Lip" stitched on the back. He was beautiful again. He was fast, sleek and 22. But, for the first and last time in his life, he was afraid.'

D 'Jonah Quigg looked like your average twelve-year-old boy, but Jonah's life was far from average. In fact he was an extraordinary young man with a shocking secret. A secret so great that, if revealed, it would alter everything we understand about our world.'

E 'Hidden away in the mountainside is the village of Mooreduck, a village populated by peculiar people with a peculiar history. Only very few are aware of its existence...'

F 'Dear Mr Bowden,
Thank you for taking the time recently on the phone to hear about our work. Not many people realise that Praxis Care is Northern Ireland's largest charity...'

Why are things written?

Everything is written for a reason. It is important that you can recognise the **purpose** of a text.

Writers of both non-fiction and literary texts are writing to **engage** and **entertain** you, so they will choose language that has the desired impact upon you as a reader.

Non-fiction writers might also aim to **inform**, to **advise**, to **explain**, to **instruct**, to **argue** or to **persuade** you, and again their language choices will help them achieve their intended purpose.

How are things written?

In the same way that an artist creates a masterpiece or an architect designs a building, a writer must craft a text. This can be a meticulous process and the writer must make deliberate decisions. Even the most talented of writers produce several drafts before a text is considered a finished piece. Texts are produced *by* writers but they are created *for* readers.

As a **reader** of a text you should be asking:

▶ **Who** is the writer's target audience?
▶ **What** is the writer's purpose?
▶ **How** has the writer crafted their text to achieve their purpose?

Writer's craft

AO3 i, ii

Style

Like musicians and artists, writers aim to create a style that will suit a particular reader or audience in order to achieve a specific purpose.

Style describes how the writer uses **words**, **sentence structure** and **sentence arrangement** to establish **mood**, **images** and **meaning** in the text. Style also describes the way in which the writer describes **events**, **objects** and **ideas**.

One easy way to understand literary style is to think about fashion styles. Clothes can be formal and dressy, informal and casual, athletic, and so forth. Just as one person might dress in several different fashions, writers can dress a single message in several different literary styles. For example:

- **Informal:** '"Nothing like that ever happened," Tony replied.'
- **Formal:** '"That happenstance did not become a reality," Tony stated.'
- **Journalistic:** '"It did not happen," Tony said.'
- **Archaic:** '"Verily, it was a circumstance, to be noted, that appeared not so much to have been a reality as to have evolved as a thing that had not yet come to be," Tony impelled.'

The style a writer uses influences how we interpret the facts that are presented. The version of a sentence that a writer chooses tells us a lot about the situation, the writer and the person being addressed (the audience).

Activity

Compare these sentences. What does each tell you about the situation, the writer and the person being addressed?
1 'He's passed away.'
2 'He's sleeping with the fishes.'
3 'He died.'
4 'He's gone to meet his Maker.'
5 'He kicked the bucket.'
6 'He's pushing up the daisies.'

Analysing how a writer has crafted their text can be a challenging task as you will need to consider and to **explain**:

- **what** the writer has done within their text
- **why** they have taken these decisions, and
- the **impact** a specific word, phrase, technique or sentence type has upon the reader.

The following spider diagram shows a number of examples of writer's craft, which we will discuss in more detail over the next few pages. Can you think of any more examples?

UNIT 4 SECTION B: READING LITERARY AND NON-FICTION TEXTS

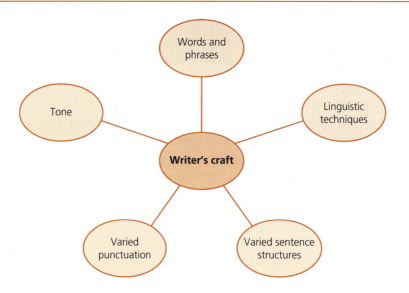

Linguistic techniques

Writers of fiction and non-fiction texts have a variety of linguistic techniques at their disposal. These are commonly used to help the writer achieve their purpose and to engage their target reader. Many of the following techniques are used by writers of fiction and non-fiction.

Figurative language

Figurative language goes beyond the literal meaning and therefore is more impactful. Common examples of figurative language include the following:

Similes allow the writer to make a comparison and are recognisable by their use of the words 'as' or 'like'. They can be an effective way of planting a vivid image within the mind of the reader. For example, a writer might state, 'Like convicts, the students shuffled slowly into the examination hall.' In this instance, the simile prompts the reader to imagine the formation of the students lined up one behind the other all dressed in the same uniform. This simile also works because it implies that the exam is a punishing and oppressive experience, like a prison sentence.

Metaphors can enhance writing by offering the reader a stronger comparison. For example, a writer might state, 'On this Monday morning, Mrs Kelly was a dragon.' The metaphor is used here to emphasise the character's bad mood.

Personification is an effective way of making descriptions more vivid and adding a dimension by comparing a thing or a concept to a person. It is commonly used by writers of fiction to add interest and depth of meaning. For example, a writer might choose to state, 'Outside it was foggy', but this is not particularly interesting or creative. Instead, they could use personification and write, 'With great stealth, fog snaked its way through the streets, choking the town and blinding all who had dared venture out.' The use of personification captures the movement of the fog, exaggerates its impact upon the city and creates a darker atmosphere.

Writer's craft

Alliteration can add interest to a text, but it is important to consider the alliterative sound as it can shape the reader's response. For example, 'He was the laziest student in Year 11, and in most lessons, would lounge lethargically across the table.' In this example the long alliterative 'l' is used to emphasise the student's extreme lack of energy and effort. In contrast, a tourist leaflet might state, 'Be prepared for a feast of fun, fantastic festivities', with the abrupt 'f' sound suggesting energy and excitement.

> ### Activity
>
> Look out of your classroom window and note the weather conditions. Write a short weather report using factual statements. Now rewrite it using figurative language.
> Swap reports with a partner. Identify which techniques the writer has used and evaluate their effectiveness.

Language to engage and connect

Sometimes writers want to connect with their readers, even address them directly, to give the impression they are conversing with them. There are several techniques commonly used to achieve this aim:

Personal and inclusive pronouns can be used to connect with the reader by establishing a conversational tone. 'You' is known as the personal pronoun as it makes the text seem personal and directly relevant to the reader. Inclusive pronouns such as 'we', 'us' and 'our' make the reader feel part of a collective group. These pronouns commonly appear in non-fiction texts where the writer wants to get the reader to feel on-side or involved, e.g. 'Join us today, you know it's the right thing to do. With your help, we can make a difference.' Fictional writers can also make use of pronouns to create a conversational tone, so that the narrator or a character seems to be talking directly to the reader. This often allows the reader to empathise, e.g. 'What you're about to read may shock you…' or 'You may be asking yourself…?'

Rhetorical questions are commonly used to keep the reader engaged or to get them thinking. They can make a point in a more powerful and emotional way, e.g. 'How long are we prepared to sit back and do nothing?' When you encounter a rhetorical question you must be able to explain specifically what the writer wants their reader to think about.

Humour arouses a response from the reader and is an effective way of engaging them in the text. In literary fiction, humour is often created through the description of characters and their situations. Puns are commonly used in non-fiction texts to add humour but they can also be used in literary texts, for example in Shakespeare's *Romeo and Juliet* the dying Mercutio exclaims, 'Ask for me tomorrow and you shall find me a grave man.'

Anecdotes or stories from personal experience add interest and engage the reader by immersing them into the world of the writer or a character within a text. In non-fiction, they are often used to demonstrate a point, for example a writer concerned about safety online might share a story from their personal experience that justifies their concern, e.g. 'Last week I looked at my bank statement and discovered £200 had been withdrawn. I had no recollection of this transaction…'

Language to induce feelings

As well as wanting to connect with their reader and make us think, writers often want to influence how we feel when we read their text. By connecting emotionally, they can leave a lasting impression upon us.

Emotive language is when the writer deliberately choses language to induce a particular emotion within their reader. Think of charity adverts you have read; they leave an emotional impact by making us feel sympathetic and try to persuade us that we can make a difference by contributing.

Hyperbole is the use of words and phrases to exaggerate. It can establish an impression or expectation within the reader, e.g. 'This experience will take you out of this world!' Writers of fiction can use exaggeration to assist with characterisation and shape the reader's reaction to characters and situations, e.g. 'Any moment now he would explode and his wrath would rain down upon me...'

Superlatives are used to influence the reader by establishing an expectation, e.g. 'It is the greatest place on earth' establishes a positive expectation, whereas, 'It was the dirtiest place on earth' has quite the opposite effect!

> **Activity**
>
> Imagine you have been asked to write a short paragraph (no more than twelve sentences) to be included on a tourist leaflet for your area. Try to use techniques to connect with your reader and induce thoughts and feelings.
>
> Swap with a partner and evaluate the success of their text by identifying what works well and how they could improve.

Language to add authority

Writers of non-fiction invest considerable time researching their chosen topic. These texts often have more than one purpose, for example they may wish to **inform** us of a problem and **persuade** us to act, and they may go on to **advise** what actions we can take to make a difference. Writers want to earn the trust of their reader and there are several techniques they can use to achieve this aim:

Facts and opinions can support a writer's point of view or argument, but you must be able to recognise bias and opinions disguised as fact.

Statistical evidence is often used to add authority and give credibility to the writer's point of view. Statistics can leave an impression upon a reader, e.g. 'On average, today's teenagers spend over four hours every day in front of a computer screen or mobile device.' In this instance the statistical evidence might shock us. Writers might also make use of statistics to impress us, alarm us, concern us or entice us.

Quotations and evidence from expert sources provide support and are often used to endorse the writer's opinions on an issue, therefore they add authority. For example, a writer who is concerned about childhood obesity might insert a quotation from a medical professional to justify their concerns.

Language for emphasis

Writers are faced with a challenge to ensure their text is memorable and their reader retains important information. With this in mind, writers often use the following techniques to emphasise ideas or points:

Imperative verbs often appear in non-fiction texts to try to encourage the reader to respond and react to what is stated, e.g. 'Stand up and do what's right!' This call to action is intended to persuade the reader to actively respond. In literary fiction characters who speak using imperative sentences are often characters of authority, e.g. '"Get up on your feet!" roared Principal Hawkins.' The imperative is used to emphasise the commanding tone of the character.

Repetition can emphasise the writer's purpose. In non-fiction texts it can help the reader retain important points. In literary fiction repetition can be used to emphasise mood or emotion.

Lists of three and triples can also be used to emphasise an idea or point. In non-fiction texts this technique can also be used to leave an impact upon a reader, especially if the triple is made up of exclusively positive or negative language, e.g. 'When the food arrived it was cold, tasteless and undercooked.' In this instance the triple emphasises how poor the dining experience was.

Contrast can be used to add emphasis and leave an impression upon the reader, e.g. in *Animal Farm* George Orwell invites the reader to contrast the characters of Napoleon and Snowball. Their plans for the farm emphasise their differing leadership styles.

Studying words and phrases

To appreciate writer's craft means you should be aware that the writer has settled on specific words or phrases for deliberate effect. When considering words and phrases used in a text it is a good idea to begin by looking at adjectives and adverbs, as sentences do not require these but they are often included for a reason, e.g. '**Tentatively**, Ben crept down the **vast empty** corridor.' Think about what the adverbs and adjectives add to this sentence.

Verbs are also important as they provide clues about how characters or individuals are feeling. In the sentence above, the verb 'crept' has been chosen deliberately to communicate the uneasiness of the character Ben.

Often writers of non-fiction share their personal experiences and concerns with their readers. Think about why a writer might choose to state, 'I was distraught' rather than writing, 'I was troubled' or 'I was upset'. The selection of words is not random!

UNIT 4 SECTION B: READING LITERARY AND NON-FICTION TEXTS

Activity

Read through the short newspaper article below and comment on the effect of the highlighted words and phrases.

Beware of the cat!

With his **big angelic eyes** and **glossy soft fur**, Heston looks like any other gentle pet cat.

So innocent is his appearance, it is easy to dismiss as a harmless joke a sign on the Robertson household's front door warning visitors to 'beware' of their tomcat.

But, as neighbours and deliverers have **unfortunately** discovered, it is nothing of the sort.

When five-year-old Heston is not nuzzling indoors with his owner Bruce Robertson, he is **terrorising visitors** to his home in Caldicot, south Wales.

So **vicious** is the cat, named after celebrity chef Heston Blumenthal, that he has injured two postwomen and a parcel delivery driver, and even **attacked** a mechanic.

Steelworker Mr Robertson, 58, who has a 21-year-old son called Shane, said the family's pet has been dubbed the 'devil cat' by locals.

'He has drawn blood from two post deliverers. One was a postwoman who after the attack was shouting at us from across the road with blood **pouring down** her arm.

'Another time a mechanic came round to give me the results from my car's MOT. He was attacked by Heston before he got through the front gate and wouldn't come in. When I went to help him Heston had his mouth **clamped** around his ankle.'

In an attempt to avoid any more **casualties**, the Robertsons have been forced to put up a sign on their front door warning people.

It was designed by Mr Robertson's wife Wendy, 51, and reads: 'Beware: Guard cat on duty. Do not put fingers through the letterbox.'

(www.dailymail.co.uk/news/article-4080624/Beware-cat-Blood-thirsty-devil-pet-leaves-two-posties-delivery-driver-mechanic-wounded-pouncing-them.html)

Studying sentence structure and punctuation

Writers also rely upon varied sentence types and sentence lengths to enhance our reading experience and hold our attention:

Long sentences may be used to exchange a lot of information or convey description. If a writer wants to argue strongly on a topic, a long sentence can convey their strength of feeling.

Short sentences can be used to create tension, convey emotion, make emphatic statements and, when they follow on from a longer sentence, they can be very impactful.

Writer's craft

Writers can also vary the types of sentences used within their text. You should be able to identify examples of the following:

- **Simple sentences** – contain one main verb.
- **Compound sentences** – are usually two simple sentences joined by 'and', 'or' or 'but'.
- **Complex sentences** – contain at least one main clause and one subordinate clause.

Of course, punctuation is an essential part of any text, but writers have the option of using punctuation for effect. Exclamation marks and ellipses can add something extra to a text and help convey the writer's tone.

Activity

Read the extract below and then the comments, which indicate how the writer has employed a variety of sentence lengths and punctuation to make the piece engaging and entertaining for the reader.

[1] Short lively sentence to establish an emphatic tone and impose the writer's opinion upon the reader.

[2] Long sentence to emphasise the extent of the writer's bewilderment. Posed as a question to get the reader thinking about why anyone would find camping appealing.

Camping is one of those things: you either hate it or you hate it. There is no other rational approach.**[1]**

Why would a sane human being in possession of a solid, brick-built house exchange hot water and central heating for the shelter afforded by a big nylon bag?**[2]** And pay for it!**[3]**

I asked myself this a fortnight ago as, stirred yet again by the cold, I awoke to find myself staring up at a patch of orange nylon illuminated by the grey light of a new day.**[4]**

Outside, the dawn chorus was clearing its throat. I was bang awake at six on a Sunday. I wanted to cry.**[5]**

(www.telegraph.co.uk/travel/campingholidays/5323901/ Eurocamp-camping-in-the-UK-Is-it-nuts-in-May.html)

[3] Short exclamatory sentence to add impact by emphasising the writer's disbelief that someone would actually pay for a camping experience.

[4] Complex sentence to make clear how a recent camping experience has influenced the writer's perspective.

[5] Series of short simple sentences to conclude, which emphasise the abrupt awakening and the writer's subsequent despair.

UNIT 4 SECTION B: READING LITERARY AND NON-FICTION TEXTS

Activity

Below are the next few paragraphs of the camping text.

Read them carefully and make one comment about each paragraph that shows your appreciation of how the writer's use of sentence structure and/or punctuation enhances meaning.

> On arrival at the tents our hearts sank: no swimming pool, no games hall, no nothing – except for an uninviting loo-and-shower block.
>
> We fired up the small barbecue, tossed on some burgers and made up the beds. The sky was cloudless and the first stars were winking in the darkening sky. We opened a bottle of wine and enjoyed, ooooh, a good twelve minutes of relaxed conversation before the girls began to moan about being cold and tired. That was when the reality of camping in Britain kicked in.
>
> In Antarctic conditions, Penny spent the night huddled with the girls in the double bed under layers of blankets, sleeping bags and coats. I shivered under a duvet brought from home, observing my breath.
>
> Eurocamp may work as a gentle introduction to camping in the Mediterranean, where the days are hot and the night air is balmy; but not in Britain in May. It's just too cold!!
>
> (www.telegraph.co.uk/travel/campingholidays/5323901/Eurocamp-camping-in-the-UK-Is-it-nuts-in-May.html)

Tone

Put simply, **tone** is the attitude of the writer. The tone of a text is conveyed through the words, phrases, techniques, sentence structures and punctuation employed by the writer. The tone of a text can change as the piece progresses and it is important to be able to identify tonal changes. In literary fiction characters speak and interact with a range of tones, which influence how the reader responds to them.

Look at these two sentences and consider *what* tone is conveyed in each and *how* the difference in tone is created:

▶ 'Boys, get your books out, please,' said the teacher.
▶ 'Boys! Get your books out now!' screamed the teacher.

In the second extract the one-word exclamatory sentence 'Boys!' establishes an aggressive tone. The second sentence begins with the imperative 'Get…', which implies an urgent tone and the substitution of 'please' with '… now!' emphasises the urgency. The inclusion of the verb 'screamed' makes the tone more threatening. As a reader, we find the teacher in the second sentence more intimidating.

Activity

Now that you are aware that writers of fiction and non-fiction give careful consideration to how they craft their texts, choose an extract from a novel, a newspaper or a magazine article and follow the instructions below:

▶ Find evidence of linguistic techniques and underline them.
▶ Place a box around words and phrases that you think have been used for deliberate effect.
▶ Highlight where the writer varies sentence length or uses punctuation to enhance meaning and leave an impact upon the reader.
▶ List the different tones you detect within the text.

Comparing literary texts

AO3 i, ii, iii

When responding to literary texts you will be expected to compare two different extracts. This means you should be able to identify *how* each writer has crafted their text and to *explain* the impact upon the reader. The task may require you to compare and contrast how a certain **atmosphere** has been created, or it might ask you to compare how **characters** have been depicted, or even how two writers craft **settings**. Whatever the task demands, you should read both texts thoroughly and:

- identify the narrative perspective – is it first or third person, what is the effect?
- consider how each writer hooks the reader at the beginning
- look at how each writer concludes their text and consider how the character, situation or effect has developed or changed since the beginning
- examine the writer's choice of words and phrases throughout the text and consider their impact upon the reader
- identify any language techniques used by the writers – remember writers can use different techniques to achieve the same effect, e.g. one might use personification to make something seem threatening while another will use a metaphor
- analyse the sentence structures used within each extract and evaluate their impact upon the reader, e.g. have short sentences been used to create tension?
- consider how each writer develops the situation – one might develop the situation rather quickly by engaging a range of senses, while another might prolong and develop the situation by gradually building up sensory awareness.

Activity

In the two short extracts below, the writers have tried to create a tense atmosphere.

Text A

John struggled to shake off the feeling that something was about to go wrong. His stomach was churning and his eyes constantly scanned ahead. At any minute he expected something unpleasant to leap out and startle him. The moon was disappearing behind heavy clouds and suddenly the only sound was that of his footsteps. He didn't like this one bit. He was afraid.

Text B

A carpet of fog seemed to rise from the ground, making it impossible to see even a few feet ahead. I switched off the radio, clutched the steering wheel tightly and fixed my eyes firmly on the road ahead. It was like civilisation had ceased to exist and I was the only human being on Earth. Guiding the car slowly and cautiously up the road, the fog looked as though it was advancing at great pace, swallowing the car up and taking pleasure in my disorientation. I had travelled these roads every day for the past six years but now they seemed alien. I regretted ever embarking upon this journey.

Below one student has started to identify the similarities and differences between the two extracts. Based on your reading, note down further ideas that you would add to this diagram:

Text A
Third person detached perspective; opens abruptly with character's feelings; focus on sights and sounds; collection of short sentences to emphasise atmosphere of uncertainty; character is walking and exposed to elements and environment

Both
Use of weather to establish tense atmosphere and establish a sense of increasing anxiety and tension; verbs and adverbs used to capture the anxiety of characters

Text B
First person perspective; opens with description of fog to establish tense and uneasy atmosphere; character/narrator is in car and forced to react to elements and environment; use of simile, exaggeration, personification; builds up to final short sentence for impact

177

UNIT 4 SECTION B: READING LITERARY AND NON-FICTION TEXTS

Language to compare and contrast

To successfully compare and contrast you should use words that show your recognition of the similarities and differences:

Language to compare	Language to contrast
Similarly…	In contrast…
Both…	Whereas…
Common to both is…	However…
Also…	On the other hand…
A shared feature is…	Unlike…

Activity

Here is the beginning of one student's response comparing the two extracts on the previous page. As you read, look at how the student analyses comparisons and contrasts.

> Both writers use descriptions of weather to establish a tense atmosphere. In Text A it states, 'The moon was disappearing behind heavy clouds', with the increasing darkness contributing to the character's feelings of unease and isolation. On the other hand, Text B opens with a description of a 'carpet of fog [that] seemed to rise from the ground', immediately immersing the reader in a tense atmosphere as we acknowledge the fog limits the character's vision; this creates tension as the car journey is challenging and potentially dangerous.
>
> Both writers convey tension through the heightened reactions of the characters. Text A states, '…suddenly the only sound was that of his footsteps'. The word 'suddenly' emphasises how the situation is changing quickly due to changes in the weather. John's reactions are shared to emphasise the tense atmosphere: 'He didn't like this one bit'. Similarly, in Text B the character's reactions to the fog enhance the tension, 'clutched the steering wheel tightly and fixed my eyes firmly on the road ahead'. The verbs and adverbs confirm that the character is feeling anxious and needs to concentrate extra hard. The reader gets the impression in both texts that the tension is only beginning and is certain to increase as each character continues their journey.

Activity

Write two further paragraphs, continuing the comparison.

Then highlight where you have used language to compare and contrast and share your response with a partner.

Responding to literary and non-fiction texts

AO3 i, ii, iii

As we read any given text we process the information. Sometimes this is a straightforward task as the writer communicates information and ideas explicitly; that is, it is stated clearly with no need for the reader to infer or deduce.

Activity

Read the extract below and write down four things explicitly stated about Marcus Dooley.

> Marcus Dooley is a fourteen-year-old genius. He has an IQ score of 129 and, unsurprisingly, he finds school boring and tedious. At this awkward age his intelligence is something of a burden as he struggles to tolerate his peers. He has a hunger for learning that they just cannot understand and he realises that he's becoming increasingly isolated with each academic year. Marcus has long given up trying to win their approval: he isn't interested in football and he has no passion at all for computer games. Marcus is fascinated by science – physics to be exact. He loves nothing more than getting home at the end of a monotonous school day and losing himself in Stephen Hawking's *A Brief History of Time*.

At GCSE it is vital that you can also handle more challenging texts, where the meaning is **implicit**. This means the writer will suggest ideas by providing clues within the text. You will need to be able to locate the clues, interpret the information and infer. To **infer** means to deduce a reasoned conclusion based on what we read.

Activity

Read the extract below and infer how the character of Emily is feeling. Copy and complete the table that follows.

Text A

> As soon as she opened the door, Emily spotted the familiar faces of her tormentors. She could feel their eyes on her, judging her. Taking a deep breath, Emily shambled across the classroom and handed the envelope to Mrs Crane. The teacher seemed to take an eternity to open the letter. Emily dared not look up. She could hear their whispering and their sniggering. Her stomach churned and she knew they were taking delight in watching her stand here awkwardly, gnawing at her lip and fidgeting her fingers.

Emily is feeling...	Evidence from the text

179

UNIT 4 SECTION B: READING LITERARY AND NON-FICTION TEXTS

Activity

Now read the extract below and identify three things you infer about the character of Steve. For each inference, provide supporting evidence.

> **Text B**
>
> Steve strolled into the canteen like he was a celebrity. He adored making an entrance. As always, the gang had already gathered; Dylan, Robert and Jack were huddled round the table by the window. Steve strutted up to the hatch, winked at the lady behind the counter and flashed a blinding smile. Obligingly, she poured extra chips on to his plate. Steve slunk into his place among the pack and they began to plan how Mr Donnell's lessons would go this afternoon.

Activity

Spend five minutes comparing and contrasting how the writers of Text A and Text B above have created characters that interest a reader.

Share your thoughts as a class.

Non-fiction texts also require us to interpret and infer. In the extract below the writer shares her experience of losing her mobile phone.

Activity

Read carefully and infer the writer's changing reactions and feelings to this situation. Copy and complete the table that follows. You may find that there is more than one piece of evidence in the paragraphs to support your inferences.

> Within a few seconds I went from casually rooting around in the bottom of my handbag to frantically patting myself down, desperately longing to feel the familiar outline of my precious phone safely secure in some secret pocket. That didn't happen!
>
> Abandoning all semblance of calmness, I squatted down right in the middle of the street and proceeded to deposit the contents of my handbag all over the pavement. Within a few seconds I was surrounded by a selection of till receipts; a rather colourful collection of sweet wrappers; a long-forgotten lipstick; two empty plastic water bottles; a badly bruised apple; my bulging make-up bag; my not-so-bulging purse; my trusty hairbrush and my car keys. Where was it? Had I been pickpocketed? Had it fallen out of my bag? I had put it in my handbag... or had I? I was certain I had put it in my bag; I would never have abandoned it at home!
>
> A wave of nausea gripped my stomach as I gathered up my things and confronted the ugly truth – I had lost my precious phone! My mind raced as I took stock of the scale of my loss... My precious phone, containing the contact details of my nearest and dearest, was gone! My precious phone with my millions of photographs and videos was no more!! My precious phone, storing the passwords for my hundreds of online accounts, might, at this very moment, be in the hands of a criminal mastermind!!!
>
> I have no recollection of how I got there, but a few minutes later I found myself sitting on a bench licking salty tears, cradling my handbag and grieving for my phone. Pathetically I pleaded to a higher deity to end my nightmare and heal my suffering. I made all sorts of ridiculous promises I had no intention of keeping; I would NEVER again store sensitive information on a phone; I vowed to back up all future photographs; I swore I would take out phone insurance and I promised to donate to a charity. Right there and then I would have done anything to be reunited with my phone, but I had to accept that was not happening. My phone was lost and I was lost without it.

Paragraph	Inference	Evidence to illustrate
1	The writer is feeling…	
2	The writer's feelings change to…	
3	The writer begins to…	
4	Finally, the writer feels…	

Responding to literary and non-fiction texts

Point. Evidence. Explanation.

When we are analysing and writing about the texts we read it is helpful to use the technique known as Point. Evidence. Explanation. (P.E.E.):

	What to do	Example
Point	Point out what **the writer** has done.	The writer uses a short exclamatory sentence.
Evidence	Introduce the **best evidence** from the text to illustrate your point. Evidence should take the form of short, relevant quotations.	Evidence of this can be found in paragraph 1, which ends with the sentence, 'That didn't happen!'
Explanation	Explain how **the reader** reacts to the chosen evidence. This might be a comment on how the reader **thinks**, how they **feel** or what they **infer**.	The reader infers that the writer feels panic. The short sentence makes the reader aware of the writer's disappointment in failing to find the phone. The exclamation mark emphasises her increasing alarm as she is forced to realise her phone is lost.

The 'Explanation' part of P.E.E can be challenging and it does require practice.

Activity

Below are a series of Points and Evidence from the mobile phone text. Copy and complete the final column with an appropriate Explanation.

Point	Evidence	Explanation
The writer uses a list of questions.	This can be seen in paragraph 2, where it states, '…Had it fallen out of my bag? I had put in in my handbag… or had I?'	The reader infers that the writer is feeling…
The writer uses repetition.	Throughout paragraph 3 the phrase 'my precious phone' appears four times.	The reader feels…
The writer uses exaggeration.	In the final paragraph, she reflects how she wanted help to, 'end my nightmare and heal my suffering.'	The reader acknowledges…

181

UNIT 4 SECTION B: READING LITERARY AND NON-FICTION TEXTS

P.E.E. can also be effective when comparing literary texts.

Activity

Re-read the extracts on pages 179 and 180 where the character Emily is sent to deliver a message to another classroom and Steve arrives in the canteen for lunch. Now read the paragraph below in which one student has used P.E.E. to compare and contrast.

[1] Point about Text A.

[4] Identifies a contrast with Text B.

[6] Evidence from Text B.

In Text A Emily is depicted as a character who is victimised by bullies.[1] This is clear when we read, 'Emily spotted the familiar faces of her tormentors.'[2] The word 'tormentors' is dramatic and makes Emily seem vulnerable as there are clearly several bullies causing her to feel uptight as she enters the classroom.[3] In contrast,[4] the character of Steve in Text B seems to feel very secure as he is part of a 'gang' and there is a suggestion they are engaged in bullying behaviour.[5] This is suggested when the writer states, 'Steve slunk into his place among the pack...'[6] The word 'pack' makes the reader think that together they are threatening and intimidating.[7]

[2] Evidence from Text A.

[3] Explanation based on Text A.

[5] Point about Text B.

[7] Explanation based on Text B.

Developing the explanation

Making a Point and finding Evidence is not particularly challenging. To show your ability to infer and analyse, you should work on providing developed Explanations. Using P.E.E.D., as shown below, can help you achieve more detailed, insightful and analytical responses to texts.

Point	Make a point about the text or about a section of the text.	'The writer hooks the reader by…' 'The writer uses…' 'The writer creates tension by…'
Evidence	Provide short, relevant evidence from the text.	'This is seen when it states…' 'Evidence of this can be seen in…' 'The best example of this can be found in…'
Explain	Consider how the reader responds.	'The reader infers…' 'The reader feels/thinks…' 'The reader acknowledges…'
Develop	Is there more to say? Have a final look at your evidence; can you zoom in on a specific word or phrase, or comment on how sentence length or punctuation enhances the overall meaning? Is there something to be said about tone?	'It also…' 'In addition…' 'Furthermore…' 'The deliberate use of … forces the reader to/implies/suggests…' 'The inclusion of two exclamation marks at the end of the sentence…' 'At this point a … tone is conveyed…'

Activity

Look back to the activity on page 181 where you completed P.E.E. responses to the mobile phone text. Select two points and practise developing your analysis using P.E.E.D.

Putting it into practice: reading literary texts

AO3 i, ii, iii

You now know that when writing about literary texts at GCSE you must be able to demonstrate an ability to:
- appreciate writer's craft
- interpret and infer meaning
- select relevant evidence from a text and explain its effect
- compare and contrast extracts.

The comparative question

Questions that require you to compare and contrast tend to carry more marks as you are expected to demonstrate an appreciation of writer's craft as well as analysing similarities and differences in two literary extracts. They often begin with 'Consider how the writer…' or 'How does the writer…?' or even 'Explain how the writer…' The word 'how' is a clue that you are required to analyse writers' craft by identifying **what** each writer has done and then to consider **why** by explaining the effect upon a reader. The marks available provide a clue that you are required to answer in more detail.

The following extract is taken from *Martyn Pig* by Kevin Brooks. Martyn lives with his father who is an alcoholic. Early in the book Martyn's father dies unexpectedly following an accident.

Here, Martyn is recounting the period immediately after his father's death and is clearly experiencing shock.

Activity

As you read the extract, focus on how the writer has crafted this text to make it interesting for the reader. Then re-read the extract carefully, considering the questions around it to help you gather ideas to answer this question:

Consider how the writer has selected language to capture the seriousness of Martyn's situation.

[1] Why has the writer used short sentences here?

[2] What technique has been employed here and what is the effect?

Text A

The harsh clatter of rain jerked me out of my trance. It was ten o'clock. I stood up and rubbed my eyes then went over to the window and pulled back the curtain. It was pouring down. Great sheets of rain lashing down into the street. I closed the curtain again and turned around. There he was. My dead dad. Still dead.**[1]** Still buckled over, sprawled across the hearth like a broken doll.**[2]** The buttons on his shirt were still undone where I'd listened at his heart. I stooped down and did them up again.

UNIT 4 SECTION B: READING LITERARY AND NON-FICTION TEXTS

An image suddenly flashed into my mind – one of those chalk outlines that detectives draw around a murder victim's body. It amused me, for some reason, and I let out a short strangled laugh, it sounded like someone else, like the sound of laughter echoing in a ghost town. **[3]**

I sat down again.

What are you going to do? I asked myself.

The telephone on the table by the door sat there black and silent, waiting. I knew what I *ought* to do. **[4]**

Wind-blown sheets of rain were rattling against the window. The room was cold. I was shivering. I shoved my hands deep down into my pockets. **[5]**

This was a sweet mess.

Then the doorbell rang. **[6]**

(Kevin Brooks, *Martyn Pig*)

[3] Explain the effect of descriptions such as 'strangled laugh' and 'like the sound of laughter echoing in a ghost town'?

[4] The writer has italicised the word '*ought*'. Why do you think this is?

[5] How is Martyn made to seem isolated and vulnerable here?

[6] Explain why this is a dramatic conclusion to the extract.

Putting it into practice: reading literary texts

Now, let's consider another section from the novel. In this passage, Martyn's Aunty Jean has arrived and Martyn is trying to conceal the fact his father is dead. He is escorting Aunty Jean up to his dad's bedroom. Martyn's friend Alex is helping him and at this moment she is hiding in the bathroom.

Text B

As I led her up the stairs my heart was pounding and my stomach felt like it was full of wasps. She kept sniffing all the time, not saying anything, just sniffing. Sniff, sniff, sniff. Like a Labrador searching for a bone. I couldn't help glancing at the bathroom door as we passed, imagining Alex in there, imagining. . . .

We stopped outside Dad's bedroom. 'He's probably still asleep,' I said. 'He was up most of the night.'

Aunty Jean rolled her eyes.

'I mean he didn't get any sleep,' I explained. 'He was up, you know, being sick all the time, in and out of bed.'

She gave me a sceptical look. 'Open the door, then.'

There are moments in your life when you have to do things you really don't want to. You have to do them, you have no choice.

(Kevin Brooks, *Martyn Pig*)

Activity

Devise eight questions that would encourage a student to consider how the writer has crafted this extract. Then swap your questions with a partner, answer theirs and discuss the answers.

Now you have an appreciation of how each extract has been crafted, it is time to think about similarities and differences.

Below is the beginning of one student's response to the task to the right. Read it carefully and identify what you think they have done well.

> In both texts a sense of drama is conveyed through the abrupt openings. In Text A it begins, 'The harsh clatter of rain jerked me out of my trance.' The adjective 'harsh' establishes an unpleasant and foreboding atmosphere, whereas in Text B the reader is immediately immersed into a situation where Martyn feels uneasy. It states, 'As I led her up the stairs my heart was pounding and my stomach felt like it was full of wasps.' The verb 'pounding' is dramatic and the description of a stomach that 'felt like it was full of wasps' makes the reader aware that whatever is happening is a painful and unpleasant experience.
>
> Text A uses short sentences to emphasise Martyn's dramatic experience. It states, 'There he was. My dead dad. Still dead.' The reader acknowledges Martyn's feelings of shock at the death of his dad, an event that is certainly dramatic and serious. In contrast Text B uses ellipses to create drama...

Activity

Make list of points you would make if answering the following question:

Compare and contrast how a dramatic experience has been depicted in the two extracts from Martyn Pig.

Putting it into practice: reading non-fiction texts

AO3 i, ii, iii

When responding to non-fiction you must also be able to appreciate a writer's craft.

Look again at the opening to this non-fiction text, which appeared on page 180. Consider how you would answer the question that follows.

> Within a few seconds I went from casually rooting around in the bottom of my handbag to frantically patting myself down, desperately longing to feel the familiar outline of my precious phone safely secure in some secret pocket. That didn't happen!

Explain how the writer grabs the reader's attention in the opening paragraph.

This student has used the P.E.E. technique in her response:

> *The writer uses contrast to engage the reader and immerse them in her experience. This is shown when she states how one minute she was 'casually rooting around' and the next she was 'frantically patting myself down' and 'desperately longing'. The actions of the writer alter quickly to convey her changing feelings. The reader infers that she quickly panicked when she realised her phone was missing.*

While this student shows they can infer, they are not analysing. They could improve their response by developing their explanation and providing a more convincing response that considers the writer's craft by commenting on the writer's choice of words and/or phrases and considering how sentence structures and punctuation enhance meaning.

Another student responded using P.E.E.D.:

> *The writer hooks the attention of the reader using contrasting adverbs to create a dramatic opening. This is evidenced when the writer recounts how she 'went from casually rooting around … to frantically patting myself down, desperately longing….'. The changing adverbs force the reader to infer her sudden panic and to realise how her emotions changed as she failed to locate her phone. In addition, the long opening sentence emphasises her frantic movements and the different emotions experienced within such a short period of time. The deliberate use of the adverb 'desperately' allows the reader to empathise with her as it exaggerates her urgent desire to locate her phone. The inclusion of a short exclamatory sentence at the end of the paragraph conveys her despondent tone.*

Putting it into practice: reading non-fiction texts

Activity

Look at the task below and answer the question using P.E.E. or P.E.E.D.

The final paragraph of this extract states:

> I have no recollection of how I got there, but a few minutes later I found myself sitting on a bench licking salty tears, cradling my handbag and grieving for my phone. Pathetically I pleaded to a higher deity to end my nightmare and heal my suffering. I made all sorts of ridiculous promises I had no intention of keeping; I would NEVER again store sensitive information on a phone; I vowed to back up all future photographs; I swore I would take out phone insurance and I promised to donate to a charity. Right there and then I would have done anything to be reunited with my phone, but I had to accept that was not happening. My phone was lost and I was lost without it.

Explain how the writer has written this paragraph to make the reader feel pity.

Below is the beginning of one student's answer to this question. Read it carefully and identify what the student has done well.

> The writer makes the reader feel pity by using exaggeration. The writer describes how she was 'licking salty tears, cradling my handbag and grieving for my phone.' The verbs used here make the reader feel pity because they suggest that the loss of the mobile phone is like experiencing a death. The verbs confirm that the experience of losing her phone has affected the writer physically, even reducing her to tears, which seems over the top but succeeds in making the reader understand her strong reactions. Words such as 'cradling' suggest that the writer now feels very protective of her possessions, but it has come too late. The verb 'grieving' makes the reader feel pity as it implies that what has been lost is more than a material item, in fact it suggests something precious and significant has been lost and that the writer is mourning, wondering how her life can continue without it. Readers who have been through a similar experience will be able to empathise with the writer's feelings here.

Activity

Write two more paragraphs to complete the analysis of the final paragraph of the non-fiction text.

187

UNIT 4 SECTION B: READING LITERARY AND NON-FICTION TEXTS

Activity

Below is a review of the Merchant Hotel. Read it carefully. As you read, think about how the writer presents her views and try to:

- identify techniques employed by the writer
- identify words or phrases that have been used for effect
- look at sentence structures and sentence lengths
- identify the writer's tone and how this is conveyed.

The Merchant is simply marvellous

Paris, Venice, Prague… Belfast? Gulp. The capital of Northern Ireland is unlikely to be a city that people instantly think of when planning a romantic weekend away. But now that the Merchant Hotel has opened, maybe they should.

It's not just the hotel, which is only Belfast's second five-star establishment. Wandering about the regenerated area by the River Lagan and into the Cathedral Quarter, it's clear the city has moved on from the depression of the Troubles and into a bright new economic dawn: there are acres of plate glass set into spankingly modern architecture, lots of twinkly lighting, wide-open plazas, soaring public artworks, funky bars on little cobbled streets and, towering over it all, vast cranes building yet more new developments.

Mind you, I wasn't that keen on leaving the hotel, which is a wonder in its own right. Heaven only knows how many millions it has cost to transform the derelict interior of the Grade A-listed building that used to be the Ulster Bank headquarters, but the answer can't be far off 'an awful lot'.

The marketing blurb calls it 'Belfast's first truly grand hotel', and to be honest, I didn't bother scouting around the city for anything better. A gleaming black Bentley does airport transfers by prior arrangement, and once guests have emerged from its soft leather interior, anyone feeling a bit peckish after an arduous journey can progress in stately fashion up sweeping stone steps and into a restaurant that is opulent beyond the bounds of reason, though thankfully not beyond the bounds of taste.

During the daytime, a graceful atrium lets light flood into the grand entrance room which is decorated in crimson, gold, black, mocha and burnt orange. At night, the lighting is mysterious and intimate. The room I stayed in – alone, sadly – was a triumph of the traditionally sumptuous combined with flashes of contemporary styling, and would be the perfect setting for a classy seduction. Anyone you brought here would know you'd spent some serious dosh.

(www.theguardian.com/travel/2006/may/15/belfast.unitedkingdom.hotels)

Practice question

Using paragraphs 2 and 3 of the review, reproduced below:

Explain how the writer has created a positive impression of Belfast and the Merchant Hotel.

> It's not just the hotel, which is only Belfast's second five-star establishment. Wandering about the regenerated area by the River Lagan and into the Cathedral Quarter, it's clear the city has moved on from the depression of the Troubles and into a bright new economic dawn: there are acres of plate glass set into spankingly modern architecture, lots of twinkly lighting, wide-open plazas, soaring public artworks, funky bars on little cobbled streets and, towering over it all, vast cranes building yet more new developments.
>
> Mind you, I wasn't that keen on leaving the hotel, which is a wonder in its own right. Heaven only knows how many millions it has cost to transform the derelict interior of the Grade A-listed building that used to be the Ulster Bank headquarters, but the answer can't be far off 'an awful lot'.
>
> (www.theguardian.com/travel/2006/may/15/belfast.unitedkingdom.hotels)

Practice question

Use only the section printed below to complete this task.

The writer has developed a lively approach in her review. Explain how she has created this lively style to capture and maintain the interest of the reader.

> The marketing blurb calls it 'Belfast's first truly grand hotel', and to be honest, I didn't bother scouting around the city for anything better. A gleaming black Bentley does airport transfers by prior arrangement, and once guests have emerged from its soft leather interior, anyone feeling a bit peckish after an arduous journey can progress in stately fashion up sweeping stone steps and into a restaurant that is opulent beyond the bounds of reason, though thankfully not beyond the bounds of taste.
>
> During the daytime, a graceful atrium lets light flood into the grand entrance room which is decorated in crimson, gold, black, mocha and burnt orange. At night, the lighting is mysterious and intimate. The room I stayed in – alone, sadly – was a triumph of the traditionally sumptuous combined with flashes of contemporary styling, and would be the perfect setting for a classy seduction. Anyone you brought here would know you'd spent some serious dosh.
>
> (www.theguardian.com/travel/2006/may/15/belfast.unitedkingdom.hotels)

UNIT 4

Reading literary and non-fiction texts: target success

Matching grades to reading literary and non-fiction texts

In Section B the essential qualities you will need are highlighted at the important grade boundaries. Read these descriptions *carefully*; they tell you what your answer should be like.

Grade C work displays:

- ✔ a competent straightforward consideration with some analysis and evaluation of how meaning and information are conveyed
- ✔ an overall understanding of the texts that is supported by appropriate explanations
- ✔ a valid interpretation of the texts that explores the writer's use of language techniques within the text.

Grade A/A* work displays:

- ✔ an assured evaluation of the linguistic and structural features of the texts. This is likely to include: style/use made of fact and opinion/the selection of words and phrases/the use made of sentence structuring and paragraphing
- ✔ a perceptive explanation/discussion of these features
- ✔ an insightful and evaluative interpretation that is supported by a range of precisely selected, appropriate evidence.

Practice question

Reading literary fiction

You have 26 minutes to read Texts A and B and respond to the task. Begin by spending 5 minutes reading the complete texts.

Text A

Trash tells the story of a discovery made by three boys who live and work in a dumpsite. In this extract one of the boys and an adult friend are visiting a prison where they hope to speak to an inmate who will help them understand the significance of their discovery.

We were led to a gate in the centre, and as the guards opened it, I became aware of the constant banging of metal on metal. Everywhere, doors were slamming, and I could hear the ratcheting of keys in locks. Suddenly we were in a strange no-man's-land, like a decompression chamber – a space in which the door behind us locked before the door in front was opened.

Under all the shouting there was laughter, and – I have to say it – it was like animal noise, with a dreadful echo. It was also, if it were possible, getting hotter, as if something was breathing on us. Orders were shouted: everyone was suddenly in a hurry. That final door was unlocked, and we were beckoned through.

'Welcome!' cried the guard receiving us.

He smiled at me. A smile of genuine interest and warmth, which seemed so wrong for the hell we were walking into.

(Andy Mulligan, *Trash*)

Text B

Bog Child is set in Northern Ireland during the Troubles. In this extract Fergus and his family are going to visit his brother Joe, who is a prisoner in Long Kesh prison.

The drive across the North was long and winding. The roads had a thoughtful quietness to them. Clouds scampered over the hills and valleys. Sun broke through fitfully. Mam sat beside him with the tart on her lap. It was three o'clock when they crossed into County Antrim.

They drew up to Long Kesh. The place, a converted RAF aerodrome, was like a low-lying colony for the miserable of the world. The sign at the main gate said HMP MAZE.

Herpes, Mastitis, Piles. A Maze of Misery. Fergus remembered reading how the Nazis had wanted to bomb the place out of existence in the Second World War. He wished they'd succeeded. When they got out of the car, all you could hear was wind and a distant lowing of cattle. The bleak and endless walls, topped with rolls of barbed wire, were barricades against the natural world.

At the entrance it was the usual routine: passports and driving licences to be shown, through the metal detector, hands up for the body search. The search was slow and deliberate. Every square inch of clothing was gone over, then a hand-held bomb detector was traced around them, as if checking their aura. Sniffer dogs were restrained on leashes. The uniformed guards were squeaky clean, with chains and keys and 'This way, sirs, this way, madams.'

Across the yard, another gate. Then down long white corridors that smelled sulphurous, almost. This way to hell, thought Fergus.

Bars caged off every doorway. The place was like a laboratory for experiments on rats.

(Siobhan Dowd, *Bog Child*)

Compare and contrast how the writers of Texts A and B have described the setting of a prison. Present supporting evidence from both texts.

UNIT 4 SECTION B: READING LITERARY AND NON-FICTION TEXTS

Sample student response

[1] Point shows appreciation of writer's craft.

[2] Selects relevant quotation to support the point made.

[4] A clear attempt to develop analysis that considers the reader's response.

Both writers make the prison seem unpleasant by using negative language to describe its appearance. **[1]** Text B states, 'The bleak and endless walls, topped with rolls of barbed wire, were barricades against the natural world.' **[2]** The adjective 'bleak' implies that this is a hopeless place and the 'rolls of barbed wire' make it seem hostile and associate it with pain as barbed wire can inflict pain upon those who get too close. **[3]** In addition, **[4]** the writer describes the walls and wire as 'barricades against the natural world', suggesting to the reader that the prison is an unnatural place, cut off from normal, civilised society. Similarly, Text A makes entering the prison seem unpleasant by describing it as 'a strange no-man's-land.' **[5]** The word 'strange' emphasises how unfamiliar the prison seems to the character. 'No-man's-land' is often associated with war and it suggests to the reader that the prison looks and feels hostile.

The writer of Text B makes the inside of the prison seem unpleasant by using varied sentence lengths **[6]** to describe the 'usual routine'. The combination of long and short sentences suggests the process to get inside and commence your visit was laborious. **[7]** Long sentences such as 'Every square inch of clothing was gone over … as if checking their aura' are used to emphasise how long this process took. Short sentences such as 'Sniffer dogs were restrained on leashes' emphasise the atmosphere of tension within the prison and force the reader **[8]** to acknowledge the intimidating presence of the dogs, which makes the prison seem an unpleasant and threatening place. In contrast, Text A focuses on the tension inside the prison by using dashes within sentences to capture the character's gradual journey through the setting. It states, '…like a decompression chamber — a space in which the door behind us locked before the door in front was opened.' The reader infers the character's awareness of tension within the prison and the fact it is a contained and controlled setting. **[9]**

[3] Valid interpretation of writer's choice of language.

[5] Effectively identifies comparison with supporting evidence from Text A.

[6] Appreciates how sentence structures convey meaning.

[7] Can select relevant evidence and arrive at an assured interpretation.

[8] Continued consideration of reader response.

[9] Continues to select appropriate material to compare and contrast

192

Target success

[10] Precise identification of language technique.

[11] Evaluates and interprets writer's craft.

> The writer of Text B also makes the prison seem unpleasant through Fergus' reactions. He describes the place as being 'like a laboratory for experiments on rats.' This simile [10] is used to make the reader imagine the horrific actions that take place within the prison. It suggests that the authorities do not regard the inmates as human beings and forces us to appreciate how people are scarred by their encounters with this place. In contrast, Text A presents the authorities within the prison in a more positive light. The guard in this extract extends a genuine 'Welcome!', which even seems to surprise the narrator who observes, 'He smiled at me. A smile of genuine interest and warmth.' The language is positive and the short sentence captures the narrator's pleasant surprise. Although Text A presents the setting as unpleasant and claustrophobic, the guard is described as a warm and sincere character whose interaction is more friendly than that of the guards in Text B, [11] who are very formal with 'This way, sirs, this way, madams.' From reading Text B the reader is encouraged to dislike the setting and the people within it.

This answer demonstrates:
- ✔ a perceptive appreciation of how the writer conveys meaning
- ✔ precise selection of material to compare and contrast
- ✔ confident analysis of the impact of language, techniques and structure upon a reader
- ✔ well-chosen and apt use of quotations.

UNIT 4 SECTION B: READING LITERARY AND NON-FICTION TEXTS

Practice question ?

Reading non-fiction

You have 24 minutes in which to read this text and respond to the **two** tasks below. Begin by spending 5 minutes reading the text.

The extract below is describing the writer's visit to Our Dynamic Earth, a centre that 'combines the latest interpretative technology and special effects with cutting edge scientific thinking'.

> Our first stop was one of the eleven scenes they call 'earthscapes'. It was supposed to be an environmental monitoring station. Anyway, this is where you get into the Time Machine. It's a sort of souped-up lift that takes you back 15,000 million years. They had rigged it so it seemed like you were moving through starfields. The lift doors opened and we staggered out into the darkness; well, there was a neon light in the far corner but it was very dark and there was a lot of bumping and 'Sorry, was that your toe?' This was the deck of a spaceship. Through viewing windows we witnessed the awesome Big Bang, which started it all off – the birth of the Solar System. Did I mention the whole thing moved? We 'flew' forward in time, which was fine until we came to an earthquake. Rather good but I nearly lost my balance and the man beside me lost his wife who kind of slid gently away to bounce off the far wall.
>
> Of course this earthquake threw up mountains and lava – spewing volcanoes, complete with blasts of air hotter than a furnace, to be dodged by our spaceship. They did it really well because when we came to the glaciers you got another blast, this time freezing cold.

Use the extract above to complete this task. Spend 12 minutes on your response.

The writer has created an entertaining and informative piece about the visit. Explain how the writer makes the text entertaining and informative.

Sample student response

[1] Descriptions discussed.

[2] Evidence to support throughout.

[3] Impact of style explored.

[4] Considers the writer's tone.

[5] Further points made and supported with evidence.

[6] Focus on sentence structure and impact explored.

[7] Quotations support points.

The writer offers detailed descriptions. They are honest, reassuring and taken directly from real-life events,[1] 'a sort of souped-up lift', 'the whole thing moved' and 'this time freezing cold'.[2] The reader can visualise the scene clearly as a result of the writer's descriptions and distinctive use of informal language. All in all, these anecdotes and observations serve to entertain the reader and give a flavour of the visit.[3]

The writer uses direct address to engage the reader and establish a conversational tone.[4] At certain points the personal pronoun 'you' is used to connect with the reader such as, '…you got another blast.' The question 'Did I mention the whole thing moved?' gives the impression they are speaking directly to the reader and, at the same time, makes the reader feel informed about the attraction. The reader can infer that the writer was not overly impressed as he calls it a 'thing' and his tone seems rather sarcastic.[5]

The writer varies sentence structure, making some short to create more impact on the reader,[6] 'This is where you get into the Time Machine', and others are longer, containing descriptions or lists, so as to provide a contrast and variety in style, preventing the piece from becoming monotone or too staccato, 'spewing volcanoes, complete with … hotter than a furnace … dodged by our spaceship.'[7] Each paragraph has a self-contained message and each takes us on a stage further in the journey, giving us the same feeling as the writer — of being taken through history in steps.

This answer demonstrates:
- ✔ developed interpretations
- ✔ clear evaluation of how details of language, grammar and structure engage and affect the reader.

UNIT 4 SECTION B: READING LITERARY AND NON-FICTION TEXTS

Practice question

Below are the final paragraphs of the writer's review of Dynamic Earth.

Use this extract to complete this task. Spend 12 minutes on your response.

> Some people in my group looked quite queasy as we left the spaceship and walked across a nasty-looking mixture with the first life-forms crawling out of it… They were almost the same shade as the heaving sludge! I'd hate to have fallen into those gooey, greenish bubbles! From here we followed a timeline through the age of dinosaurs to the appearance of Early Man before climbing into a yellow submarine and exploring the ocean.
>
> There were loads of other areas, in fact it was a lot to take in. But we all loved the tropical rainforest, which was full of animated animals and snakes. One big snake appeared suddenly and threateningly from the undergrowth. They even laid on a thunderstorm and real rain! No, you don't get wet but it's very convincing.

Explain how this section is intended to make the reader feel that a visit to Dynamic Earth is worthwhile.

Sample student response

This section makes the reader feel the attraction is worth visiting because the exhibits seem to induce strong reactions from visitors and are very authentic as the writer states, 'some people in my group looked quite queasy as we left the spaceship.'**[1]** This makes the reader think that the spaceship has been an energetic experience and will appeal to thrill-seekers.**[2]**

The writer also suggests a visit is worthwhile as the attraction will appeal to those interested in history and exploration. The writer recounts, 'we followed a timeline through the age of dinosaurs to the appearance of Early Man before climbing into a yellow submarine and exploring the ocean.' Verbs such as 'climbing' and 'exploring' give the impression this is an interactive experience that offers the visitor an opportunity to immerse themselves in the past.**[3]**

The writer assures the reader that it is worth visiting as there was 'a lot to take in', which makes the reader think it offers value for money and a range of things to see and do. The writer's excited tone comes across at the end when he states, 'we all loved the tropical rainforest'. This makes the reader think this

[1] Makes appropriate inference with relevant supporting evidence.

[2] Explains using own words and considers audience appeal.

[3] Evaluates the impact of specific verb choices upon the reader.

Target success

attraction is popular and worth seeing.**[4]** The fact he writes 'we all' adds to the positive impression of the place overall as it suggests all the customers were satisfied and enjoyed the rainforest. The reader begins to believe this attraction is worth seeing as it transports them to a range of exotic and historic locations.**[5]**

Finally the writer implies that even he was surprised by how impressive the attraction was as 'They even laid on a thunderstorm and real rain!' The exclamation mark confirms his surprise**[6]** and the expression 'They even laid on' makes this seem like a privileged treat, which suggests the staff want to please their customers.**[7]**

[4] Considers the writer's tone with appropriate supporting evidence.

[5] Offers detailed and valid explanation.

[6] Recognises how punctuation enhances meaning.

[7] Makes assured comment, appreciating the writer's purpose.

This answer demonstrates:
- ✔ valid and convincing explanations that recognise the impact of the writer's craft upon a reader
- ✔ an evaluative approach to some selected language features.

Reading literary and non-fiction texts: key to success

POINTS TO REMEMBER

Read these key pointers:

▶ Use the following **W, W, W, H** questions to help you with your analysis:

1. **What?** Subject matter – what is the piece all about?
2. **Who?** Audience – exactly who is being targeted?
3. **Why?** Purpose – what is the ultimate aim? To sell something/inform/entertain/persuade/amuse/be provocative?
4. **How?** Style, structure and language – the 'nuts and bolts' that are employed to successfully achieve the desired outcome.

▶ Don't fall into the trap of judging a piece of writing aimed at a different kind of reader from yourself by seeing it only through teenage eyes; instead, try to 'become the text's reader' when you judge its style and appropriateness.

Checklist for success: working towards Grade C	
Have you focused on the demands of the set task?	
Have you kept the focus on how the writer has achieved their effects?	
Have you developed an answer that considers the response of the reader?	
Have you clearly constructed your answer so that points are supported by evidence from the text?	
Have you tried to keep your focus on the writer's purpose and on the techniques that they have used to accomplish their goals?	

Checklist for success: working towards Grade A/A*	
Does your analysis sustain its focus on the demands of the set task?	
Have you presented a range of relevant evidence that supports perceptive conclusions on how the writer has achieved their effects?	
Does your answer present a perceptive and evaluative analysis of what the writer has achieved and how the reader responds?	
Have you focused your analysis throughout on the writer's purpose and the techniques that they have deployed to accomplish their goals?	

Exam practice
Putting your skills into practice

This section will help you assess how your reading and writing skills are developing. You are likely to use this resource:

▶ for practice once you have finished the learning and preparation around a particular unit or section. For example, you would complete the Unit 1 Section A task after you have completed the work and activities based on the skills of Writing for purpose and audience

▶ as exam preparation, completing a full unit under timed conditions. So, you will complete all the Unit 1 tasks in 1 hour and 45 minutes. This approach is most useful when you are close to taking the actual GCSE and will benefit from answering under timed pressure, as well as from comparing your responses in detail against the Mark Schemes (pp.208–23).

Regardless of when you approach the tasks in this section, you should welcome every opportunity to identify your personal strengths and weaknesses in reading and writing tasks so that you are fully aware of what you are doing well and where you can improve.

You might use this section to:

▶ assess your skills and determine how prepared you are for each section of Unit 1 and Unit 4

▶ provide yourself with opportunities to complete tasks under timed conditions

▶ get familiar with the types of questions that are set and even practise producing your own

▶ review the Mark Schemes and assessment descriptors to help you self-assess your work to identify how you can further develop your reading and writing skills

▶ use the assessment descriptors to practise being an examiner by assessing the work of other students.

The following pages offer guidance and resources for all the examined elements of the English GCSE course: Unit 1 Sections A and B and Unit 4 Sections A and B.

EXAM PRACTICE

Unit 1 Section A: Writing for purpose and audience

Section A of Unit 1 is a test of your writing, so you must carefully consider both *what* you write and *how* you write. This response will attract two separate marks, one for the quality of the content, and a separate mark for sentence variation and accurate spelling, punctuation and grammar.

Read the sample task below. It has been annotated to help familiarise you with the process of producing your response.

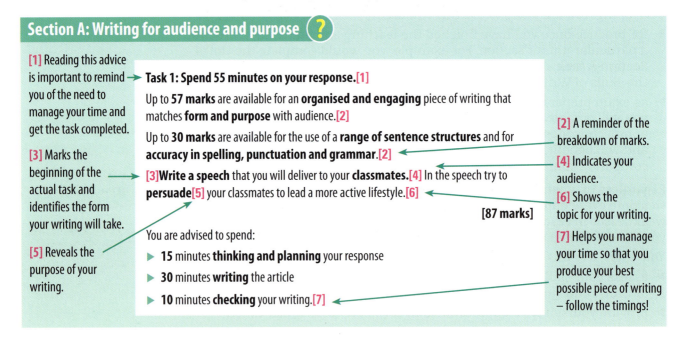

Unit 1 Section B: Reading to access non-fiction and media texts

Section B of Unit 1 is a test of reading. You are required to complete four tasks. The practice tasks below will assist you in preparing for this section and allow you to gain experience of answering under timed conditions.

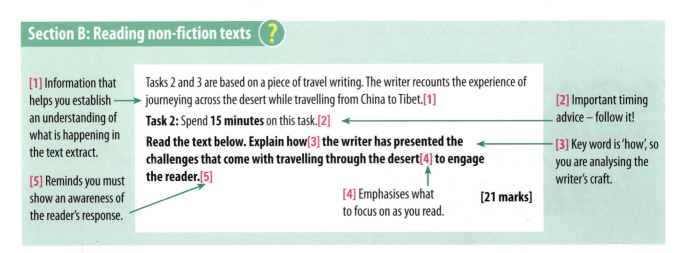

Putting your skills into practice

After an hour's descent I reach the desert. Sweat pours from my body and evaporates in seconds. My water is half-finished, and the lake has sunk from view. I must rely on my compass from now on.

The sun is still overhead. As I breathe the hot air in and out, my mouth becomes as dry as dust. The compass in my hand burns like the gravel underfoot. The dry noodles have reached my stomach and seem to be sucking the moisture from my blood. I long to reach the shore of the lake and plunge my head in its cool water. For brief moments, refracted through the heat waves on the right, I see villages, moving trucks, or a sweep of marsh. If I didn't have a compass, I might be tempted to walk straight into the mirage.

(Ma jian, *Red Dust*)

Section B: Reading non-fiction texts

Task 3: Spend **10 minutes** on your response.[1]

The writer is forced to think about the uncertainty of his surroundings.[2]

Read the text below. In your own words[3] **write down TWO reasons the writer gives to explain why he is uncertain about his exact location. Present supporting evidence.**[4]

[1] Crucial timing advice – follow it!

[2] Offers brief contextual information to give you an idea of what is happening in the text extract.

[3] Signals that it is vital to show your understanding of the text by summarising using your own words.

[4] Reminds you always to select relevant evidence from the text to support your point. Direct quotations should always be placed inside quotation marks.

Four or five hours go by. At last I see clumps of weed rise from the gravel. The land starts to dip. I check the compass. Sugan should be right in front of me now, but all I see is the wide stony plain.

Suddenly it dawns on me that distances can be deceptive in the transparent atmosphere of the desert. The lake that from the pass seemed so near could be a hundred kilometres away. After all, what looked like a tiny blue spot is in fact a huge lake. It is too late to turn back now though – my bottle is empty. I have no choice but to keep walking towards the water. Where there is water there are people, and where there are people there is life. There is no other path I can take.

(Ma jian, *Red Dust*)

a	First reason	[1 mark]
	Supporting evidence	[5 marks]
b	First reason	[1 mark]
	Supporting evidence	[5 marks]

EXAM PRACTICE

Section B: Reading media texts

[1] A reminder that Tasks 4 and 5 are based on your reading of a set media text. So be specific in what you say.

[2] Important timing advice – follow it!

[3] You won't cover every aspect so focus on selecting evidence that you can confidently explain.

Tasks 4 and 5 are based on a book cover.**[1]**

Task 4: Spend **17 minutes** on your response.**[2]**

Below is some of the text used in this book cover.

Comment on how language[3] has been used to develop a sense that this would be an interesting book to read.[4] Present supporting evidence.[5]

[4] Indicates what you must focus on when deciding what to write about.

[5] Reminds you to offer evidence – select short, relevant quotations and avoid copying out large sections.

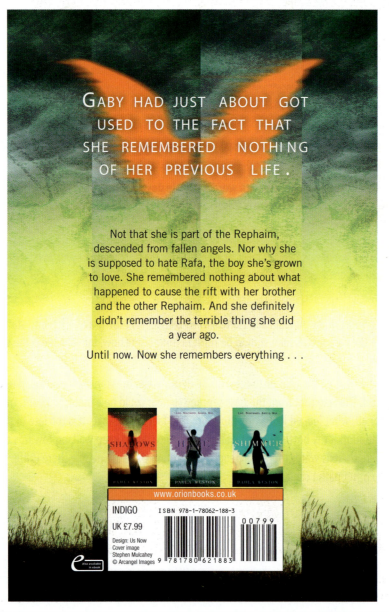

Putting your skills into practice

[1] Important advice about timing – follow it!

[2] Indicates to write about only two presentational devices.

[4] Reminder to be specific. What does the presentational device make the reader think or feel about the subject, in this case the book itself?

Task 5: Spend **8 minutes** on your response.[1]

Study the front cover of the book.

Select two[2] presentational features used on the front cover to support the idea that this is an interesting book to read. Explain the intended effect[3] of these two presentational features on the reader.[4]

[3] When writing about your chosen two presentational features, be very sure to explain their impact upon the reader.

LOVE. NIGHTMARES. ANGELS. WAR.

BURN

PAULA WESTON

a	First feature	[4 marks]
	Explanation	[2 marks]
b	First feature	[4 marks]
	Explanation	[2 marks]

203

EXAM PRACTICE

Unit 4 Section A: Personal or creative writing

Section A of Unit 4 is another test of your writing. Two tasks are set, one **personal writing task** and one **creative writing task**; you will select one and write a response. The creative writing task will provide an image to help stimulate your creative thinking.

Section A: Personal or creative writing

Task 1

Spend 55 minutes on your response. **[1]**

Mark allocation: 88 marks

Up to **58 marks** are available for an **organised** piece of personal/creative writing that matches **form with purpose to engage the specified audience.[2]**

Up to **30 marks** are available for the use of **a range of sentence structures** and **accuracy in spelling, punctuation and grammar.[2]**

Complete only ONE task.[3]

Either

a **Write a personal blog** in which you tell your readers about a memorable summertime.**[4]**

Or

b **Write a creative story** to be published in a collection of young people's writing.**[5]** The picture below is to be the basis for your story. Provide your own title.**[6]**

[88 marks]

You are advised to spend:
- **15** minutes **thinking and planning**
- **30** minutes **writing** your response
- **10** minutes **checking** your writing.

[1] Remember that this includes 15 minutes to think and plan, 30 minutes to write and 10 minutes to check over.

[2] Indicates that your response will attract two separate marks: both content and accuracy are important.

[3] Offers important advice (along with 'Either' and 'Or') to read both tasks carefully before deciding which one you will answer.

[4] Concentrate on writing something that is interesting and that you yourself would enjoy reading.

[5] Indicates your audience; be sure to write something that will hook and hold their interest.

[6] The title can be decided after completing your story, but don't forget to add it.

Putting your skills into practice

Section B: Reading literary and non-fiction texts

[1] Timing advice – follow it!

[2] Reminder to use language that shows you are comparing and contrasting, e.g. *Both*, *Similarly*, *In contrast*, *Whereas*…

Task 2

You have **26 minutes**[1] in which to read **both texts** and respond to the **task** below.

Compare and contrast[2] how the writers of Texts A and B convey a sense of panic.[3] **Present supporting evidence from both texts.**[4]

[3] Signals clearly what to focus on as you read the texts.

[4] Highlighting or underlining key part of the extracts can help you locate your supporting evidence quickly.

Text A

The children aren't anywhere near the ice-cream van.

'I'll just see where they are,' he says casually but then breaks into a run. Fran calls something after him but he can't hear. He's panicking, telling himself not to be so bloody stupid, but there are so many streams and lakes round here, it's no place for a toddler to be on his own. But he's not on his own, he's with Gareth and Miranda. He asks the man in the ice-cream van whether he's seen a fair-haired toddler with an older boy and girl. A woman standing nearby, swirling her tongue around an ice-cream cone, points to a path that leads down to the largest lake.

Nick careers down the hill, jumping on the verge to avoid an elderly couple. The path's uneven, shelving down steeply between the roots of trees. A hundred feet below there's a stream, its water blackish-brown, flowing over black rocks. Sometimes it flashes white over miniature waterfalls, or opens into deep pools with pebble promontories. Every hundred yards or so wooden bridges span the stream. There's a path on the other side too, narrower than this, bordered by glistening ferns that are almost as wet as the rocks. Nick crosses over and thinks he sees them, two taller figures holding a small boy by the hand. He opens his mouth to call their names then realises it's a couple with their child. The children are nowhere to be seen.

The fir trees tower over him. Even the roots are above his head. Only by craning his head back can he see glints of sunlight on the uppermost branches. A warm, dark, wet enclosed place. It reminds him of the garden at Lob's Hill. All the trees and bushes are evergreens, their dead leaves forming a weed-killing mulch that kills everything else as well.

And then he sees them. Comes round a corner of the twisting path and sees them, Jasper with his trainers and socks off, paddling; Miranda sitting on a rock sucking out the last drop of ice cream from the bottom of a cone; Gareth standing on a rock in the middle of the stream, the turbulent water chafing around him.

(Pat Barker, *Another World*)

EXAM PRACTICE

Text B

The passage below is set during the First World War. Robert and a group of soldiers are searching large craters to try to recover Morrison, a missing comrade.

There was no reason for crawling anymore. The night was clear. And they would have to hurry. And the other two stood up as well when they saw him doing so. He couldn't leave a man to die in the pit of green slime.

'We'll run,' he said. And they ran to the first one and listened.

They cried fiercely. 'Are you there?' But there was no answer.

Then they seemed to hear it from the next one and they were at that one soon too, peering down into the green slime, illuminated by the moonlight. But there was no answer. There was one left and they made for that one. They screamed again, in the sound of the shells, and they seemed to hear an answer. They heard what seemed to be a bubbling. 'Are you there?' said Robert, bending down and listening. 'Can you get over here?' They could hear splashing and deep below them, breathing, frantic breathing as if someone was frightened to death.

'It's all right,' he said, 'if you come over here I'll send my rifle down. You two hang on to me,' he said to the others. He was terrified. That depth, that green depth. Was Morrison down there after all? He hadn't spoken. The splashings came closer. The voice was like an animal's, repeating endlessly a mixture of curses and prayers.

(Ian Crichton Smith, *The Crater*)

[32 marks]

Tasks 3 and 4

You have **24 minutes** in which to read and respond to the **two tasks** based on the **non-fiction blog 'Mid-term trauma.'**

Task 3: Spend **12 minutes** on your response.[1]

The extract below is the beginning of the blog.[2]

Explain how[3] **the writer has tried to engage the interest of the reader.**

---

[2] Contextual information helps set up the task that follows. The extract may also be taken from the middle or end of a full text.

[1] Important timing advice – follow it!

[3] Indicates that you will be analysing the writer's craft.

Mid-term trauma

I consider myself a reasonably good mum who actually enjoys the company of her children, but my heart sinks every mid-term as my children force me to suffer a torturous day at the swimming pool. For me this really is a traumatic experience, but one I have been surviving for the past eleven years for the sake of my beloved babes.

My trauma begins in the changing room, sorry: the 'village changing area'. As usual all the family changing areas have been taken up by gangs of youths with no sign of a parent among them. 'They can't all be family, I mean how many are in there? Sixteen? Where are the staff?' I'm afraid I protest rather too loudly, as my eleven-year-old rolls her eyes in mortification and drags me off to a quieter corner where we squeeze ourselves into coffin-sized cubicles and, like contortionists, attempt to get ourselves ready for swimming. Of course, with superhero speed my younger son has already removed his clothes and abandoned them all over the soaking wet floor. I want to cry!

[15 marks]

Task 4: Spend **12 minutes** on your response.[1]

The extract below is the next four paragraphs of the writer's blog.[2]

Explain how[3] the writer has created a negative view of her experience in the swimming pool itself.[4]

[1] Important timing advice to follow.

[2] Provides contextual information that shows how this extract links with the one in Task 3.

[3] Indicates that you will be analysing the writer's craft.

[4] Shows what you should be concentrating on when explaining the effect of chosen words, phrases, techniques or structural features.

The swimming pool has undergone considerable refurbishment since our last ordeal, I mean, 'family swim'. Delightedly, the children leap towards 'Kiddie-Splash'. This is complete torture! Whoever designed this clearly does not have children; it is a multi-coloured, water-squirting, eye-stinging health and safety hazard!

We head to the 'Lazy River'. I quickly discover that the 'lazy' part of this attraction is that it takes so much effort and energy to get out of it that you end up just going around in circles. The 'wave effect' sends my son hurtling away from my grip and smashes him against the wall. I freeze. He roars with laughter. Soon I am dizzy doing laps and am determined to succeed in my mission to get out of here safely and still with two children.

Finally, we settle into the 'jacuzzi pool', where it's calmer and safer. That is until one foolish parent thinks this is the perfect place to begin a game of splash. I can't stand it! Once again we're on the move. I am longing for the orange light to flash and signal an end to our session and this trauma.

'How long is left, Mum?' asks my son. 'Too long,' I want to reply but instead I smile through gritted teeth and look forward to tomorrow's trip to the cinema.

[15 marks]

Mark schemes

Unit 1 Section A: Writing for purpose and audience

Task 1

Response time: 55 minutes
Total marks: 87 marks

Write a speech to persuade your classmates to lead a more active lifestyle.

1(a)	Form, content and style	Use of language and structure	Sense of audience and purpose	
Light bronze	• Nothing to reward.	• Nothing to reward.	• Nothing to reward.	
Dark bronze	• Communicates ideas with limited success. • May not acknowledge form.	• May use simple/few language techniques. • Limited evidence of structural features.	• Limited awareness of audience and purpose.	
Light silver	• Some successful communication and development of ideas to promote a point of view or compel the reader. • Some recognition of form.	• Some successful attempts to use language techniques. • Sensible organisation of ideas that, in places, might be linked by structural features.	• Some conscious awareness of audience and purpose. • Some evidence of language choices that are fitting for audience and purpose.	
Dark silver	• Successful communication of ideas in a way that can hook, hold and engage or compel the reader. • Recognition of form in the content of the writing.	• Uses language techniques with increasing success. • Successful organisation of ideas with evidence of a variety of structural features.	• Clear identification of audience and purpose. Evidence of a variety of language choices that are fitting for audience and purpose.	
Light gold	• Communicates ideas in a way that is increasingly convincing and compelling. • Evidence of an engaging style is obvious throughout the response. • Confident recognition of form.	• Deliberately and successfully uses a variety of language techniques throughout the response. • Skilful organisation of ideas with structural features used to enhance meaning and/or engagement.	• Emerging confidence in the awareness of audience and purpose. This is obvious throughout the response where language is deliberately selected with consideration of audience and purpose.	
Dark gold	• Assured development of ideas in a style that is highly engaging and compelling. • Assured recognition of form.	• Skilfully employs a full range of language techniques that are consciously selected for effect. • Assured organisation of ideas with structural features.	• Assured and sustained awareness of audience and purpose. This is obvious through the use of precise language consciously chosen in recognition of audience and purpose.	

Mark schemes

1(b)	Variation in sentence structuring	Employment of punctuation	Accuracy in spelling and selection of vocabulary	
Light bronze	• Nothing to reward.	• Nothing to reward.	• Nothing to reward.	
Dark bronze	• Some evidence of sentence structuring.	• Some evidence of simple punctuation such as full stops, but may not be consistently used with accuracy.	• Some accuracy in spelling of simple words. • Limited range of vocabulary.	
Light silver	• Evidence of straightforward sentence structuring.	• Mostly accurate use of simple punctuation, such as full stops and commas, to achieve straightforward communication.	• Mostly accurate spelling of uncomplicated words. Some evidence of vocabulary used to enhance the response.	
Dark silver	• Evidence of some variation in sentence structures.	• Sound use of full stops, commas, question marks and exclamation marks, with some evidence of punctuation deliberately used to add impact.	• Accuracy in the spelling of straightforward words and some more complex words. • Evidence of attempts to use a wide and varied vocabulary, including some ambitious words.	
Light gold	• Evidence of deliberate variation in sentence structures to enhance meaning.	• Successfully employs a range of punctuation throughout the response to maintain precision in expression and engage the audience.	• Accurate spelling of the majority of words with only occasional errors in the use of challenging words. • Evidence of a precise and varied vocabulary.	
Dark gold	• A full range of sentence structures are used to enhance the overall response.	• Confidently uses a full range of punctuation that helps improve the overall quality of the writing and keeps the audience engaged.	• Virtually all spellings are accurate with only one-off errors that are likely to occur as an attempt to use more ambitious and complex language. • Evidence of sophisticated vocabulary.	

MARK SCHEMES

Unit 1 Section B: Reading to access non-fiction and media texts

Task 2

Response time: 15 minutes   Total marks: 21 marks

Explain how the writer has presented the challenges that come with travelling through the desert to engage the reader.

Below is a checklist that identifies material you may refer to in your answer to this task:

- The writer begins by sharing the fact he has been travelling for some time, which makes the reader realise how vast the land is: 'After an hour's descent I reach the desert.'
- The writer draws the reader's attention to how hot the desert is: 'Sweat pours from my body and evaporates in seconds.' Dramatic choice of verb 'pours' makes the reader appreciate the intensity of the heat and its impact upon the human body.
- He forces the reader to acknowledge the importance of water and hydration in the desert and hints that he will have to manage his water intake: 'My water is half-finished, and the lake has sunk from view.'
- The writer stresses the need to have some guidance and direction while travelling through the desert: 'I must rely on my compass from now on.' The expression 'I must' makes him seem dependent upon the compass.
- The short sentence emphasises the intensity of the heat and his increasing fatigue: 'The sun is still overhead.'
- The humidity of the desert and its effect upon him is emphasised through the use of adjective 'hot' and the simile 'as dry as dust': 'As I breathe the hot air in and out, my mouth becomes as dry as dust.'
- The heat is clearly stifling and inescapable, making him experience discomfort: 'The compass in my hand burns like the gravel underfoot.'
- Personification exaggerates his increasing discomfort and dehydration: 'The dry noodles have reached my stomach and seem to be sucking the moisture from my blood.'
- The writer confesses 'I long to reach the shore of the lake and plunge my head in its cool water.' Through the contrasting descriptions of his present location and his desired location, the reader detects his desire to be somewhere cooler, with expressions such as 'I long' and 'plunge' confirming his present discomfort.
- The writer acknowledges how disorientating it can be travelling through the desert: 'For brief moments, refracted through the heat waves on the right, I see villages, moving trucks, or a sweep of marsh. If I didn't have a compass, I might be tempted to walk straight into the mirage.' The word 'or' makes us appreciate he is disorientated. In the final sentence he makes the reader aware of his total reliance upon his compass to stay safely on course.

Mark schemes

2	Ability to explain and analyse the writer's craft	Ability to interpret the intentions of the writer	Extracting meaning and selecting evidence	
Light bronze	• Nothing to reward.	• Nothing to reward.	• Nothing to reward.	
Dark bronze	• A simple attempt to offer some basic comments on the writer's craft.	• Some simple understanding of the writer's intentions.	• Simple understanding that may offer some selection of relevant evidence.	
Light silver	• A straightforward recognition of writer's craft that considers some language choices and/or language techniques.	• Demonstrates an overall understanding of the writer's intentions with some awareness of how intentions have been communicated.	• Straightforward understanding with some attempt to select relevant evidence to support interpretations.	
Dark silver	• A generally focused consideration of the writer's craft with appropriate explanation and some analysis of language.	• A generally focused interpretation of the writer's intentions with recognition of how some of the writer's intentions have been communicated through language choices.	• Generally accurate selection of evidence linked to appropriate interpretations and explanations.	
Light gold	• A more analytical consideration of the writer's craft that explores and evaluates some language strategies.	• A secure interpretation that displays sound understanding of how the writer's intentions are conveyed through language choices.	• A range of mostly accurate evidence that is used to explore in some detail the methods and intentions of the writer.	
Dark gold	• An assured analysis that examines and evaluates the writer's craft. Confidently able to identify appropriate features worthy of analysis.	• An assured and analytical interpretation that shows insightful recognition of how the writer's intentions are conveyed through language choices.	• An assured selection of precise evidence that is used to support confident analysis of the writer's methods and intentions.	

MARK SCHEMES

Task 3

Response time: 10 minutes   Total marks: 12 marks

In your own words write down TWO reasons the writer gives to explain why he is uncertain about his exact location. Present supporting evidence.

The order in which reasons are stated is unimportant.

Accept any of the following reasons and supporting evidence:

Reason	Supporting evidence
The writer is not even sure how far he has been travelling and seems to have lost track of time and location.	'Four or five hours go by.'
The writer seems relieved to see signs of life growing in the ground and it is as though he has not been prepared for this.	'At last I see clumps of weed rise from the gravel.'
The terrain is deceptive and he relies on his compass to try to work out where he is.	'The land starts to dip. I check the compass.'
The sight in front of him is not what he was expecting to see and it offers no clues about where he is or how far he is from Sugan, his intended destination.	'Sugan should be right in front of me now, but all I see is the wide stony plain.'
He realises the land is deceptive and that therefore he cannot rely on his own sense of direction to determine where he is.	'Suddenly it dawns on me that distances can be deceptive in the transparent atmosphere of the desert.'
He cannot be certain about distance and seems unsure exactly how far away he is from the lake.	'The lake that from the pass seemed so near could be a hundred kilometres away.'
He no longer seems in control of his movements and is pressing on through necessity rather than through choice.	'I have no choice but to keep walking towards the water … There is no other path I can take.'

Task 4: Media text – Use of language

Response time: 17 minutes   Total marks: 20 marks

Comment on how language has been used to develop a sense that this would be an interesting book to read. Present supporting evidence.

Below is a checklist identifying points which you may refer to in your answer:

- ▶ Intriguing opening sentence, 'Gaby had just about got used to the fact that she remembered nothing of her previous life' introduces a sense of curiosity and mystery around the character of Gaby.
- ▶ The blurb suggests the central character will make several life-changing discoveries, which prompts the reader to think that the plot is intricate and intriguing through the repetition of 'remembered nothing.'
- ▶ Particular words suggest this is a fantasy text which will have particular interest for fans of this genre: '…she is part of the Rephaim, descended from fallen angels.'
- ▶ The plot seems intricate as the blurb lists different things which Gaby is unsure of: for example, 'why she is supposed to hate Rafa, the boy she's grown to love.' Contrasting words 'hate' and 'love' confirm a central conflict. The reader is also intrigued by the prospect of a romantic sub-plot.

Mark schemes

▶ The structure of the blurb builds up to the sentence beginning with 'And she definitely didn't remember…'. This creates the impression that the action develops rather quickly to hold the reader's interest.
▶ Dramatic language of 'the terrible thing she did a year ago' increases the reader's interest in the character of Gaby. The emotive language whets the appetite of the reader who is keen to discover the character's backstory and read how her past impacts upon her present.
▶ Abrupt dramatic sentence 'Until now.' The reader infers Gaby's memory has returned unexpectedly, creating a complication and a gripping storyline.
▶ Final sentence of blurb, 'Now she remembers everything…' is teasing. The word 'everything' seems dramatic and forces the reader to expect revelations which will hold their attention.
▶ The inclusion of ellipsis to conclude the blurb is intended to hook the reader by creating anticipation. The writer intends to encourage the reader to open the book and immerse themselves in the story.

4	Ability to explain and analyse the writer's craft	Ability to interpret the intentions of the writer	Extracting meaning and selecting evidence	
Light bronze	• Nothing to reward.	• Nothing to reward.	• Nothing to reward.	
Dark bronze	• A simple attempt to offer some basic comments on the writer's craft.	• Some simple understanding of the writer's intentions.	• Simple understanding that may offer some selection of relevant evidence.	
Light silver	• A straightforward recognition of writer's craft that considers some language choices and/or language techniques.	• Demonstrates an overall understanding of the writer's intentions with some awareness of how intentions have been communicated.	• Straightforward understanding with some attempt to select relevant evidence to support interpretations.	
Dark silver	• A generally focused consideration of the writer's craft with appropriate explanation and some analysis of language.	• A generally focused interpretation of the writer's intentions with recognition of how some of the writer's intentions have been communicated through language choices.	• Generally accurate selection of evidence linked to appropriate interpretations and explanations.	
Light gold	• A more analytical consideration of the writer's craft that explores and evaluates some language strategies.	• A secure interpretation that displays sound understanding of how the writer's intentions are conveyed through language choices.	• A range of mostly accurate evidence that is used to explore in some detail the methods and intentions of the writer.	
Dark gold	• An assured analysis that examines and evaluates the writer's craft. Confidently able to identify appropriate features worthy of analysis.	• An assured and analytical interpretation that shows insightful recognition of how the writer's intentions are conveyed through language choices.	• An assured selection of precise evidence that is used to support confident analysis of the writer's methods and intentions.	

MARK SCHEMES

Task 5: Media text – Presentational features/devices

Response time: 8 minutes Total marks: 10 marks

Select two presentational features used on the front cover to support the idea that this is an interesting book to read. Explain the intended effect of these two presentational features on the reader.

Below is a checklist of appropriate comments that you may refer to. You will be awarded marks for:

- Striking central image to imply the plot will revolve around this character who is obviously female but her dress could be described as unisex implying she is an edgy and modern heroine.
- Sense of mystery and intrigue is conveyed by the fact the character's face is concealed.
- The use of dark colours suggests she is a character who lives in the shadows and leads a rather dark life.
- The character is holding a sword, which suggests conflict. The sword and the character's gaze are aimed downwards, which intrigue the reader.
- The image of an individual in an isolated setting suggests the character is involved in some individual or personal battle that will hold the interest of the reader.
- The character's dress appears modern whereas the sword is a weapon associated with ancient warfare, so the reader expects a clash of modern and ancient worlds.
- The strong orange and yellow colours are associated with fire, which link with the title and further the idea of an intense and explosive storyline.
- The orange colour is arranged to look like wings, hinting at the fantasy genre of the book and creating interest in the character who may actually be something more than she appears. Also links to the word 'Angels' at the top of the cover.
- The sunlight is peeking out below the orange. The infusion of optimistic and warm colours with darker colours furthers the idea of a clash or conflict.
- The idea of conflict is also suggested by the image of the sun and darker shadows leading the reader to expect some conflict between the forces of good and evil.
- The dark colours suggest the storyline will deal with some dark secrets and dark forces.
- Dark colours hint that this will appeal to mature readers.
- The dramatic title is centrally positioned in the centre of the text to imply this is a dramatic read and it seems to relate to the character.
- The font style is distinctive, with a tribal look, hinting at themes of identity. The title appears as if it has been branded onto the cover.

Mark schemes

Unit 4 Section A: Personal or Creative Writing

Task 1

Response time: 55 minutes Total marks: 88 marks

Either

a Write a **personal blog** in which you tell your readers about a memorable summertime.

Or

b Write a **creative story to be published in a collection of young people's writing**. The picture below is to be the basis for your story. Provide your own title.

1(a)	Form, content and style	Use of language and structure	Sense of audience and purpose	
Light bronze	• Nothing to reward.	• Nothing to reward.	• Nothing to reward.	
Dark bronze	• Communicates ideas with limited development.	• May use simple/few language techniques. • Limited evidence of structural features.	• Limited awareness of audience and purpose.	
Light silver	• Some successful communication and development of ideas to write from experience or write creatively. • Some recognition of form.	• Some successful attempts to use language techniques. • Sensible organisation of ideas that, in places, might be linked by structural features.	• Some conscious awareness of audience and purpose. • Some evidence of language choices that are fitting for audience and purpose.	
Dark silver	• Successful communication of ideas that is developed in places to hook, hold and engage the reader in Personal or Creative Writing. • Recognition of form.	• Uses language techniques with increasing success to gain the interest of the audience. • Successful organisation of ideas with clear evidence of structural features.	• Clear identification of audience and purpose. Evidence of a variety of language choices that are fitting for audience and purpose.	
Light gold	• Communicates ideas in a way that is increasingly convincing and compelling. • Evidence of an engaging style is obvious throughout the response. • Confident recognition of form.	• Deliberately and successfully uses a variety of language techniques throughout the response to enhance the engagement of the reader. • Skilful organisation of ideas.	• Emerging confidence in the awareness of audience and purpose. This is obvious throughout the response where language is deliberately selected with consideration of audience and purpose.	

215

MARK SCHEMES

Dark gold	• Assured development of ideas in a style that is highly engaging and successfully maintains the interest of the reader when writing from experience or writing creatively. • Assured recognition of form.	• Skilfully employs a full range of language techniques that are consciously selected for effect and to sustain a connection with the reader. • Assured organisation of ideas with structural features.	• Assured and sustained awareness of audience and purpose. This is created through precise selection of language.

1(b)	Variation in sentence structuring	Employment of punctuation	Accuracy in spelling and selection of vocabulary
Light bronze	• Nothing to reward.	• Nothing to reward.	• Nothing to reward.
Dark bronze	• Some evidence of sentence structuring.	• Some evidence of simple punctuation such as full stops, but may not be consistently used with accuracy.	• Some accuracy in spelling of simple words. • Limited range of vocabulary.
Light silver	• Evidence of straightforward sentence structuring.	• Mostly accurate use of simple punctuation, such as full stops and commas, to achieve straightforward communication.	• Mostly accurate spelling of uncomplicated words. Some evidence of vocabulary used to enhance the response.
Dark silver	• Evidence of some variation in sentence structures.	• Sound use of full stops, commas, question marks and exclamation marks, with some evidence of punctuation deliberately used to add impact.	• Accuracy in the spelling of straightforward words and some more complex words. • Evidence of attempts to use a wide and varied vocabulary, including some ambitious words.
Light gold	• Evidence of deliberate variation in sentence structures to enhance meaning.	• Successfully employs a range of punctuation throughout the response to maintain precision in expression and engage the audience.	• Accurate spelling of the majority of words with only occasional errors in the use of challenging words. • Evidence of a precise and varied vocabulary.
Dark gold	• A full range of sentence structures are used to enhance the overall response.	• Confidently uses a full range of punctuation that helps improve the overall quality of the writing and keeps the audience engaged.	• Virtually all spellings are accurate with only one-off errors that are likely to occur as an attempt to use more ambitious and complex language. • Evidence of sophisticated vocabulary.

Mark schemes

Unit 4 Section B: Reading literary and non-fiction texts
Task 2

Response time: 26 minutes   Total marks: 32 marks

Compare and contrast how the writers of Texts A and B convey a sense of panic. Present supporting evidence from both texts.

You may refer to the following to make points of comparison and contrast:

- Text A uses the reactions of a central character to emphasise the growing panic that comes from a sense of responsibility – Nick in Text A feels responsible for the children. Similarly, Robert in Text B feels responsible for his comrade, but in Text B Robert is accompanied by other comrades who seem to feed off his panic and at the end of Text B the writer conveys the panic of the fallen comrade.

- In both texts the onset of panic is clear from the beginning. In Text A Nick's words are spoken 'casually' but the description of his actions where he 'breaks into a run' establishes his brewing panic. In Text B the panic is conveyed in the first paragraph with 'they would have to hurry' and 'He couldn't leave a man to die in the pit of green slime.'

- In Text A the writer emphasises Nick's increasing panic through the use of long sentences to give the impression of his quick running and his mind tortured with thoughts: 'He's panicking, telling himself … it's no place for a toddler to be on his own.' The word 'toddler' helps the reader understand how awareness of the vulnerability of the child and the potential dangers of the environment intensify Nick's panic.

- Similarly in Text B, the landscape is dangerous and increases Robert's panic: 'He couldn't leave a man to die in the pit of green slime.' The reader accepts that in both texts Nick and Robert are involved in a race against time.

- In Text A verbs emphasise how Nick's panic manifests itself in his actions as he 'careers down the hill' and is moving at such a quick pace that he finds himself 'jumping on the verge to avoid an elderly couple.' In Text B adverbs capture how the feeling of panic is apparent in the shouts of Robert and his men who 'cried fiercely', with 'fiercely' making clear their desperation to locate their comrade.

- In Text A the writer gives some description of the setting, which gives the impression that everywhere he looks Nick sees potential danger: 'the path's uneven, shelving down steeply…', 'A hundred feet below…', 'flowing over black rocks.'

- In Text A Nick 'thinks he sees them' and his panic causes him to react instantly as he 'opens his mouth' but quickly 'realises it's a couple'. The reader senses that panic is changing to despair through the short sentence, 'The children are nowhere to be seen.'

- Likewise, in Text B the writer describes how the characters 'seemed to hear…', which gives momentary hope as they react at once, 'they were at that one soon too, peering down…'. The short sentence, 'But there was no answer.', however, captures their disappointment and feeling of failure as they make their way towards the last crater, 'There was one left…' The writer is leading the reader to expect that panic will turn to despair.

MARK SCHEMES

- In Text B the final efforts of the men are conveyed through the writer's verb choices, 'They screamed again…' Their panic returns as they 'seemed to hear an answer' and the repeated use of questions captures the sudden increase in panic once more as they must determine for certain if their comrade is inside the final crater.
- In Text A the density of the forest seems to increase Nick's panic and the descriptions of the sights around him induce dark, foreboding feelings: 'The fir trees tower over him' makes the reader appreciate his challenge of finding small children when an adult feels dwarfed by the trees: '… their dead leaves forming a weed-killing mulch that kills everything else as well.' Through suspending the paragraph here and using ominous language such as 'dead' and 'kills everything else' the writer is implying that Nick is beginning to fear the worst.
- In Text B the reader is suddenly focused on the panic felt by the fallen comrade: 'They could hear splashing and deep below them, breathing, frantic breathing as if someone was frightened to death.' The reader infers the intense panic of the soldier but the words 'deep below' suggest that getting him out will not be straightforward.
- Text A ends with a resolution and the panic is replaced with relief as 'then he sees them.' The short sentence emphasises his relief and the description of the children makes it clear they are completely unaware of any danger or panic and instead seem content, 'Jasper … paddling; Miranda sitting … sucking out the last drop of ice cream…; Gareth standing…' The final description, however, suggests that Nick's awareness of danger has not completely disappeared as the water still seems dangerous, 'the turbulent water chafing around him.'
- In contrast, Text B concludes with increasing panic from both Robert and his fallen comrade. The writer uses a short sentence to capture the intensity of Robert's panic and fear as he must now attempt to rescue his comrade: 'He was terrified.'
- Robert's panic is internalised at the end of the extract as he wonders, 'Was Morrison down there after all? He hadn't spoken.'
- The final sentence concludes Text B in dramatic and unresolved fashion as the panic of Morrison, the fallen comrade, seems to have consumed him and engaged a survival instinct: 'The voice was like an animal's, repeating endlessly a mixture of curses and prayers.' The inconclusive ending makes Text B highly dramatic.

Mark schemes

2	Ability to interpret the intentions of the writer	Ability to explain and analyse aspects of writers' craft	Extracting meaning and selecting material to compare and contrast	
Light bronze	• Nothing to reward.	• Nothing to reward.	• Nothing to reward.	
Dark bronze	• A basic understanding of the texts that is demonstrated through simple comments on the writers' language.	• May be reliant on copying or paraphrasing the texts. Some awareness of obvious language features that may consider the impact on a reader.	• Simple comments or reflections on one or both texts.	
Light silver	• A straightforward understanding of the texts that is demonstrated through general comments based on some selection of textual evidence OR a straightforward recognition of some obvious intentions.	• Straightforward explanations that consider some language features and their impact in an uncomplicated way.	• Straightforward understanding with some selection of evidence. An attempt to connect evidence to an explanation about the writers' craft. • Some success in identifying uncomplicated comparisons and/or contrasts.	
Dark silver	• Overall, a secure understanding of both texts with appropriate interpretation of the writers' ideas supported by comments on language.	• Generally relevant explanations based on a selection of textual evidence and a clear attempt in places to assess the impact upon a reader.	• Generally relevant selection of evidence from both texts with appropriate explanation and, in places, interpretation. • Appropriate comparing and contrasting.	
Light gold	• Demonstrates clear understanding of the texts with emerging evidence of evaluation. • Overall interpretations are accurate and supported by examination of language.	• A range of relevant explanations with several attempts to develop comments by evaluating the writers' craft.	• A range of relevant evidence selected from both texts for the purpose of comparing and contrasting inferences or interpretations about the writers' choice of language.	
Dark gold	• Confident understanding of the texts with assured analysis of how the writers shape the reader's response through deliberate selection of language.	• Confident examination of the writers' craft with evaluative explanations that show assured appreciation of the intended effect.	• An assured selection of precise evidence from both texts to support skilful comparing and contrasting and precise analysis of the writers' craft.	

MARK SCHEMES

Task 3

Response time: 12 minutes   Total marks: 15 marks

Explain how the writer has tried to engage the interest of the reader.

- Dramatic title to intrigue the reader and lead them to expect that the text will deal with serious subject matter: 'Mid-term trauma'.
- Anecdotal style to engage the reader at the beginning: 'I consider myself…'
- Confessional tone makes the reader feel connected to the writer: '…my heart sinks every mid-term…'
- Emotive language to develop the idea that a visit to the swimming pool is a painful experience for the writer: 'force me to suffer a torturous day at the swimming pool.'
- Exaggeration for humorous effect: 'surviving'.
- Alliteration 'beloved babes' – the reader admires the writer's devotion to her children.
- Repetition of 'trauma' (title and Paragraph 2) to make the visit seem painfully emotional.
- Structural features to take the reader on the journey and to suggest the ordeal is prolonged: 'My trauma begins in…'
- Sarcastic tone to convey the writer's disapproval of the communal changing area: 'begins in the changing room, sorry: the "village changing area".'
- Use of direct speech to show the writer's humorous and exaggerated reaction to the youths. Repeated use of questions emphasises her frustration and annoyance: 'I mean how many are in there? Sixteen? Where are the staff?'
- The writer's heightened emotions and her daughter's reaction force the reader to realise the writer is a source of embarrassment for her children: 'my eleven-year-old rolls her eyes in mortification and drags me off to a quieter corner…'
- Long sentence to emphasise the unpleasant nature of the changing room experience: 'I'm afraid I protest rather too loudly … attempt to get ourselves ready for swimming.'
- Exaggeration: 'coffin-sized cubicles' creates humour and the harsh alliteration of 'c' emphasises the discomfort inside the cramped changing room.
- Simile: 'like contortionists…' creates humour for the reader by making them imagine the challenge of changing in such a cramped space.
- Conversational tone to engage the reader: 'Of course,…'
- Further humour created through the description of the writer's son, who undresses with 'superhero speed' and 'abandons' his clothes on the wet floor.
- Writer follows with reaction: 'I want to cry!' Short blunt sentence and exclamation mark emphasises her emotional distress.

3	Extract meaning and select evidence	Ability to interpret the intentions of the writer	Ability to explain and analyse the writer's craft	
Light bronze	• Nothing to reward.	• Nothing to reward.	• Nothing to reward.	
Dark bronze	• Simple understanding of the text. May include textual evidence, some of which may be relevant.	• Simple recognition of the writer's intentions may be evident.	• Simple comments on parts of the text that might remark on how they achieve effect.	
Light silver	• Some understanding of the text, with efforts to select some relevant textual evidence.	• A straightforward explanation of the writer's intentions.	• A straightforward examination of some language devices used within the text.	
Dark silver	• General understanding of the text. Will include some relevant supporting evidence.	• A general interpretation that recognises how some of the writer's intentions have been communicated through language choices.	• A generally effective examination of writer's craft with evidence of an ability to analyse writer's craft.	
Light gold	• Secure understanding of the text with relevant selection of material.	• A secure interpretation that clearly recognises how the writer's intentions are reflected through language choices.	• A secure evaluation of writer's craft that explores the use of some aspects of language and structural features.	
Dark gold	• Confident understanding of the text with precise selection of textual evidence that enables analysis of the text.	• A confident and analytical interpretation that demonstrates an insightful understanding of how the writer's intentions are apparent through language choices.	• A confident and precise analysis of relevant aspects of writer's craft.	

MARK SCHEMES

Task 4

Response time: 12 minutes Total marks: 15 marks

Explain how the writer has created a negative view of her experience in the swimming pool itself.

- The **personal style** of the writing and its conversational style encourages the reader to adopt the writer's perspective.
- The use of **negative language** such as 'ordeal' reinforces the negative experience.
- **Exclamatory sentence** and **emphatic tone** encourage the reader to feel convinced by the writer's recount and to share her negative perspective: 'This is complete torture!'
- Suggests the attraction is badly designed and there is clear evidence of a **critical tone**: 'Whoever designed this clearly…'
- The writer **lists** the faults found in 'Kiddie-Splash' to defend her negative perspective and the exclamation mark emphasises her disapproving tone: 'it is a multi-coloured, water-squirting, eye-stinging health and safety hazard!'
- Challenges the suggestion that the swimming pool is a relaxing and safe environment: 'that it takes so much effort and energy to get out of it that you end up just going around in circles.' and 'sends my son hurtling away from my grip and smashes him against the wall.' **Dramatic and violent verbs** suggest it is unsafe and help the reader understand the writer's concerns.
- **Short dramatic sentence**: 'I freeze.' to capture her feelings of panic and the anxiety that she experiences during the visit to the swimming pool.
- 'determined to succeed in my mission to get out of here safely': **words** like 'determined', 'mission' and 'safely' suggest that this is not something to be taken for granted and reinforce the writer's belief that the swimming pool is dangerous.
- Description of the jacuzzi pool and **use of comparatives** 'calmer' and 'safer' to give the impression that other areas are less calm and less safe.
- **Anecdote** to highlight the irresponsibility of other adults to give the impression that relaxation and safety cannot be taken for granted anywhere in the swimming pool: 'one foolish parent…'
- **Emotive language** to emphasise her desire to leave: 'I am longing for the orange light to flash and signal an end to our session and this trauma.'
- **Confessional anecdote** and **contrast** between her inner thoughts and her outward experience give the impression that the pressure to pretend she is enjoying herself, for the sake of her children, only adds to the writer's displeasure: '"Too long" I want to reply but instead I smile through gritted teeth and look forward to tomorrow's trip to the cinema.'

Mark schemes

4	Extract meaning and select evidence	Ability to interpret the intentions of the writer	Ability to explain and analyse the writer's craft	
Light bronze	• Nothing to reward.	• Nothing to reward.	• Nothing to reward.	
Dark bronze	• Simple understanding of the text. May include textual evidence, some of which may be relevant.	• Simple recognition of the writer's intentions may be evident.	• Simple comments on parts of the text that might remark on how they achieve effect.	
Light silver	• Some understanding of the text, with efforts to select some relevant textual evidence.	• A straightforward explanation of the writer's intentions.	• A straightforward examination of some language devices used within the text.	
Dark silver	• General understanding of the text. Will include some relevant supporting evidence.	• A general interpretation that recognises how some of the writer's intentions have been communicated through language choices.	• A generally effective examination of writer's craft with evidence of an ability to analyse.	
Light gold	• Secure understanding of the text with relevant selection of material.	• A secure interpretation that clearly recognises how the writer's intentions are reflected through language choices.	• A secure evaluation of writer's craft that explores the use of some aspects of language and structural features.	
Dark gold	• Confident understanding of the text with precise selection of textual evidence that enables analysis of the text.	• A confident and analytical interpretation that demonstrates an insightful understanding of how the writer's intentions are apparent through language choices.	• A confident and precise analysis of relevant aspects of writer's craft.	

ACKNOWLEDGEMENTS

Acknowledgements: p.11: NHS: from https://www.nhs.uk/smokefree/why-quit/smoking-health-problems Used with permission from Patient available at http://patient.info/health/smoking-the-facts © 2017, Egton Medical Information Systems Limited. All Rights Reserved; **pp.34 and 35: Bill Bryson:** from *Notes from a Small Island* (Doubleday, 1995); **pp.36–7 and 38: Bear Grylls:** from *Mud, Sweat and Tears: The Autobiography* (Channel 4, Transworld Publishers, 2011); **p.37: Joe Simpson:** from *Touching the Void* (Vintage, 1988); **p.40: Malala Yousafzai:** from *I am Malala* (Weidenfeld & Nicolson, Orion Publishing, 2013), reprinted with permission. Copyright © 2013 Salarzai Limited; **pp.58 and 59: Priscilla Higham:** from 'Angels of the Slum' (*London Daily Telegraph*, 18 November 2000), reprinted with permission of Priscilla Higham (www.africansolutions.org); **p.93: Barack Obama:** extract of transcript from Barrack Obama's Farewell speech (10 January 2017), public domain; **pp.94–5: David Beckham:** extract of transcript from interview with David Beckham, https://www.youtube.com/watch?v=glncXTp3ezU (1992); **p.96:** extract of transcript of commentary between Clive Tyldesley and Ron Atkinson from European cup final 1999 between Manchester United and Bayern Munich, https://www.youtube.com/watch?v=0xX570dVnOc (26 May 1999); **p.97: Jamie Oliver:** extract from transcript with Jamie Oliver, https://www.youtube.com/watch?v=2O05boE-tWA (15 November 2010), published with fair use; **p.98: Michael Parkinson:** extract from transcript from interview between Parkinson and David Beckham, *Parky's People: The Interviews* (Hodder & Stoughton, 2010); **pp.106 and 107: J.B.Priestley:** from *An Inspector Calls* (Heinemann, 1945); **pp.112, 139 and 149: John Steinbeck:** from *Of Mice and Men* (Heinemann, 1937); **p.116: Jessie Pope:** from 'Who's for the Game?', public domain; **p.128: Jennifer Johnston:** from *How Many Miles to Babylon* (Hamish Hamilton, Penguin Group, 1974), published with fair use; **p.131: Bill Bryson:** from *Neither Here Nor There: Travels in Europe* (Black Swan, 1991); **p.137: Andy Weir:** from *The Martian* (Del Ray Publishing, 2011); **p.138: Bram Stoker:** from *Dracula* (Archibald Constable and Company, 1897); **p.138: Robert Swindells:** from *Stone Cold* (Heinemann, 1993), published with fair use; **p.146: Barry Hines:** from *A Kestrel for a Knave* (Heinemann, 1968); **p.148: Alan Gibbons:** from *The Edge* (Orion, 2002), first published in the UK by Orion Children's Books, an imprint of Hachette Children's Books, Carmelite House, 50 Victoria Embankment, London imprint, EC4Y 0DZ. Reprinted with permission; **p.150: Teresa Breslin:** from *Whispers in the Graveyard* (Egmont, 1994); **p.151: Louis Sachar:** from *Holes* (Bloomsbury Publishing, 1998), used with permission © Louis Sachar, 2000, Holes, Bloomsbury Publishing Plc; **p.153: Susan Hill:** from *The Woman in Black* (Hamish Hamilton, Penguin Group, 1983); **p.156: Khaled Hosseinin:** from *And the Mountains Echoed* (Bloomsbury Publishing, 2013), published with fair use; **p.174: Inderdeep Bains:** from 'Beware of the Cat!', http://www.dailymail.co.uk/news/article-4080624/Beware-cat-Blood-thirsty-devil-pet-leaves-two-posties-delivery-driver-mechanic-wounded-pouncing-them.html (Daily Mail, 1 January 20017), used with permission © Dail Mail; **p.176: Neil Tweedie:** from 'Camping: is it nuts in May?', http://www.telegraph.co.uk/travel/campingholidays/5323901/Eurocamp-camping-in-the-UK-Is-it-nuts-in-May.html (The Telegraph, 15 May 2009), used with permission © Telegraph Media Group Limited 2009; **pp.183–4 and 185: Kevin Brooks:** from *Martyn Pig* (Chicken House, 2004), Text © Kevin Brooks 2004, Reproduced with permission of Chicken House Ltd. All rights reserved; **pp.188 and 189: Louise Tickle:** from 'The Merchant Hotel: Belfast', https://www.theguardian.com/travel/2006/may/15/belfast.unitedkingdom.hotels (The Guardian, 15 May 2006), used with permission Copyright Louise Tickle; **pp.190–91: Siobhan Down:** from *Bog Child* (David Fickling Books, 2008); **p.191: Andy Mulligan:** from *Trash* (David Fickling Books, 2010); **p.201: Ma Jian:** from *Red Dust* (Vintage, Random House, 2002); **p.205: Pat Barker:** from *Another World* (Penguin, 1998); **p.206: Ian Crichton Smith:** from 'The Crater', *Red Door, The: The Complete English Stories 1949-7* (Birlinn Ltd, 2001), reproduced with permission of Birlinn Limited via PLSclear.